READING
ROMANS
THROUGH THE
CENTURIES

READING ROMANS
THROUGH THE
CENTURIES

From the Early Church to Karl Barth

JEFFREY P. GREENMAN
AND TIMOTHY LARSEN, EDITORS

BrazosPress

Grand Rapids, Michigan

© 2005 by Jeffrey P. Greenman and Timothy Larsen

Published by Brazos Press
a division of Baker Publishing Group
P.O. Box 6287, Grand Rapids, MI 49516-6287
www.brazospress.com

Printed in the United States of America

Unless otherwise marked, scripture is taken from the New Revised Standard Version of the Bible, copyright 1989, Division of Christian Education of the National Council of the Churches of Christ in the United States of America. Used by permission. All rights reserved.

Library of Congress Cataloging-in-Publication Data
Reading Romans through the centuries : from the early church to Karl Barth / [edited by] Jeffery P. Greenman and Timothy Larsen.
     p.   cm.
   Includes bibliographical references.
   ISBN 1-58743-156-4 (pbk.)
   1. Bible. N.T. Romans—Criticism, interpretation, etc. I. Greenman, Jeffrey P.
II. Larsen, Timothy, 1967– III. Title.
BS2665.52.R38 2005
227′.106′09—dc22   2005016878

For Roy C. Matheson
Scholar, Teacher, Pastor, Colleague, Friend

CONTENTS

Notes on Contributors

Gerald Bray
Dr. Gerald Bray is Anglican Professor of Divinity at Beeson Divinity School of Samford University, Alabama, where he teaches church history, historical theology, and Latin. An ordained Anglican minister with a doctorate from the Sorbonne, before coming to Beeson he lectured in theology and philosophy at Oak Hill College in London, England. He is the editor of three volumes in the Ancient Christian Commentary on Scripture series (InterVarsity Press), including the volume on Romans, as well as the author of many books, including *Creeds, Councils and Christ, Doctrine of God,* and *Biblical Interpretation: Past and Present.*

Christopher A. Hall
Dr. Christopher A. Hall is Dean of Templeton Honors College at Eastern University (formerly Eastern College) in Pennsylvania, where he has taught since 1992. His Ph.D. dissertation at Drew University focused on John Chrysostom's treatise *On Providence,* and he has continued to work in patristics as the associate editor of many volumes in the Ancient Christian Commentary on Scripture series (InterVarsity Press). In that series, he edited, along with Thomas Oden, the volume on Mark (1998). His books *Reading Scripture with the Church Fathers* and *Learning Theology with the Church Fathers* are companion volumes to the series.

Pamela Bright
Dr. Pamela Bright is Chair of Theological Studies, and graduate program director, at Concordia University in Montreal, and a former president of the Canadian Society for Patristic Studies. Her interests include questions of hermeneutics, asceticism, and ecclesiology, and especially how the Bible has been understood in early Latin-speaking Christian communi-

ties. She is well known for her work on Augustine, including editing a new edition of *De Doctrina Christiana* as well as editing *Augustine and the Bible*, which is the second volume in the Bible through the Ages series, which she is producing with her husband, Charles Kannengeisser.

Steven Boguslawski, O.P.

Fr. Steven Boguslawski is Rector and President of Sacred Heart Major Seminary in Detroit. Previously he was Vice-President and Academic Dean of the Pontifical Faculty at the Dominican House of Studies in Washington, D.C. He completed his Ph.D. dissertation at Yale University on the subject of Aquinas's commentary on Romans 9–11, and has an ongoing interest in exegetical, theological, and historical issues related to Romans in particular, and to Paul in general.

Timothy George

Dr. Timothy George is the founding Dean of Beeson Divinity School of Samford University, Alabama, and chairs the Commission on Theological Education of the Baptist World Alliance. He was awarded his Th.D. degree from Harvard University. A prolific author, he has written and edited numerous articles and books, including *The Theology of the Reformers, John Calvin and the Church, Baptist Theologians,* and the volume on Galatians in the New American Commentary. He also serves as a senior editor of *Christianity Today*.

Jeffrey P. Greenman

Dr. Jeffrey Greenman is the Associate Dean of Biblical and Theological Studies and Professor of Christian Ethics at Wheaton College, Illinois. His Ph.D. dissertation at the University of Virginia dealt with seventeenth-century Anglican practical divinity, and his research interests include theological ethics, the English Reformation, and Anglican intellectual history.

David Demson

Dr. David Demson is Professor of Systematic Theology, emeritus, at Emmanuel College of Victoria University, University of Toronto, where he taught from 1962 to 2001. His D.Phil. thesis at Oxford University explored Calvin's theology of the Word of God. In addition to his book *Hans Frei and Karl Barth: Different Ways of Reading Scripture,* he has written a number of articles related to Luther, Calvin, and Barth, as well as on issues in hermeneutics. He has been the general secretary of the Karl Barth Society of North America since 1972 and is a past president of the Canadian Theological Society and a past chair of the theology department at the Toronto School of Theology.

Victor Shepherd

Dr. Victor Shepherd is Professor of Systematic and Historical Theology at Tyndale Seminary in Toronto. He was awarded the Th.D. degree from Emmanuel College, University of Toronto, and is the author of numerous articles and books, including *The Nature and Function of Faith in the Theology of John Calvin*. His areas of research include systematic theology, Reformation studies, Puritanism, and John Wesley.

Mark Noll

Dr. Mark Noll is the Carolyn and Fred McManis Professor of Christian Thought, and the co-founder of the Institute for the Study of American Evangelicals at Wheaton College, Illinois. He obtained his Ph.D. in the History of Christianity from Vanderbilt University. He is the author of numerous books, including *A History of Christianity in the United States and Canada, The Princeton Theology, 1812–1921,* and *America's God: From Jonathan Edwards to Abraham Lincoln.*

Timothy Larsen

Dr. Timothy Larsen, a fellow of the Royal Historical Society, is Associate Professor of Theology at Wheaton College, Illinois. His most recent monographs are *Christabel Pankhurst: Fundamentalism and Feminism in Coalition* and *Contested Christianity: The Political and Social Contexts of Victorian Theology*, and he is the editor of the *Biographical Dictionary of Evangelicals*. His areas of research include religion and society in Victorian Britain, the history of evangelicalism, and the history of biblical interpretation and criticism.

John Webster

Dr. John Webster is Professor of Systematic Theology at the University of Aberdeen. After Ph.D. work on Eberhard Jüngel at Cambridge University, he taught at the University of Durham, Wycliffe College in Toronto, and Oxford University. He is the author of numerous articles and books dealing with systematic and historical theology, including *Barth's Ethics of Reconciliation, Barth's Moral Theology, Barth,* and *Word and Church*. Widely recognized as a leading authority on Karl Barth, he has also edited *The Cambridge Companion to Karl Barth*.

1

INTRODUCTION

Jeffrey P. Greenman and Timothy Larsen

If one were to endeavor to excise the influence of the apostle Paul's Letter to the Romans from the history of Christian thought, it would be difficult to set any limit on how radical the surgery would have to be, or to guarantee what would be left over once it had been completed. Indeed, James Dunn has claimed that Romans is "the first well-developed theological statement by a Christian theologian which has come down to us, and one which has had an incalculable influence on the framing of Christian theology ever since—arguably the single most important work of Christian theology ever written."[1] In every epoch, the church's leaders and teachers have been preoccupied with Romans. They have engaged intently with the central themes of Romans and have attempted to articulate a careful interpretation of its text. Their diligence has generated a rich, expansive corpus of commentaries, sermons, and treatises.

As the eminent New Testament scholar Richard Longenecker has observed, "whenever the church has felt itself (1) threatened by some new teaching that differed from the norm, (2) rejuvenated by some new approach to Christian understanding, or (3) confused as to what

---

1. J. D. G. Dunn, "Romans, Letter to the," in *Dictionary of Paul and His Letters*, ed. Gerald F. Hawthorne and Ralph P. Martin (Downers Grove, IL: InterVarsity Press, 1993), 838.

to believe in light of competing ideologies or methodologies—or, perhaps, some combination of all three of the above—it has turned back to its foundational documents, in particular to Paul's Letter to the Romans."[2] In this light, Longenecker avers that the work of interpreting Romans and offering detailed commentary upon it has ever been an expression of "spiritual vitality, intellectual vigor, and moral courage."[3] These comments by Dunn and Longenecker suggest that Romans has a place in the history of Christianity unlike any other biblical book. Moreover, because Christians are a "people of the book," a valuable window through which to view the experience of Christians throughout history is an examination of the ways they have read the Epistle to the Romans. The prominence and centrality of Romans in Christian thought and experience is captured succinctly by Joseph Fitzmyer, a leading modern Roman Catholic biblical scholar: "One can almost write the history of Christian theology by surveying the ways in which Romans has been interpreted."[4]

The purpose of this volume is to explore the ways in which a broad range of important or suggestive Christian leaders and theologians have "encountered" the Epistle to the Romans throughout history. The chapters presented here ask questions such as: How do major Christian thinkers engage the letter? What place did Romans occupy in their life, ministry, and theological development? What approaches to reading the text have they taken? How does their interaction with Romans reflect the needs and interests of their historical era? In addressing these questions, this volume is making a contribution to the resurgence of scholarly interest in the history of biblical interpretation.

During the past twenty years, scholars in a range of fields—notably biblical studies, theology, and church history—have given increasing attention to the leading figures and diverse traditions of biblical interpretation. For example, a comprehensive reference work analyzing the thought of "major biblical interpreters" from the early church, the medieval period, the sixteenth and seventeenth centuries, and through the twentieth century has been published.[5] A growing stream of monographs and textbooks are appearing in this subject area.[6] Two major publishing projects are under way that seek to recover the church's precritical patterns of biblical interpretation, documenting the tradition of classical

2. Richard Longenecker, private correspondence, March 2, 2001.
3. Ibid.
4. Joseph Fitzmyer, *Romans* (New York: Doubleday, 1993), xiii.
5. *Historical Handbook of Major Biblical Interpreters*, ed. Donald K. McKim (Downers Grove, IL: InterVarsity Press, 1998).
6. Including a notable one by one of our contributors, Gerald Bray, *Biblical Interpretation: Past and Present* (Downers Grove, IL: InterVarsity Press, 1996).

Christian exegesis in order to offer resources to contemporary preachers, scholars, and students.[7] Other scholars are exploring the history of biblical interpretation in an effort to recover "theological exegesis."[8] Still others are seeking to identify the contributions of women interpreters to the tradition, or to locate the distinctive approaches of various denominational traditions. This volume uses the Epistle to the Romans as a particularly promising door into this whole inviting tradition of Christian thinkers encountering the biblical text in diverse times, places, and intellectual and theological contexts.

The different figures selected for discussion in this book include several writers, such as John Calvin and Karl Barth, who are well known for their formal commentaries on the Letter to the Romans. Other chapters explore the interaction of prominent Christian thinkers, for example, Augustine and William Tyndale, who engaged Romans vigorously but never wrote a formal commentary. The operative principle has been to focus on thinkers whose engagement with Romans has been substantial and whose work illuminates wider movements in the church's theological development. No attempt has been made to track each step in the history of major commentaries on Romans. Therefore, this study is representative, but not exhaustive: an equally viable alternative set of figures could have been chosen, including, for example, Origen, for the patristic period, and Martin Bucer and Philipp Melanchthon, for the Reformers. Our aim has been to be suggestive, rather than comprehensive.

The book flows chronologically, beginning with explorations of the engagement with Romans in the work of three major patristic figures. Gerald Bray shows that Ambrosiaster "set a model" of commentary for Augustine and the subsequent Western tradition. Bray documents Ambrosiaster's strong interest in the Jewish background to Paul's treatment of law and covenant, his clear exposition of the doctrine of justification by faith (calling it "clearer and more detailed than any patristic writer['s]" apart from John Chrysostom), and his unusually clear and detailed interpretation of Christ's atoning death as a "nullification of the sentence of death" brought on by sin.

Christopher Hall analyzes John Chrysostom's homilies on Romans, paying special attention to certain themes in Romans, including the grace of God, the relation of Jews and Gentiles, and justification by

7. These two projects are the Ancient Christian Commentary on Scripture series by InterVarsity Press, Thomas Oden, general editor, and "The Church's Bible" by Wm. B. Eerdmans Publishing Company, Robert L. Wilken, general editor. Another of our contributors, Timothy George, has recently agreed to edit a series of biblical commentary by the Reformers for InterVarsity Press.

8. For example, *The Theological Interpretation of Scripture: Classic and Contemporary Readings*, ed. Stephen Fowl (Cambridge, MA: Blackwell, 1997).

faith. Hall focuses in detail upon Chrysostom's understanding of sin and human freedom, exploring the theological perspective represented by the affirmation of a "synergism" between divine grace and human choice in salvation.

Pamela Bright contextualizes Augustine's engagement with Romans throughout the many phases of his long ministry. She shows how Augustine, who never completed a commentary on Romans, handled different aspects of Romans at different stages of his life and in an enormous range of literary works. Augustine unmistakably was "a man of the Bible," and Bright shows how he interacts with Romans, primarily in relation to pressing issues of Christian confession and ministry. She concludes that he is best seen as "a man of conversation," whose life was permeated by constant interaction with scripture.

Medieval thought is represented in our volume through Thomas Aquinas, whose presence casts the longest shadow into the future in Roman Catholic theology. Steven Boguslawski claims that Aquinas saw chapters 9–11 as the theological center of Romans, and he proceeds to expound Aquinas's reading of those passages as discussed in major works such as the *Summa Theologia* and the *Commentary on Romans*. Boguslawski presents Aquinas's method of biblical interpretation as a "hermeneutical helix" and shows the complex interplay between systematic and theological concerns, on the one hand, and exegetical precision and experiential factors, on the other. This chapter also examines how Aquinas interpreted Romans 9–11 on the subjects of election, predestination, and divine providence.

The next major section of this volume studies the thought of three prominent figures of the Protestant Reformation. Martin Luther's belief that Romans is "really the chief part of the New Testament, and is truly the purest Gospel" provides a point of departure for Timothy George's analysis of the *Lectures on Romans*. After describing the reappearance of the missing *Lectures*, and situating these lectures within Luther's teaching duties, George examines the impact of Romans on the shape of Luther's emerging Reformation theology, with special attention to Luther's concepts of sin, justification by faith, and humility.

David Demson's chapter argues that the theme of God's mercy in Christ as the central meaning of the gospel is the organizational center of John Calvin's *Commentary on Romans*. Demson shows that Calvin found the mercy of God in Christ to be the focus of Paul's teaching on the knowledge of God, divine judgment, the issue of law and works, and original sin. Demson also suggests, however, that Calvin's discussion of election in Romans 9 substitutes the category of "God's secret will" for God's mercy in Christ, and he goes on to judge this an unfortunate departure from Calvin's primary interpretative theme.

Jeffrey Greenman presents William Tyndale as a skilled biblical theologian whose constructive theology is shaped significantly by Romans. Greenman offers a nuanced rendering of Tyndale's reading of Romans by demonstrating both Tyndale's indebtedness to Luther's understanding of Romans and Tyndale's own distinctive theological voice. Tyndale's insistence upon the necessity of "love for the law," his view of the relation between law and gospel, and his emphasis upon the activity of the Holy Spirit are clear indicators that it is "quite inaccurate" to consider his thought as nothing more than a series of footnotes to Luther.

The final section of the book deals with figures from the eighteenth century through the twentieth century. Victor Shepherd examines John Wesley, whose faith was enlivened when he heard a public reading from the preface of Luther's *Commentary on Romans.* Shepherd expounds Wesley's own interpretation of Romans, especially Romans 3:31 and 7:12, as expressed in his three major tracts on the law of God. Wesley's understanding of these two verses is indicative of his understanding of the totality of the gospel. Shepherd argues that Wesley believed Jesus Christ is "the substance of the law," which is holy, just, and good. He also demonstrates how exegetical findings in Romans enabled Wesley to avoid the twin dangers of moralism and antinomianism.

Mark Noll discusses nineteenth-century America's leading Calvinist theologian, Charles Hodge. Noll analyzes Hodge's commentary on Romans in light of its historical setting, paying special attention to the theological crises in his Presbyterian circles. Hodge's writings on Romans reasserted Calvinist orthodoxy on the doctrines of sin and atonement, in response to rival interpretations put forward by Moses Stuart and Albert Barnes. Noll argues that what emerged here were distinctively American theological developments.

John William Colenso, bishop of Natal, would appear to be the only Anglican bishop to have received a sentence of excommunication in at least the last three hundred years. This peculiar status, together with the scandal centered around his commentary on the Pentateuch (which was widely considered to be heretical), has caused Colenso's commentary on Romans to be neglected. Timothy Larsen recovers it in his chapter, arguing that it was not the work of a rogue heretic, but rather a telling expression of liberal Anglican thought in the mid-nineteenth century. Colenso offered a rendering of the epistle that took Romans 5:18 as its theological center. From that starting point, he expounded justification in Christ as having already come to all human beings, even "the heathen." This universalistic instinct the missionary bishop then applied to numerous other doctrines, including hell, which he suggested was perhaps more akin to what is usually meant by purgatory, a place of punishment that was temporary and remedial. Colenso's reading of Romans was also explicitly anti-Calvinist.

The final chapter is devoted to Karl Barth's *Commentary on Romans*. John Webster reminds us of the centrality of biblical commentary and exegetical writings within Barth's massive output and seeks to redress the lack of attention to Barth's work as a commentator. Webster interprets Barth's *Commentary* precisely as a commentary, in line with Barth's own intentions, rather than as any attempt to develop a new theology of his own. In this light, this chapter argues that Barth's work on Romans was driven not by "dogmatic principles," but rather by a commitment to listening to "the divine Word in the text's words." Having located Barth's approach to the task of biblical commentary within the classical theological tradition and highlighted the influence of Calvin's exegesis upon Barth, Webster claims that what is happening in *Romans* is a "rediscovery" of a "commentarial mode of theology."

Taken as a whole, this volume affords insights into the function of scripture in Christian thought across the centuries. First, we gain a deeper appreciation for the ongoing, contextualized task of biblical interpretation as central to the Christian tradition. The greatness of the "great figures" of the church's life, such as some of those studied here, is comprehensible only when we see that they have been men and women of the Bible, first and foremost. Their lives have been indelibly shaped by an engagement with the scriptures: their ministries have been concerned with the transmission of the message of the Bible, and their theological development is the story of their growing understanding of its claim upon the church. Each figure studied in this book sought, amidst the pressing demands and challenges of their day, to hear the message of Romans addressing their situation. Augustine turns to Romans again and again over the decades for guidance on a wide range of pastoral and theological issues. As first-generation Reformers, Luther and Tyndale found in Romans what they perceived to be the key to recovering the meaning of the gospel. Wesley drew deeply upon Romans as he sought to articulate the way forward for members of his movement who were at risk of being driven into either the Scylla of moralism or the Charybdis of antinomianism. Hodge expounded what he believed to be the great themes of Romans in the face of emerging doctrinal alternatives from prominent revisionists. What we see, therefore, is a fresh picture of Christian theology as the ongoing practice of the contextual exposition of scripture.

Second, this volume provides a glimpse of the multilayered connectedness of the Christian tradition. Ambrosiaster's pioneering work sets in place a continuous tradition of exegesis on Romans. We see the influence of Luther upon Tyndale and Wesley, and that of Calvin upon

Hodge and Barth. Augustine, the "man of conversation," appears as a conversation partner over and over again in subsequent chapters of this volume. Moreover, the conversation sometimes turns to debate. Calvin's reading of Romans is very different from John Chrysostom's, and Colenso expounded the epistle in a way that made it quite clear that Calvinists do not have a monopoly on its meaning. As any teacher knows, if all the students have read the same material, then you have a good basis for a fruitful discussion. In Christian thought, Paul's Letter to the Romans has served as that common, required text.

Finally, taken as a whole, this volume allows us to see the same themes emerge in different contexts, surprising us by both the comparisons and the contrasts. For example, we encounter the theme of the Jews in the very first chapter, on Ambrosiaster, only to have it reemerge strongly in the chapter on Thomas Aquinas. The idea of the universal scope of the atonement, present in both Ambrosiaster and John Chrysostom, has its boldest exposition in the chapter on Colenso. Likewise, the notion of love of the law that emerges, for example, in the thought of William Tyndale, has an even greater flowering in that of John Wesley. The commentaries on Romans by Charles Hodge and John William Colenso were published within a few years of each other, yet the former wrote to defend, and the latter to debunk, both Calvinism and the idea of substitutionary atonement. Nevertheless, in a strange convergence, they both drew on commonsense instincts as an authority when developing their theological claims. These comments are merely indicative; the reader will be able to continue this process of comparison, contrast, affinity, and counterpoint along numerous additional lines.

This volume originated with a conference entitled "Reading Romans," sponsored by Tyndale Seminary, Toronto, in cooperation with the Canadian Society of Patristic Studies, held in Toronto on 28–29 May 2002 during the annual meeting of the Congress of the Social Sciences and Humanities. The chapters in this volume were selected from the papers presented to a receptive audience of scholars, pastors, and students at that conference. We are grateful to Dr. Nancy Calvert-Koyzis and Dr. William Klassen for also having presented papers on that occasion. We acknowledge with gratitude the generous support of the Maranatha Foundation, whose grant in support of the conference made it possible to include an international roster of presenters. Special thanks are also due to Sherrilyn Hall, who provided efficient organization of the conference and assisted skillfully in the preparation of this volume for publication.

The "Reading Romans" conference in 2002 marked the occasion of the retirement of Dr. Roy Matheson, Professor Emeritus of New Testament at Tyndale Seminary, Toronto. This volume is a token of appreciation for his thirty years of exemplary service to his institution as teacher, scholar, administrator, mentor, and colleague. During his teaching of the full range of New Testament studies, the Epistle to the Romans has held a place of special significance in his work—he taught a semester-length, focused study of Romans probably thirty times in his career. As a pastor-scholar who maintains an active ministry in leadership at Chartwell Baptist Church, Dr. Matheson has modeled for a generation of students a rare capacity to expound the meaning of "the gospel of God" (Rom. 1:1) with a clarity and conviction that nurtures, orients, and sustains pastoral ministry and congregational mission.

2

AMBROSIASTER

Gerald Bray

His Identity

In the history of the interpretation of Paul's Epistle to the Romans, Ambrosiaster is unique. He is the only one of the major commentators who is completely unknown, even though he lived in Rome and made a significant contribution to biblical exegesis in an age of theological giants. How could such a man have vanished from sight? In particular, how could his great work, a commentary on the entire Pauline corpus (of which the Romans section takes up about half), have been subsumed under the name of Ambrose of Milan, whose own style of commentary is so very different? Ambrose is florid and allegorical where Ambrosiaster is succinct and literal; who could possibly have put them together as one? And why did Erasmus, who discovered our anonymous author, think fit to give him a derogatory name that has effectively condemned him to the second rank of patristic writers, when he ought to be out in front? For such has been the prejudice against anonymity that even a man like Lactantius or Minucius Felix is given greater recognition than the so-called Ambrosiaster, who by any objective standard ought to stand head and shoulders above them.

Whoever Ambrosiaster was, he was at least a well-educated Roman writing during the pontificate of Pope Damasus I (366–84). More than a century ago, Dom Germain Morin suggested that he might have been a layman or consular rank called Decimus Hilarianus Hilarius, and this suggestion was adopted by Alexander Souter.[1] If correct, it would tie in with Augustine's attribution of the commentary to a certain Hilary,[2] and might also explain why so little is known about him, since laymen often got overlooked in ecclesiastical histories.

His Philo-Semitism

He was unusually well-informed about, and sympathetic to, Judaism, which has led some people to suggest that he was a converted Jew. But educated Romans were trained in the elements of Roman law, and that might have given Ambrosiaster an interest in Judaism sufficiently unusual to stand out from the fourth-century norm. At one point he even goes so far as to claim that the name *Jew,* which derives from *Judah,* was given to the people of Israel because it was out of Judah that Christ came in the flesh. This was prophesied in the Old Testament and recognized by the other Israelite tribes, who praised Judah for it. In fact, so much was Judah's destiny bound up with that of Christ that the two figures merged in Ambrosiaster's mind, and he ended up claiming that the word *Jew* really meant "belonging to Christ," although the Jewish people themselves naturally failed to recognize this fact (Rom. 2:17). That blindness led to their destruction, because by failing to see Christ in the scriptures they were emptying them of their meaning and destroying themselves at the same time.

The nature and extent of this Jewish bias can be gauged from the way in which Ambrosiaster treats the opening salutation of Romans. On the one hand, he says that Paul called himself a "servant of Jesus Christ" in order to emphasize his belief that Jesus was God. This was signified by the addition of the word *Christ,* and Paul supposedly did this in order to distance himself from Judaism. On the other hand, he claims that Paul says that he has been "set apart for the Gospel of God" because he had already been "set apart" as a Pharisee and given a teaching post among the Jews. The use of this expression, says Ambrosiaster, harks back to Paul's Jewish days and must be understood in conjunction with them.

Of course, it is easy for us to say that he was wrong in making these statements, and there were ancient commentators like Origen who

1. Alexander Souter, *A Study of Ambrosiaster* (Cambridge: Cambridge University Press, 1905), 183–5. For the original suggestion, see Dom G. Morin, "L'Ambrosiaster et le juif converti Isaac," *Revue d'histoire et de littérature religieuses* IV (1899), 97–121; especially 111–14.

2. St. Augustine of Hippo, *Contra duas epistolas Pelagii,* 4.4.7, quoting Romans 5:12.

were superior to him in this respect. But nobody else in the ancient world was as concerned as Ambrosiaster was to explore Paul's Jewish background in such detail. Furthermore, he was the only ancient commentator to notice that Paul's missionary zeal was remarkably similar to his zeal as a Jew and to ascribe this to a calling which was transformed but not fundamentally altered by the new dispensation of the covenant.

At the same time, Ambrosiaster was careful not to let the new covenant be subsumed under the old. When discussing the nature of apostleship (Rom. 1:5), he remarks that it was a gift of divine grace quite independent of Judaism, and adds that its appearance annoyed the Jews because they discovered that not only Jesus, whom they had rejected, but also his main followers were endowed with a divine power that was foreign to their experience. Ambrosiaster thus maintains a balance between the testaments by allowing a sacred form to the former while at the same time reserving spiritual power to the latter. The significance of power as the main difference between the old and the new covenants is a theme that recurs constantly in Ambrosiaster's commentary. For instance, when the apostle Paul says that he wants to come to Rome to impart some spiritual gift to the Romans (Rom. 1:11), Ambrosiaster assumes that until that time, the Roman Christians had been content with the law of Moses as their guide—not bad as far as it went, but not enough for salvation. The mission of the apostle was therefore to bring a spiritual gift, namely the power of the gospel, to bear on their lives and to transform their spiritual experience.[3]

Later on in the commentary, Ambrosiaster returns to this theme and says that the nobility and dignity of the Jewish people lies in the nature of the promises made to them. But by rejecting the Savior, they lost this advantage and became worse than the Gentiles, because to lose a dignity is worse than never to have had it, a view that was common in antiquity and in essence defined the nature of patristic anti-semitism (Rom. 9:5). Ambrosiaster reads the conflict between Jews and Gentiles in the Roman church in a way that presupposes that a Judaizing form of Christianity was what the Romans had been taught, and that the apostle Paul's mission was to take them to a higher stage, even as he himself had been rescued from the Jewish law to a higher calling in the gospel. He even goes so far as to claim that the Romans' preaching had previously lacked the power of God, because there were no signs and wonders to accompany it (Rom. 1:16).

3. All quotes from Ambrosiaster are taken from G. L. Bray, ed., *Romans*, Ancient Christian Commentary on Scripture, New Testament VI (Downers Grove, IL: InterVarsity Press, 1998), occasionally with minor adjustments made to fit the overall flow of the text.

Furthermore, Ambrosiaster understands that Paul presented his theology in a way that only a Jew speaking to other Jews could have done. He may perhaps be accused of having made Paul more Jewish than he really was, but there can be no doubt about the general tendency of his commentary, and surely we can agree that Ambrosiaster was fundamentally right in his perception of Paul, which would receive general endorsement today. What is remarkable is that he said this at a time when it went against the grain for most Christians, who knew little about Hebrew culture and who were trying to distance themselves from Judaism as much as they reasonably could. Later on in his commentary, we get echoes of this as Ambrosiaster has to uphold the legitimate place of Jewish Christians in the church and insist that not all the Jewish people have been rejected (Rom. 3:3). His greatness as a commentator is thus revealed as twofold. He understood where Paul was coming from, and he was not afraid to give full weight to his outlook even when it was not politically correct to do so.

From there Ambrosiaster moves on to discuss the Old Testament, which Paul says promised the coming of Christ. He mentions the unity of the covenant dispensations, but this is more or less in passing. His most interesting comment is about the prophets, whom he regards as great men on the ground that only great men would be chosen to herald the coming of the Messiah. By itself, this is an unremarkable statement, but in the context, it underlines the inspired character of the Old Testament, which Ambrosiaster is subtly recommending to his readers. We must remember that the Old Testament had not been fully translated into Latin when he was writing, and so his recommendation may be seen as an exhortation to the Roman church to make the whole of the scriptures readily available to Latin-speakers. As we know, Ambrosiaster's contemporary, Pope Damasus I, commissioned Jerome to do just that, and it is at least possible that it was encouragement of this kind that persuaded him of the urgency of the task.

His Orthodoxy

As a Christian theologian, Ambrosiaster understood the foundational importance of right belief, and he himself was fully orthodox, sometimes in ways that were in advance of the church of his day. Commenting on Romans 1:3, for example, he notes that Jesus was truly man, as well as God, "for he would not be truly man if he were not of flesh and soul." When we remember that this was when the Apollinarian controversy was raging in the Eastern church, and when it was by no means generally agreed that Jesus had a human soul, Ambrosiaster's quiet assurance on that point is quite remarkable. He also includes a clear, if general, statement about the atonement and indicates that it was the primary purpose of the incarnation. Though there is nothing startling here from our point of view, Ambrosiaster states the matter with a clarity that surpasses even the ancient creeds. He even ties the incarnation to the doctrine of the Trinity by interpreting the phrase "Spirit of holiness" as a reference to the Holy Spirit. This interpretation may be contested by some, but there can be no doubt that Ambrosiaster had a functioning systematic theology, which he brought to bear on his reading of Romans, and that in doing this he was generally in advance of his time.

Ambrosiaster never denies the literal sense of the biblical text, but he finds spiritual purposes in it that may go beyond what the apostle originally intended and thus leaves modern readers feeling somewhat uneasy. For example, on Romans 1:10, where Paul speaks about his desire to make a successful journey to Rome, Ambrosiaster claims that by "successful," Paul meant "spiritually fruitful." Of course Paul wanted that as well, but the text rather suggests that Paul was primarily concerned with getting to Rome—something that he had not yet been able to do—and not with what he hoped would happen once he got there. Similarly, Ambrosiaster sees Rome as the spiritual heart of the Gentile world, and so he interprets Paul's letter as a kind of final assault on the pagan citadel of opposition to the gospel. Once again, modern readers may be somewhat uneasy with so bold an assertion, though here Ambrosiaster may well be revealing something of a mentality that was common in ancient times, but which escapes us today. The Bible attached spiritual power to cities like Nineveh and Babylon, and Babylon is a type of Rome in other parts of the New Testament. Is Ambrosiaster's sense of the city's spiritual significance perhaps more in tune with this way of thinking, and therefore more accurate as an interpretation of Paul, than most modern scholars are willing to allow?

Justification by Faith

On the great theological theme of justification by faith, Ambrosiaster is clearer and more detailed than any patristic writer, apart from his younger contemporary John Chrysostom. He states quite clearly that righteousness belongs to God alone, and that it is revealed in the gospel by God's gift of justifying faith to man. When a man believes, then God's righteousness is revealed in him, and he becomes a witness of the fact that what God promises, he fulfills. Ambrosiaster did not have to face the complex issues surrounding justification by faith alone that confronted Martin Luther, but there can be no doubt that the two men are on the same wavelength. Man's faith is not his own but belongs to

God, who has freely given it to him. It is therefore clear to Ambrosiaster
that any righteousness or faith that might be found in man is a gift of
God, without any connection to, or dependence on, works, so that no
human being can claim to have earned or deserved his salvation. This
is Luther *avant la lettre,* and shows incidentally just how deeply rooted
in patristic thought the German Reformer's theology was.

When it comes to the ungodly, Ambrosiaster draws a parallel between
them and believers. He claims that just as God's faith and righteousness
are revealed in the latter, so ungodliness and unrighteousness are revealed
in the former. They are the natural consequence of the spiritual state of
the person concerned. What is more, the ungodly are guilty before God,
because they have the natural law to guide them. It is interesting to note
that where other ancient writers tend to think in intellectual terms, and
regard the sinful state of fallen man as confusion and blindness, Ambrosiaster prefers to speak of guilt, of which the sinner is fully aware and
for which he alone is responsible. Ambrosiaster is in no doubt that the
ungodly person is fully able to comprehend the structure of the world,
and that that structure reveals enough about God for him to feel suitably
convicted of his sin. "They were so far from being ignorant," he says, "that
they confessed that there was a single principle from which all things
in heaven, and on earth and under the earth derive their origin" (Rom.
1:21). The foolishness of these people does not consist in any inability to
understand the workings of the universe, but in their failure to acknowledge the God who created it. In this respect, Ambrosiaster is remarkably
close to the theology of Abraham Kuyper and the Dutch neo-Calvinists,
with their emphasis on so-called common grace, though, of course, the
latter have developed their theology over against atheistic humanism,
not pagan idolatry. Nevertheless, it is striking how, in both cases, unbelievers tend to deify dead men instead of turning their eyes toward the
living God. Ambrosiaster's catalog of the abuses to which unbelievers
subjected nature is fairly standard, though it is perhaps worth pointing
out that on the matter of unnatural sexual relations, it is lesbianism, not
male homosexuality, that he singles out for condemnation.

Ambrosiaster regarded Paul's list of the evil things that result from
unbelief as systematic in the apostle's presentation. All of them proceed
from inside a man and are revealed in his external actions. Thus, envy,
murder, strife, and deceit are but the visible consequences of a latent
malice, just as gossip and slander are the manifestations of an already
existing, though concealed, malignity. We may well be skeptical of his
exegesis here, but Ambrosiaster's theological insight is of the first order.
He knew that Jesus had taught that the evil a man does comes from
within him, and he was determined to find this principle in these verses,
whether they state it clearly or not.

The notion of inherited guilt that Ambrosiaster held is foreign to the Eastern tradition, and it is virtually certain that Ambrosiaster was the first commentator on Romans to write in such terms. Augustine adopted him as his guide on this point, and so his view became standard in the Western church. It is therefore important for us to realize that Ambrosiaster understood inherited guilt as a necessary consequence of human sin in a world made by God. In his view, a good creator could not abandon his creation once it was made, and the existence of a divine providence upholding the universe is proof that guilt must be part of the human inheritance of sin. It was not only Adam and the first creatures who had to deal with God; we must all do so, whether we realize this or not. We are therefore not the helpless victims of a past mistake that cannot now be rectified, but rather disordered, and therefore disorderly, beings living on sufferance in God's world.

God's judgment on sin is both universal and just. In Ambrosiaster's eyes, its justice is only increased by God's willingness to be so patient and tolerant now. Every day that goes by without retribution for sin means that when punishment finally comes, it will be all the more severe. Indeed, Ambrosiaster even suggests that the biblical picture of eternal punishment in the fires of hell (Rom. 2:6) is a guarantee that the final reckoning will be delayed as long as possible, because the eventual reckoning will be so terrible. In fairness to Ambrosiaster, he sees the logic and justice of this most clearly in the fact that the righteous will inherit immortality (Rom. 2:6). To the very end there is an inverted symmetry at work in his mind; the greater the rewards for the saints are, the more horrible the fate of the damned must be in order to balance them. The individual will get his due, but whatever that is, it will fit perfectly into the overall harmony of the created universe.

In this connection, it is worth remembering that Ambrosiaster regarded the punishment reserved for unbelieving Gentiles not only as just, despite the fact that the Gentiles did not have the law of Moses to guide them, but as even more severe than that which will befall the Jews. His reasoning is that whereas Jews had the opportunity to assent to both the natural and the Mosaic law, Gentiles were restricted to the natural law only, which was greatly inferior to the Mosaic one. Since they had less protection against sin to begin with, they would be more likely to fall into it. To our minds, this is a curious argument, which seems to go against what the apostle Paul was trying to say, but it probably reflects Ambrosiaster's legal background and training. For him, the mere existence of law was beneficial and brought civilization out of chaos. The Jews were privileged to be spiritually civilized to a unique degree, and therefore they had a better chance of escaping the worst consequences of sin. We must also bear in mind what Ambrosiaster thought "keeping the law" was all about. It did

not entail fulfilling every commandment in detail, but acknowledging
the Creator, something that the Jews had undoubtedly done from the
beginning (Rom. 2:14). Their fault lay in not accepting Christ, the one to
whom the Jewish law bears witness. It was the fact that they had neither
accepted Christ nor acknowledged the Creator that put the pagans in a
fundamentally worse position as far as judgment was concerned.

On the other hand, it is a higher thing to act according to conscience,
which is an internal virtue, than merely to do what the external law pre-
scribes, whether one really believes in it or not. It is this conscientious
behavior that put the Gentiles ahead of the Jews in the quest for salvation.
Like most people in antiquity, Ambrosiaster does not seem to have considered that the conscience might be dulled or corrupted, except perhaps by
some form of demon possession. He therefore does an about-face halfway
through his argument and says that, in the final analysis, honest Gentiles will have an easier time of it on the day of judgment than dishonest
Jews—which of course is the point Paul was trying to make! In the end, it
is that view that wins out in Ambrosiaster's mind, and it is the Gentile who
has known Christ only by nature who is being prepared for heaven, not
the Jew who knew him neither by nature nor by the law (Rom. 2:27).

Ambrosiaster's view of the Jewish law does not surprise us, but the amount
of attention that he pays to it is unusual in the ancient world. Much of this
can probably be ascribed to Ambrosiaster's own legal background, which
gave him a special interest in legal questions. This in turn brings justification
to the fore, and Ambrosiaster discusses it to a depth not found elsewhere in
antiquity. In commenting on Romans 3:20, for example, Origen says only
that through the law we learn what is and what is not sin. The law functions
like a medicine in that it helps us to pinpoint the disease inside us and start
to cure it. Ambrosiaster, by contrast, eschews the medical imagery, perhaps
because he did not think it particularly appropriate, and concentrates on
the reward that will be given to those who keep God's law. He argues that
because the law was conceived within time, keeping it will bring only a
temporal reward. The law is thus ontologically incapable of giving us salvation, which is not temporal but eternal. That is why we can be justified only
by Christ, the eternal Son of God, and why the temporal law is abolished
once Christ comes. Ambrosiaster also distinguishes three different aspects
of the law, one of which is eternal in the sense that it discusses the mystery
of God's divinity, and one of which is purely temporal, because it concerns
only rites and ceremonies. In the middle, however, there is another aspect,
which corresponds to what Gentiles would call the "natural law." It is here
that Jews and Gentiles meet on common ground, and that the inadequacy
of both their traditions is exposed. For the natural law, whether it is given to
Jews through Moses or to Gentiles through some other lawgiver, is still time-
bound and therefore defective on the key point of salvation. Jews who boast

in the law and claim superiority to the Gentiles because of it may have some reason to do so, but from the Christian point of view, both Jews and Gentiles stand on the same footing—they both need the saving power of God's grace, which can be dispensed only by eternal, spiritual means.

The Christian revelation of the righteousness of God is in fact a revelation of the first aspect of the Jewish law, which focuses on God's divinity. Unfortunately, the Jews had obscured this aspect of their law by concentrating too much on those parts of it that are purely temporal and ceremonial. They even believed that it was these ceremonies that made them superior to the Gentiles, when in fact the true greatness of the law was all along being obscured. Knowledge of God's divinity was precisely what the Gentiles did *not* have, but until Christ came, the Jews were blind to this aspect of their law and so failed to realize what its true merits were. The apostle Paul could therefore weigh in with both a condemnation of the law and an affirmation of its greatness. The condemnation applies to the third aspect (rites and ceremonies), and the affirmation to the first (the nature of God). By arguing in this way, Paul could overturn Judaism as it actually was, while at the same time insisting that he was doing no more than uncovering the law's true greatness. For when the nature of God's divinity is understood, the only meaningful response is one of faith—absolute trust and dependence on him for salvation. In this way, says Ambrosiaster, Paul was able to claim that the law contained the principle of faith within itself, depriving the Jews of any excuse for not having known that fact. There is therefore no contradiction in the law between justification by works and justification by faith, since the law contains only the latter. It was only because the Jews regarded the third and most inferior aspect of the law as its highest and most fundamental point that they were led to develop the belief that they could be saved by their works.

Ambrosiaster is as clear as can be that faith is not only incompatible with works, it is also the only basis for our salvation. As he describes believers, whom he calls the saints: "They are justified freely because they have not done anything nor given anything in return, but by faith alone they have been made holy by the gift of God" (Rom. 3:24). Later in the commentary, he discusses the place of good works in the Christian life, and it is quite clear that they are the works intended for those who have already been made righteous by faith; in no sense can they be regarded as meritorious in their own right (Rom. 6:13).

His Doctrine of the Cross

Ambrosiaster is also much clearer and more detailed than other ancient commentators when it comes to describing the nature of Christ's atoning death, which he describes as a nullification of the sentence of death that had been passed on the human race because of sin. Like most patristic writers, Ambrosiaster speaks in what today would be regarded as universalist terms. Christ died for the entire human race, both those on earth and those in hell. Of course, this must be understood in context. What Ambrosiaster is trying to say is that salvation is now offered to the Gentiles as well as to the Jews, and it is in that sense that it is universal. But he also specifies that it is given only to those who believe, which saves him from universalism as we would now understand it (Rom. 3:25). This is made quite clear later in the commentary, when Ambrosiaster refers to the universalists of his time and says quite specifically: "Some people think that because the condemnation was universal, the acquittal will also be universal. But this is not so, because not everyone believes" (Rom. 5:18).

It is important to understand that for Ambrosiaster, it was the sentence of death that was nullified by Christ's sacrifice, not the law as such. He brings this out in his commentary on Romans 3:31, where he says that the nullification of the sentence entails the fulfillment of the law, because the law contained that promise within it. Therefore, the obsolescence of the law follows naturally from its having been fulfilled in Christ, and is not the result of its own inadequacy. Ambrosiaster goes on to add that it is impossible to earn merit for keeping the law, whether it be the law of Moses or the law of nature. Keeping the law is an obligation, and so the one who does it is merely paying off his debt to God, not earning extra merit with him. Faith is superior to this because it is not an obligation, but a choice. Nobody is forced to believe, but the person who does so has made the right decision, and it is this rightness that glorifies God.

Moreover, faith is so powerful that it can justify even Gentiles who are bound by sin and cut off from the law, so that they cannot obey it even if they want to. But if faith can overcome this problem and justify even a Gentile, what further need is there for the law? However good it may be in itself, in practice it is merely a barrier to salvation, which ought to be dispensed with before it can cut even more people off from the Savior. The law says that there are different kinds of sin, of which the first is denial of the Creator. The second kind covers the more serious sinful acts, and the third the less serious, a distinction that would later give rise to the classic medieval distinction between "mortal" and "venial" sins. But faith in Christ wipes away all three kinds of sin, so that the distinction between them no longer matters. As Ambrosiaster puts it, Christ is sufficient to meet every human need, however great or serious that need may seem to mere mortal observers (Rom. 4:11).

Law, Wrath, and Faith

Unlike some other ancient commentators, and notably Origen, Ambrosiaster has no hesitation about affirming that the law of Moses brought wrath into the world (Rom. 4:15). He makes it clear that he does not regard the law as *being* wrath, but only as *bringing* it, because it lays down what the punishment for sin will be. Conversely, once the guilty have been removed from the law's power and have been forgiven, the transgression has been wiped out and there is no more room for wrath. Note that what we today see as applying to the time before the giving of the law, Ambrosiaster understands as referring to the present age, after the coming of Christ. The reason for this is that, with the abolition of the law of Moses, the faith of Abraham is once more relevant to the believer. His faith, without the works of the law, rests on the same foundation as our faith, and that similarity makes us his children and heirs of his promise. Furthermore, Ambrosiaster is quite clear that the greatness of Abraham's faith was that he believed the impossible, viz., that he would have a son when his wife was past childbearing age. The resurrection of Jesus Christ is also "impossible" in this sense, because it too goes against the law of nature. But that is what true faith is. Nature is no barrier to God, and those who believe in him will all transcend it—first, by not living according to the flesh in this life, and next, by being born again with a new, spiritual body in the next world. Impossible for us, says Ambrosiaster, but perfectly normal and natural for God!

The belief that the law belongs to this world but faith to the next is fundamental to Ambrosiaster's interpretation of Romans and determines his whole approach to chapters 5 to 8. It is the key to understanding how he views Christ's sacrificial death and the benefit that has accrued to us as a result. The Son of God came into the world to take on the burden of the law, to pay the price for our sins and to make it possible for us to rise with him into his heavenly kingdom. Ambrosiaster says that if Jesus did as much for us when we were still sinners, how much more will he do for us now that we have been saved? The blessings that will be given to the righteous stand in the same relationship to the blessings we have already received as heaven does to earth, or as faith does to the law.

The fundamental distinction between law and faith also determines his approach to the famous Romans 5:12. Ambrosiaster was apparently the first person to say that the human race sinned in Adam as in a "lump," the so-called *massa damnata*, which became a staple of medieval thought after it was picked up by Augustine. But Ambrosiaster believed that the sin of Adam led only to physical death, because to his mind it was a transgression of an earthly law. Elsewhere (Rom. 6:12) he states that if Adam had not sinned, he would have lived forever, because he would have been immortal by nature. He therefore interprets what we would call original sin to mean that by Adam's sin, the human race has lost its original nature and become mortal. But he adds that there is a second death, the one that is spiritual. As he says:

> Death is the separation of body and soul. There is another death as well, called the second death, which takes place in Gehenna. We do not suffer this death as a result of Adam's sin, but his fall makes it possible for us to get it by our own sins. Good men were protected from this, as they were only in Hades, though they were still not free, because they could not ascend to heaven. They were still bound by the sentence meted out in Adam, the seal of which was broken by the death of Christ. The sentence passed on Adam was that the human body would decompose on earth, but the soul would be bound by the chains of Hades until it was released.

It is hardly necessary to add that this interpretation raises more questions than it answers. Who, for example, were the "good" men, and what was it that entitled them to that designation? Are we really to believe that Adam's sin did not have eternal, spiritual consequences? And are we on the verge of an incipient doctrine of limited atonement, according to which Christ would have died for those in Hades, but not for those in Gehenna? Ambrosiaster left these questions dangling; they probably never occurred to him. But even Augustine could not leave matters there, and although he picked up Ambrosiaster's notion of the *massa damnata,* he was forced to rework it in a way that would bring spiritual consequences to bear on Adam's sin. Ambrosiaster's analysis was to prove fruitful, but mainly because it invited those who came after him to turn it inside-out in order to make sense of it.

Another very curious conclusion that Ambrosiaster draws, still following his basic division between heaven and earth, is that before the coming of the law, mankind would not be punished for its sins against God, because people were unaware of them, but they would be punished for sins against each other, since they had the natural law, which told them that what they were doing was wrong. Yet punishment for breaking the natural law was not eternal, because the natural law itself was not eternal. Thus Paul could say that when the law came, sin sprang to life and he died, because he was talking about sin against God, which brought eternal death, and not sin against one's neighbor, which incurred only temporal punishment (Rom. 5:13). It is a curious notion to our minds, but a salutary reminder of how a preconceived theory can distort our exposition of particular passages of scripture if we allow it to control our interpretation.

Sin and Guilt

Ambrosiaster was unique in the ancient world in his appreciation of the deeper issue raised by Romans 5:12–14: the underlying question was whether Adam's sin was the prototype of ours or not. If it was, then the reign of death that we now experience is both logical and inevitable, since we have all died in Adam. But if it was not, we have to try to explain how it is that death reigns even over those who have not sinned in the way that Adam did. Must we argue, as Ambrosiaster claimed, that Satan extended his sway to cover those who had not sinned in the way that Adam had, because his jealousy would not allow them to escape his clutches?

We can see, of course, that the issue is between the concept of a universally inherited sin and guilt, which Western Christianity has come to accept as orthodox, and particular sin and guilt, which each person falls into because of Adam's disobedience but which are the personal responsibility of each individual, and not something inherited from Adam. This view, which was based on the Greek text, has become the standard Eastern Orthodox interpretation, and Ambrosiaster is a witness to the fact that this divergence already existed in the mid-fourth century. He interprets it as follows:

> There is a textual difference between the Latin and some of the Greek manuscripts. The Latin says that death reigned over those whose sins were like the sin of Adam, but some Greek manuscripts say that death reigned even over those whose sins were *not* like Adam's. Which of the two readings is the correct one? What has happened is that somebody who could not win his argument altered the words of the text in order to make them say what he wanted them to say, so that not argument but textual authority would determine the issue. However, it is known that there were Latin-speakers who translated ancient Greek manuscripts which preserved an uncorrupted version from earlier times. But once these problems were raised by heretics and schismatics who were upsetting the harmony of the church, many things were altered so that the Biblical text might conform to what people wanted. Thus even the Greeks have different readings in their manuscripts. I consider the correct reading to be the one which reason, history and authority all retain. For the reading of the modern Latin manuscripts is also found in Tertullian, Victorinus and Cyprian.

In other words, the doctrine of inherited sin and guilt is the true one, which got corrupted in the Greek textual tradition because of heretical influence. Ambrosiaster does not say it, but the subtext here is that heresy is a Greek thing, not present in the Latin world. The Romans have preserved the faith as they received it, and since they received it from the apostles, it has been preserved in all its original purity. This anti-Greek stance was

common in the Roman world and was to be a factor in church relations
into modern times. Today we can take a more dispassionate view of the
matter, but although the textual argument has been resolved in favor of
the Greeks, the Western churches have not followed them in the theology
that they have based on it. Instead, they have continued to prefer the view
expounded by Ambrosiaster, basing it on the broader logic of scripture
and not on the testimony of a single verse in Romans.

Lastly, Ambrosiaster believed that God gave the law in order to show
Satan who was boss. As the prince of this world, Satan believed that he
had complete control over the destinies of his subjects, the human race,
but God intervened to demonstrate that this was not the case. In doing
so, he actually caused sin to abound all the more, since those who were
in bondage to Satan merely reacted against this intrusion and rejected
it (Rom. 5:20)! Once again, the fatal flaw in Ambrosiaster's argument is
his insistence that the law belongs exclusively to the temporal sphere,
so that its spiritual character refers only to its divine origin, and not
to its eschatological purpose—a consistent error that shapes his whole
presentation of the subject.

The Christian Life

When he turns to a discussion of the nature of the new life we have in
Christ, Ambrosiaster does little more than follow the standard lines laid
down in antiquity and followed by virtually all the fathers of the church.
Baptism is the death of the old man and the beginning of the new life in
which we are being transformed into the likeness of Christ in a spiritual
sense. We cannot become God by nature, but by grace we can act in the
way that God wants us to, which for Ambrosiaster is the sum of Christian obedience. He recognizes (Rom. 6:11) that it is necessary to read
the word *flesh* in two different ways, as both a physical and a spiritual
principle, and assumes that it will be clear from the context which sense
is intended. Nowadays we might think that this is a bold assumption to
make, but there was a common understanding of the matter in ancient
times, and Ambrosiaster never questions or deviates from it.

In discussing the Christian life, Ambrosiaster makes the interesting observation that the apostle Paul told the Romans to protect their
members, rather than their whole bodies, against the wiles of the devil
(Rom. 6:13), because the devil no longer has complete control over us.
He still has power to use parts of us for his purposes, but not the whole.
Later on, Ambrosiaster nuanced this by saying, along with Paul, that
our bodies must become a living sacrifice, but even so, he insisted that
this was because the sins of the body had to be put to death; the body

was not to be regarded as sinful in itself (Rom. 12:1). This is an important distinction, because it shows that Ambrosiaster was well aware of the Platonic notion that all matter is essentially evil, and also that he rejected it. Elsewhere in his commentary he returns to this theme and develops it more carefully (Rom. 7:18). He says:

> Paul does not say that the flesh is evil, as some think, but that what dwells in the flesh is not good, i.e., sin. How does sin dwell in the flesh when it is not a substance, but the perversion of what is good? Since the body of the first man was corrupted by sin and became dissolvable, this same corruption of sin remains in the body because of the state of transgression, retaining the strength of the divine judgment given in Adam, which is the sign of the Devil, at whose prompting Adam sinned. Because of this, sin is said to dwell in the flesh, to which the Devil comes as if to his own kingdom. For the flesh is sinful and sin remains in it in order to deceive man by evil temptations, so that man will not do what the law commands.

However, he goes on to add that a Christian who sins falls back under the power of the law, showing that he believes that the only way to escape the law's power is by leading a sinless life, something that he clearly believed was not only possible, but normal for believers. Ambrosiaster is even capable of saying that the mind delights in the teachings of the law, because sin does not dwell in the mind but in the flesh (Rom. 7:22). For him, the spiritual struggle of the Christian is between an outer self, the flesh or the members of the body, which are subject to sin, and the mind, which is naturally equipped with the law of God, but which is subjected to constant pressure from the flesh (Rom. 7:23). Furthermore, for him, the "law of God" could mean either the law of Moses or the law of Christ, or even the law of nature, implanted in man by God at the creation.

Ambrosiaster uses Romans 13 as an opportunity to emphasize the last of these, and says that God had gone so far as to delegate the administration of his law to human authorities—including those who did not know or acknowledge him. For Ambrosiaster, Paul's commands in that chapter were merely a way of bringing the natural law into conformity with the revelation of the gospel, by emphasizing that in the new dispensation, the divine love that underpinned the whole system was to be shown to our enemies as well as to our friends and neighbors (Rom. 13:10). It was therefore theoretically possible to avoid sin, merely by the right kind of mental exertion. This shows that his concept of sin was essentially legalistic and superficial, and reveals that his thinking was basically that of a Roman magistrate. Nevertheless, he does understand that the law does not create sin but merely reveals what is already there. The law was given to those who were living under the power of the devil, as a way of demonstrating to them just how far from God's will they were.

The fact that it condemned sinners to death shows how righteous it was, because the punishment was fully justified. The only thing wrong with it was that it could do nothing to save its victims, and therefore it appeared to be a curse, rather than a blessing (Rom. 7:6).

For this reason, it was necessary to move on from the law of Moses to the law of the Spirit of life, which sets us free from the law of sin and death and gives us a sense of security that we will not sin (Rom. 8:2). To effect this change, God sent his Son in the "likeness" of sinful flesh (Rom. 8:3), which Ambrosiaster interprets to mean that Christ came with a body like that of Adam before the fall. The devil could attack this body and even put it to death, but because it had not sinned and did not deserve death, the body of Christ came back from the dead, triumphing over sin and the devil as it did so. It was in this sense that God condemned sin in the flesh, making it possible for us to be forgiven the sins of our flesh and to become friends of the law. The Christian who has been set free from sin can use his mind to observe the law of God in its fullness. This is what Ambrosiaster understands by walking according to the Spirit, and not according to the flesh (Rom. 8:4).

Predestination

On the vexed subject of predestination, Ambrosiaster shows himself to have been fully "Augustinian" *avant la lettre*. He accepts that the destruction of large numbers of Jews was foreordained and says that although Paul grieved for them, his grief was limited by that knowledge (Rom. 9:13). As Ambrosiaster puts it:

> There was no point in grieving over those who were not predestined to eternal life, for God's foreknowledge had long ago decreed that they would not be saved. For who would cry over someone who is long dead? When the Gentiles appeared and accepted the salvation which the Jews had lost, Paul's grief was stirred, but this was mainly because they were the cause of their own damnation.

In working this out, Ambrosiaster made a crucial distinction between God's justice and his foreknowledge. To illustrate the difference, he used the words of Jesus in Luke 10:20, addressed to the seventy-two disciples who later abandoned him. Jesus said to them: "Your names are written in heaven." Ambrosiaster claimed that this was just, since the seventy-two were good people who deserved their reward. But they fell away, and so, as God said to Moses: "If someone sins against me, I shall delete him from my book" (Exod. 32:33). Having one's name written in heaven was therefore no guarantee of ultimate salvation, and God knew before-hand whose names he would have to delete from the heavenly roll. Thus Ambrosiaster managed to accommodate not only those who were saved, but more importantly, from a pastoral point of view, those who initially appeared to be saved but who later fell away. That too was foreordained by God and was fully consonant with his justice, which punished the apostasy of the privileged even more than the unbelief of the ignorant.

In the case of the Jews, however, the logic of predestination worked the opposite way, and ultimately in their favor. The unbelief into which the Jews have now fallen is not permanent. Ambrosiaster distinguished two different kinds of blindness, the temporary and the permanent, and claimed that Paul taught that it was the second kind that afflicted the Jews (Rom. 11:8). Their blindness was not so severe as to preclude their ultimate conversion, and when that happened the world would be a better place for it. He interpreted their present plight as a kind of purgatory, in which they were working off the sin that they had incurred by rejecting Christ. When that sin was fully paid for, they would recover the free exercise of their will and be reconciled to God (Rom. 11:15). Ambrosiaster went on to insist that the unbelief of the Jews, though it provided an opportunity for the conversion of the Gentiles, was not primarily intended for that purpose. God condemned the Jews not in order to save Gentiles, but because his justice had to punish their unbelief. Therefore, although Gentiles have benefited from the condemnation, they have no grounds for boasting and no right to insult the unfortunate Jews because of it. In saying this, Ambrosiaster reveals that his anti-semitism, if that is the word for it, was strictly theological and applied only to Judaism insofar as it had rejected Christ. Jews themselves were to be pitied, and every effort to win them for their Savior was to be encouraged. In particular, the seriousness of their sin was no barrier to the grace of God, which could—and would—overcome it (Rom. 11:28–9).

Conclusion

It is not necessary to delve into Ambrosiaster's remarks on the last chapters of Romans, with their practical exhortations and list of believers in the Roman church. There is nothing in what he says about these things that stands out as exceptional, and everything he says may be regarded as more or less standard, both then and now. For example, he has no difficulty with the controversy over the Jewish food laws, believing that Christians are free to eat anything, but that to eat something against one's better judgment is wrong. The Jews of his day continued to observe the laws of *kashrut,* of course, as they still do, but since the controversy was no longer a matter that divided the church, it could be passed over with little comment. On the members of the Roman church listed in chapter 16, Ambrosiaster has nothing to say that does not come from the text itself; like other ancient commentators, he had no inside knowledge of who these people were and is reduced to speculation, just as we are.

In conclusion, therefore, it can be said that Ambrosiaster had a clear picture in his mind of what Romans was all about, and that he developed this consistently in his commentary. Fundamentally, it was a book about the law of God, which had been given to man in two forms—one through Moses, to the Jews, and the other through nature, to the Gentiles. In both cases, the law had the effect of defining human sin more clearly, and therefore of increasing human guilt and the condemnation that inevitably followed it. Christ had come to fulfill both laws, and in doing so, he had transcended both of them. The Christian now has the law of the Spirit of life living in him, and this new law makes it possible to stop sinning altogether. The main difficulty that the believer now faces is the temptation to fall back under one or another of the earlier laws, and so to be captured by sin once more. He must therefore rely on the Spirit of God, who has been poured out into his heart, and have faith in the God who has justified him in and through Christ. He must also understand that his salvation is part of God's plan, which will eventually reconcile both Jews and Gentiles, though at the same time he must not presume on God's goodness. Even those whose names are written in the Lamb's Book of Life can be struck off, if they fall away, and the only assurance we have comes from a constant and total obedience to Christ's commands.

On exegetical points, Ambrosiaster is often perceptive, but with occasional lapses, as we have seen. However, it is as a theologian that he stands out, not as an exegete. His systematic approach to Romans set a model for Augustine and the later Western tradition, even if some of his solutions to apparent difficulties raised more questions than they answered. Modern readers will naturally want to go further than he did, and discuss any number of points that he either glossed over or answered unsatisfactorily. But at the same time, it is clear that Ambrosiaster stands at the head of the tradition of scriptural commentary that we have inherited. His continuing place in any study of Romans is well deserved, and his thoughts continue to stimulate us even after so many centuries. That is his greatness, and the main reason that his contribution deserves to be remembered and honored in the life of the church today.

3

JOHN CHRYSOSTOM

Christopher A. Hall

St. John Chrysostom deeply loved the apostle Paul. Paul is the "spiritual trumpet" whose music rouses and warms Chrysostom's desire. For Chrysostom, to read Paul's epistles is to recognize "the voice so dear to me," "to fancy" Paul as "all but present to my sight, and to behold him conversing with me."[1] Hence, as Chrysostom begins his series of homilies on Paul's Epistle to the Romans, probably preached in Antioch, he exhorts his audience to listen more carefully to the voice of the apostle. "But I grieve and am pained, that all people do not know this man, as much as they ought to know him; but some are so far ignorant, as not even to know for certainty the number of his Epistles."[2]

Chrysostom inaugurates his sermons on Romans much like a modern scholar might, commenting on the date of the Roman letter and its place in the chronology of Paul's writing. For instance, Chrysostom observes that "it is not, as most think, before all the others, but before all that were written from Rome, yet subsequent to the rest, though not to all

1. John Chrysostom, "The Argument," in *Homilies on the Epistle of St. Paul the Apostle to the Romans*, A Select Library of the Nicene and Post-Nicene Fathers of the Christian Church (NPNF) 11, vol. 1 (Grand Rapids: Eerdmans, 1980), 335.
2. Ibid.

ōf thēm.   Ïhē Lōrïnthïan cōrrēspōndence, for example, Chrysostom
reckons to be earlier than Romans.[3]

The Grace of God

As we move into the main body of the homilies on Romans, a number
of significant themes begin to emerge. Think, for instance, of the grace
of God. In his extended discussion of Paul's character and apostleship,
Chrysostom emphasizes that Paul's calling as an apostle was rooted
in the grace of God, as was true of all the apostles (Rom. 1:5). "For
it was not by having toiled much and labored much that we had this
dignity allotted to us, but we received grace (ἀλλὰ χάριν ἐλάβομεν), and
the successful result is a part of the heavenly gift. . . . It was not the
Apostles that achieved it, but grace paved the way before them (ἀλλ᾽ ἡ
προοδοποιοῦσα χάρις αὐτοῖς). For it was their part to go about and preach,
but to persuade was of God, who worked in them."[4] Just as the apostles
were called in grace, so were the Roman Christians. "For even you were
called and did not come over of yourselves" (καὶ γὰρ ὑμεις ἐκλήθητε, καὶ
οὐκ ἀφ᾽ ἑαυτῶν προσήλθετε).[5]

Chrysostom reiterates the importance of grace as he ponders Paul's
desire to "impart" to the Roman church "some spiritual gift" so that
they might be deeply "established" (Rom. 1:11). "This then also comes
of grace," (Ἄρα καὶ τοῦτο χάριτος) John comments, "namely, the being
unwavering and standing fast."[6] Yet, grace and human freedom are
inextricably linked in John's thinking. Yes, the Roman community will
remain firmly established because of God's grace, but they must not
think grace displaces the need for "our part." The "labor of resolve" (τὸν
ἐκ τῆς προαιρέσεως πόνον) is still necessary. "Do not become apathetic,
then, because Paul has called this a gift of grace. For he knows how, in
his great candor, to call even good deeds, graces; because even in these
we need much influence from above."[7] In the same way, Paul's voice
as an apostle effectively "shone forth above the sun, and he abounded
more than all the rest in the word of doctrine," because "he labored more
abundantly than they" and by doing so "also drew upon himself a large

3. Ibid., 336.
4. Ibid., 340, Homily 1.
5. Ibid., 342. Cf. PG 60.400D. Chrysostom comments: "Strange! How mighty is the
love of God! We which were enemies and disgraced, have all at once become saints and
sons."
6. Ibid., 345, Homily 2.
7. Ibid., 345. I have slightly modified the NPNF translation.

measure of the Spirit's grace" (ἐπειδὴ γὰρ περισσότερον αὐτῶν ἐκοπίασε, πολλὴν καὶ τὴν τοῦ Πνεύματος ἐπεσπάσατο χάριν).[8]

Interesting, too, will be Chrysostom's treatment of Paul's argument in Romans 9 that the potter possesses the right to form the clay into whatever shape he chooses. Already in his second homily Chrysostom highlights a consistent theme he will develop tirelessly (Rom. 1:13). Do not pry into matters that are too high for human understanding! To attempt to plumb the depths of God's wisdom and inscrutable providence will only lead to spiritual and exegetical disaster. Paul had often desired to visit the Romans, but God's providence had prevented him from doing so. Paul, Chrysostom comments, wisely yielded "to the incomprehensibleness of Providence, thereby both showing the right tone of his soul, and instructing us all never to call God to account for what happens, even though what is done seem to trouble the minds of many."[9] After all, "shall the thing formed say to him that formed it, 'Why have you made me thus?'" (Romans 9). Indeed, Chrysostom insists, "a main feature of faith" is the willingness to accept what God chooses to reveal and not reveal of his providential purposes.[10]

Gentile and Jewish Sin

As Chrysostom moves into Paul's analysis of the dynamics of Gentile and Jewish sin in Romans 1–2, he emphasizes that God had placed the knowledge of himself within human beings "from the beginning." God had paraded this knowledge before humanity in creation itself, "so that both wise, and unlearned, and Scythian, and barbarian, having through sight learned the beauty of the things which were seen, might mount up to God."[11] The "order," "beauty," and "grandeur" of creation were purposely designed to bring human beings to the knowledge of God. Humanity, though, through the misuse of its reason, had descended into idolatry. Reason misused had turned everything upside-down. Conceptions of God that humanity "ought to have had," such as that "he is God, that he is Lord of all, that he made them which were not, that he exercises a providence," had dissipated in the "darkness" of human reasoning. The result was a disastrous search for the incorporeal God in the corporeal bodies of idols, "a most rueful shipwreck."[12]

8. Ibid., 335.
9. Ibid., 346, Homily 2.
10. Ibid., 347.
11. Ibid., 352.
12. Ibid., 352–53.

God had done more than enough to provide human beings with the guideposts to knowledge of the divine. The world itself was "a form of doctrine." In addition, God "gave them reason, and an understanding capable of perceiving what was needful." Humanity had possessed, Chrysostom is convinced, both the innate rational capacity and surrounding environment for cultivating the knowledge of God. What God would not do, however, was to force this knowledge upon human beings. How could God do so? Coercion and "force" would rob us of the possibility of cultivating virtue.[13]

Chrysostom then turns his attention to the Jews in his interpretation of Romans 2. Noting Paul's words that "there will be anguish and distress for everyone who does evil, the Jew first and also the Greek" (Rom. 2:9), Chrysostom comments that neither social class nor national background offers a wall of protection against God's judgment. Humanity's "disease" is great, caused by "the carelessness of the disordered." Chrysostom believes the remedy is "easy," but the punishment severe. As for the Jews, they will receive an even more severe punishment than the Gentiles, precisely because they have received a "larger share of instruction." "The wiser or mightier people we are, the more are we punished if we sin. For if you are rich, you will have more money demanded of you than of the poor; and if wiser than others, a stricter obedience; and if you have been invested with authority, more shining acts of goodness; and so in the case of all the other things, you will have to bring in measures proportioned to your power."[14]

Chrysostom asks what Paul means when he speaks of glory, honor, and peace coming to those who work good, to "the Jew first, and also to the Greek" (Rom. 2:10). Somewhat surprisingly, Chrysostom argues that Paul is pointing back to the Jews and Gentiles who had lived "before Christ's coming." At this point in the letter to the Romans, Paul has not yet "come to the times of grace, but . . . was still dwelling upon the earlier times." Why? Paul wanted to show that even in the earliest periods of Jewish and Gentile history, God had dealt with Jews and Gentiles on exactly the same basis. "For if in the earlier times when this grace had not shone forth in such greatness, when the estate of the Jews was solemn and renowned and glorious before all people, there was no difference, what could they say for themselves now after so great a display of grace?"[15]

There had always been, for instance, Gentiles who had "adored God" and "obeyed the law of nature, who strictly kept all things, except for

13. Ibid., 354.
14. Ibid., 562–63, Homily 5. Cf. PG 60.426B. I have slightly modified the translation.
15. Ibid., 363.

the Jewish observances." People such as Melchizedek, Job, the Ninevites, and more recently Cornelius were apt examples. The distinction between the circumcised and uncircumcised had already been severed from afar, and would be made even more clearly in the present. The issue of the genuinely circumcised and uncircumcised had never been, at least in Chrysostom's interpretation of Paul, one of national identity. Rather, the key issue was obedience. Thus, the Jew who led a disobedient life had no advantage over the obedient Gentile, for "it is upon works that both punishment and reward depend, not upon circumcision and uncircumcision."[16]

Chrysostom agrees that Gentiles experience God's judgment because of their refusal to amend their lives in light of the teaching of nature and reason. Jews, though, experience an even greater judgment, because they possess an additional revelation, that of God's law. If the Jew is apt to condemn Gentile sins, how much more so is the Jew liable to the same judgment? "For here, as I said before, Paul shows not only the equality of the Jew and the Gentile, but that the Jew was even deeply burdened by the gift of the Law." What is the key principle? The greater attention and benefit one receives from God, the greater the punishment if obedience fails to result. "See how much greater is the necessity which he lays upon the Jews of a speedy recourse to grace! For in that they said, they did not need grace, being justified by the Law, he shows that they need it more than the Gentiles, considering they are liable to be punished more."[17]

Yes, "circumcision truly profits, if you keep the law. If you break the law, your circumcision has become uncircumcision" (Rom. 2:25). Chrysostom understands Paul to be speaking of two circumcisions, two uncircumcisions, and two laws. There is, for example, a "natural law" and a "written law." In fact, Chrysostom refers quickly to a third law, that of "works." When the Gentiles, who do not have the written law, do by nature the things of the law, they are obeying the "law of works." They are "a law to themselves" by "using the natural law" and by doing so demonstrate their obedience to the law of works or "actions." "For that which is by writing lies outside; but this is within, the natural one, and the other is in actions."[18] In short, the first two laws, the written law and the law of nature, exist for the sake of the law of works. Apart from the existence of the third law of works or actions, the operation of the first two laws is actually harmful, inevitably bringing punishment.

16. Ibid.
17. Ibid., 364.
18. Ibid., 370, Homily 6.

What of the two uncircumcisions and the two circumcisions? As for the two uncircumcisions, one is from nature and the other from conduct. In the same pattern, there is a circumcision of the body and a circumcision of the will (ἡ ἀπὸ προαιρὲσεως).[19] Paul does not reject circumcision in itself, Chrysostom believes, but rather the Jew who is physically circumcised but rejects the obedience required by the law. Thus, we can clearly have the possibility of a Gentile who is uncircumcised by nature but circumcised in the will as demonstrated by obedience, and a Jew who is circumcised in nature but uncircumcised in will. In the latter case, circumcision has become uncircumcision. In a word, for Chrysostom circumcision equals obedience; "circumcision is well doing and uncircumcision is evil doing."[20]

When Paul writes that he is a Jew who "is one inwardly; and circumcision is that of the heart, in the spirit, and not in the letter" (Rom. 2:29 KJV), Chrysostom understands Paul to be explicitly setting aside "the sabbaths and the sacrifices and purifications" of Judaism. He is paving "the way for the conduct of the Church" on the basis of faith.[21] The only thing that matters, for both Jew and Gentile, is faith leading to an obedient life. As Chrysostom puts it, ". . . when this is agreed upon, of necessity the circumcision of the flesh is set aside, and the need of a good life is everywhere demonstrated."[22] Chrysostom acknowledges that Paul underscores the many "advantages" given the Jews by God (Rom. 3:1–2), but sees these as only increasing their punishment because of Jewish unbelief. All the gifts given to the Jews were gifts of grace. What is the true fundamental principle for Chrysostom? Grace must lead to obedience. The two are inseparable. If grace fails to engender obedience, judgment is the inevitable result.

Paul has clearly demonstrated that both Jew and Gentile are in need of God's grace, for both are equally sinful. "He had accused the Gentiles, he had accused the Jews; it came next in order to mention the righteousness which is by faith (τὴν δικαιοσὺνην λοιπὸν τὴν διὰ τῆς πὶστεως). For if the law of nature availed not, and the written Law was of no advantage, but both weighed down those that used them wrongly, and made it plain that they were worthy of greater punishment, then after this the salvation which is by grace was necessary" (ἀναγκαία λοιπὸν ἡ διὰ τῆς χάριτος σωτηρία).[23] Paul's argument is specifically designed to pave the way for faith. "So close is the relationship of the Old Testament with

19. Ibid., 370.
20. Ibid.
21. Ibid., 371.
22. Ibid.
23. Ibid., 375, Homily 7.

the New, since even the accusations and reproofs were entirely with a view to this, that the door of faith might open brightly upon them that hear it."[24] All have disobeyed. All are guilty. All "need the assistance of another, and such was the plight of all of us, in that we had lost the things pertaining to salvation."[25]

Justification by Faith

How, then, can one escape the "vengeance" of God? Chrysostom observes "two high points" in Paul's presentation: we can be justified by faith and obtain this blessing "without the law," principles that Chrysostom understands to be operative under both the old and new covenants.[26] Chrysostom carefully lists the "proofs" of God's love manifested in Jesus Christ:

1. We can know we are justified and redeemed on the basis of the "worthiness" of the source of our redemption and righteousness, God himself.
2. The law and prophets attest to God's love toward humanity as manifested in salvation "without the law."
3. The sacrifices "under the old dispensation" point toward the greater efficacy of the sacrifice offered by Christ. "For if the sacrifices of things without reason . . . cleared from sin, much more would this blood. And he does not say barely λυτρώσεως but ἀπολυτρώσεως, entire redemption . . . for this same reason he calls it a propitiation, to show that if the type had such force, much more would the reality display the same."[27]

Chrysostom then asks a key question: what does Paul mean when he declares the righteousness of God? Chrysostom makes a number of comparisons to capture the meaning of Paul's statement: God is rich and can make other people rich. God is alive and can "make the dead to live." God is powerful and can "make the feeble powerful." Paul declares God's righteousness, "not only that He is Himself righteous, but that He does also make them that are filled with the putrefying sores of sin suddenly righteous." It is to explain this dynamic of salvation, "viz. what is 'declaring,' that he has added, 'That he might be just, and the

24. Ibid., 376.
25. Ibid.
26. Ibid., 377.
27. Ibid.

justifier of him who believes in Jesus.'" How so? ". . . it is not of works,
but of faith . . . for it is a blessing in two ways; because it is easy, and
also open to all people."[28]

Interestingly, Chrysostom warns his audience not to be "abashed"
or "shamefaced" over the salvation offered to them, as though the ease
or simplicity of salvation was beneath them. For if God finds delight
in the redemption he offers, why wouldn't those who receive it? God
had acted on humanity's behalf when "there was no longer any hope
of recovering health, but as the paralyzed body needed the hand from
above, so does the soul which has been deadened." Indeed, at the very
point when we had given ourselves over to sin and fully deserved God
to pronounce sentence against us, when our sins "were in their full, God
displayed His own power, that we might learn how great is the abundance
of righteousness with Him."[29] All are convicted of sin. All are saved by
grace. God "had waited a long time" to accomplish fully his salvation,
precisely to demonstrate humanity's "inability to help themselves." God
"then saved them by His grace." What is "the law of faith" (Rom. 3:27)?
"It is being saved by grace (Διὰ χάριτος σώζεσθαι). Here Paul magnifies
God's power, in that He has not only saved, but has even justified (ἀλλὰ
καὶ ἐδικαίωσε), and led them to boasting, and this too without needing
works, but looking to faith only" (πίστιν ζητήσας μόνον).[30]

Chrysostom sums up Paul's argument in Romans 3 under three main
points:

1. One can be justified by faith "without the Law."
2. The law itself could justify no one.
3. Faith is not opposed to the law.[31]

The great patriarch Abraham had himself modeled the fundamental
pattern of grace and faith. While the Jews looked to Abraham as the first
of those who were circumcised, Paul wished to "show that it was by faith
that he too was justified." Abraham is particularly noteworthy, because
he of all people had many good works. "But for a person richly adorned
with good deeds, not to be made just from hence, but from faith, this
is the thing to cause wonder, and to set the power of faith in a strong
light."[32] The pattern of Abraham's response of faith, one that occurred
before his circumcision, clearly demonstrated that his righteousness

28. Ibid., 378.
29. Ibid.
30. Ibid., 379.
31. Ibid., 380.
32. Ibid., 385, Homily 8.

before God was based on his faith rather than on his many good deeds. Why, then, was Abraham circumcised? Abraham's circumcision sets him off as father of both Jew and Gentile. "For he says that the reason Abraham received circumcision was that either of us two parties might have him for a forefather, and that those in the uncircumcision might not thrust aside those in the circumcision."[33]

προαίρεσις and the Chrysostomic Synergism

We now come to a crucial juncture in Chrysostom's interpretation of Paul. For both Paul and Chrysostom must answer the questions, "Why has sin continually troubled human existence? What is sin's source? And, of course, what of death?" Overarching all these questions is perhaps an even more fundamental one: what is a human being? Further, what enables a human being to respond to God, choose the good, reject evil, and live a life pleasing to God?

It is time to direct our attention to a fundamental aspect of Chrysostom's analysis of human nature, ability, and choice or προαίρεσις. Chrysostom, in his interpretation of Romans, and in the wider Chrysostomic corpus, is insistent that creation is good, and that the beauty and utility of creation demonstrate its goodness. Rather, the true source of evil is to be found in a perverted or disobedient choice or προαίρεσις. The classical definition of προαίρεσις was the choice of one thing in preference to another. Aristotle, as Edward Nowak observes, defined προαίρεσις as a choice formed by reflection and specifically referred to προαίρεσις as a choice between good and evil.[34] W. A. Oldfather normally translates Epictetus's use of προαίρεσις as "freedom of choice" or "moral purpose."[35]

Church fathers, particularly in the Eastern tradition, considered προαίρεσις a property and privilege of human nature. It is what distin-

33. Ibid., 388.
34. Cf. Edward Nowak, *Le chrétien devant la souffrance: Étude sur la pensée de Jean Chrysostome* (Paris: Beauchesne, 1972), 37. In my discussion of Chrysostom's understanding of προαίρεσις I am freely drawing upon my doctoral work found in Christopher A. Hall, *John Chrysostom's* On Providence: *A Translation and Theological Interpretation* (Ann Arbor: U.M.I., 1991), 17–49. I have also found Metropolitan Demetrios Trakatellis's comments on προαίρεσις in Chrysostom's exegesis of Romans to be quite helpful and am obligated to Metropolitan Trakatellis for his insights. See Metropolitan Demetrios Trakatellis, "Being Transformed: Chrysostom's Exegesis of the Epistle to the Romans," *Greek Orthodox Theological Review* 36, nos. 3–4 (1991): 215–18.
35. See Epictetus, *The Discourses*, vol. 1, trans. W. A. Oldfather (Cambridge: Harvard University Press, 1925), Book 1, 4.2; Book 1, 1.23; Book 1, 4.18.

guishes human beings from animals or inanimate beings. Nowak notes that προαίρεσις is opposed to both necessity (ἀναγκη) and astral determinism. Human προαίρεσις is associated with the act of sin and is that element which creates genuine moral responsibility for moral choices and actions. It is a human attribute that must be exercised for an act to be considered truly moral. Indeed, "virtue's web," Chrysostom writes in his homilies on Matthew, is woven from the interaction between our "willingness," human choice, and the grace of God: ". . . a man's willingness (προθυμιας) is not sufficient, unless any one receive the succor from above; and that again, we shall gain nothing by the succor from above, if there is not a willingness . . . For indeed of these two things is virtue's web woven."[36]

Chrysostom's comments on Matthew's Gospel clearly reflect a synergism that is also present throughout Chrysostom's exegesis of Romans. Metropolitan Demetrios Trakatellis draws our attention to a number of key comments in Chrysostom's exegesis where the synergism between the grace of God and the προαίρεσις of human beings is evident. For instance, Chrysostom comments on Romans 1:11: "When you hear of grace, think not that the reward of deliberate choice (προαιρέσεως μισθός) on our part is thereby cast aside; for Paul speaks of grace, not to disparage the labor of προαίρεσις, but to cut off the haughtiness which comes from an insolent spirit. Do not, therefore, fall back because Paul has called this a gift. For he uses, out of a fullness of gratitude, to call gifts even our achievements, because even in these we need a good deal of assistance from heaven."[37]

In Chrysostom's comments on Romans 1:18–25, he employs the example of Daniel as an illustration of the importance of exercising one's προαίρεσις well. "We also are attacked by lions in the form of anger and desires of passions, with fearful teeth tearing asunder those who fall among them. Become then like Daniel and let not these passions plant their teeth into your soul. But Daniel, you will object, had the whole of grace assisting him. Correct; (this happened) because προαίρεσις preceded grace. So that if we be willing to train ourselves to a similar character, even now the grace is at hand."[38] Grace, then, does not precede the exercise of προαίρεσις but works with it. Hence, Chrysostom's insistence in his exegesis of Romans and throughout almost all his works that the present life is an arena to be used for the strengthening of προαίρεσις.

36. John Chrysostom, *Homilies on the Gospel of Saint Matthew*, NPNF 4, vol. 10, First Series, 494–95; cf. PG 58.742D.
37. See Metropolitan Trakatellis's translation, "Being Transformed," 216.
38. Ibid.

Chrysostom's synergistic viewpoint is best understood against the broader background of his theological anthropology. He distinguishes προαίρεσις from the soul (ψυχή), body (σῶμα), and the will (βούλησις). In other words, the faculty of the will is to be distinguished from the event or act of willing, προαίρεσις itself. Chrysostom, for instance, comments in his thirteenth homily on Romans: "Now the essence of the soul and body and of that choice (προαίρεσις) are not the same, for the first two are God's works, and the other is a motion from ourselves towards whatever we please to direct it. For willing is indeed natural (ἔμφυτον), and is from God: but willing on this wise is our own, and from our own mind."[39]

The goal, then, of the Christian is to exercise, train, and cultivate the gifts God has given to us, that is, our soul, mind, body, and will, so that the good and true choice can be made in the midst of the perplexities and turmoils of this present life.

Chrysostom's comments on three key texts in Romans illustrate well his thoughts on προαίρεσις:

- On Romans 8:7–10—What is "walking in the Spirit"? "The gift (of the Spirit) was not put into us by natural necessity, but the freedom of choice (ἐλευθερία προαιρέσεως) placed it in our hands. It rests with you, therefore, to become this or that (i.e., to walk according to the Spirit or to walk according to the flesh)."[40]
- On Romans 9:22–23—"Whence they are some vessels of wrath and some vessels of mercy? Of their own free choice (ἀπὸ προαιρέσεως οἰκείας)." ". . . It is not on the potter that the honor and the dishonor of the things made of the lump depends, but on the use made by those that handle them, so here also it depends on the free choice" (ὅπερ οὖν καὶ ἐνταῦθα ἀπὸ τῆς προαιρέσεως).[41]
- On Romans 11:24—"When you hear the expression 'contrary to nature,' do not suppose that Paul means this nature which is unchangeable. . . . For the good things and the bad are not such by nature, but by opinion and deliberate choice alone" (γνώμης καὶ προαιρέσεως μόνης).[42]

If deliberate choice plays such a significant role, rather than nature itself, it should not surprise us that in Chrysostom's exegesis of Ro-

39. John Chrysostom, "Homily 13," in *The Epistle to the Romans*, 429; cf. PG 60.510C.

40. Trakatellis's translation, "Being Transformed," 217.

41. Ibid., 217–18.

42. Ibid., 218.

mans 5 he does not see the sin of Adam as fundamentally crippling or
distorting human nature itself. Rather, as we also see in Chrysostom's
comments on other Pauline Epistles, it is the προαίρεσις rather than
ούσία (human nature itself) that determines our ultimate destiny. For
instance, in Chrysostom's homilies on Colossians he states: "The moral
choice does rather determine one than the substance, and is rather
'man' than the other. For his substance casts him not into hell, nor
leads him into the kingdom, but men themselves."[43] To be free to choose
is to be fully human. If so, Chrysostom's insistence that human judgment and the underlying disposition that influences judgment must
be trained to view and respond to life in a healthy and life-promoting
manner—that is, to judge things correctly and not simply on the basis
of appearances—takes on greater coherence. Many aspects of human
suffering, Chrysostom is convinced, can be traced to ignorance, i.e.,
a failure to form a proper judgment concerning the affairs and circumstances of this life.[44]

Chrysostom's understanding of faith and its relationship to προαίρεσις
reflects a fundamental synergism. On the one hand, Chrysostom understands faith to be a contribution human beings make to salvation
itself. In his exegesis of Romans 3 Chrysostom writes: "In order that
no one should say, how can we be saved without ourselves contributing
anything, Paul demonstrates that we contribute no small matter toward
this, I mean faith."[45] He comments on Romans 5:21: "See how in all
instances God presents both what he does and what we do! On God's
part, however, there be things varied and numerous and diverse. . . .
What we contribute is only faith."[46] Metropolitan Trakatellis helpfully
reminds us of Chrysostom's comment in his exegesis of Romans 4: it is
"the one who believes" who "does much more than the one who works,
and that the one who believes needs much more power and abundant
strength and sustains no common degree of labor."[47]

What characterizes such faith? As Abraham responds in faith to God's
promises, he "displays sincere love," "the noblest soul," a "philosophic
spirit" or Christian disposition, and a "lofty mind." For "to believe that
it is possible for God to do things impossible requires a soul of no mean

43. John Chrysostom, "Homily 8," in *Homilies on Colossians*, NPNF, vol. 13, first series,
294; cf. 62.353A, referenced in Nowak, *Le chrétien devant la souffrance*, 63.
44. Chrysostom writes: "There are many things which from ignorance alone cause us
sorrow, so that if we come to understand them well, we banish our grief." John Chrysostom, "Homily 7," in *Homilies on 1 Thessalonians*, NPNF, first series, 352; cf. PG 62.435A,
referenced in Nowak, 64.
45. Trakatellis's translation, "Being Transformed," 218.
46. Ibid.
47. Ibid., 218–19.

stature, and earnestly affected towards Him; for this is a sign of sincere love."[48] The ability to believe God's promises, particularly that God justifies the ungodly, highlights not only the glorious nature of Abraham's faith, but the faith of all believers. "For reflect how great a thing it is to be persuaded and have full confidence that God is able on a sudden not to free one who has lived in impiety from punishment only, but even to make him just, and to count him worthy of those immortal honors" (Ἐννόησον γὰρ ἡλίκον ἐστὶ πεισθῆναι καὶ πληροφορηθῆναι, ὅτι δύναται ὁ Θεὸς τὸν ἐν ἀσεβείᾳ βεβιωκότα τοῦτον ἐξαίφνης οὐχὶ κολάσεως ἐλευθερῶσαι μόνον, ἀλλὰ καὶ δίκαιον ποιῆσαι, καὶ τῶν ἀθανάτων ἐκείνων ἀξιῶσαι τιμῶν).[49] The contribution believers make to their own salvation, their own faith exercised in response to God's acts on their behalf, is itself surrounded and supported by the grace of God. "For this is the very thing that makes the believer glorious; the fact of his enjoying so great grace, of his displaying so great faith."[50]

The Dynamics of Salvation

Chrysostom's exegesis of Romans 6 illustrates his understanding of the dynamics of salvation. In the waters of baptism believers have died to sin. "For this baptism effected once for all, it made us dead to it [sin]." What does baptism into death mean? It is a manner of dying similar to Christ's death on the cross. It is "with a view to our dying as he did. For baptism is the cross. What the cross then, and burial, is to Christ, that baptism has been to us, even if not in the same respects."[51] Both Christ and the believer have died, Christ in his body on the cross, the believer in his or her death to sin. And what is the result of our baptism and consequent death to sin? It is a life free from sin. "But this must of our own earnestness thenceforth continually be maintained, so that, although sin issue countless commands to us, we may never again obey it, but abide unmovable as a dead man does" (δεῖ δὲ λοιπὸν παρὰ τῆς ἡμετέρας σπουδῆς κατορθοῦσθαι αὐτὸ διηνεκῶς, ὥστε, κἂν μυρία ἐπιτάττῃ, μηκέτι ὑπακούειν, ἀλλὰ μένειν ἀκίνητον ὥσπερ τὸν νεκρόν).[52]

If this death to sin is to be "real," believers must be diligent to contribute their own part, largely through the formation of new habits. By a "change of habits" (ἐκ τῆς τῶν τρόπων μεταβολῆς γινομένην), "the forni-

48. Chrysostom, "Homily 8," 386. Cf. 60.455C.
49. Ibid., 386.
50. Ibid.
51. Ibid., 405.
52. Ibid.

cator becomes chaste, the covetous man merciful, the harsh subdued," demonstrating that even in this present life a "resurrection has taken place, the prelude to the other."[53] In fact, in our baptism "the old life has been made to vanish, and this new and angelic one is being lived in. But when you hear of a new life, look for a great alteration, a wide change."[54]

Of course, the problem Chrysostom faces is the reality of post-baptismal sin in his congregation, attitudes and behavior he attributes to "listlessness" and the failure to cultivate the dispositions or habits that facilitate righteous living. The opposite of the listless soul is one that is "youthful and well-favored . . . in the very prime of life, ever ready for any fight or struggle." Think of the prodigal son, Chrysostom exhorts his congregation. Even he, "who wasted out all his share, and was reduced to the greatest wretchedness, and was in a feebler state than any imbecile or disordered person," was able to change. How so? By exercising his will. "But when he was willing, he became suddenly young by his decision alone and his change." In the same way, Christians can change. ". . . even if we have gotten carried beyond the boundary, let us go up to our Father's house, and not stay lingering over the length of the journey." "For if we be willing, the way back again is easy and very speedy. . . . Do but put a beginning upon the business, and the whole is done." Again, Chrysostom emphasizes the relationship between willing and habit formation. If one avoids sinful behavior "for two days, you will keep off on the third day more easily; and after three days you will then add ten, then twenty, then a hundred, then your whole life."[55]

Love plays a special role in cultivating the will to live a holy life, Chrysostom believes. When we have "no strong feeling about a person," we will not desire his friendship. If we love another "warmly and really," as believers are called to love Christ, the esteem that love engenders will produce changed behavior. To lovingly respond to love received, even when our responses result in suffering, is to be "right-minded." What results is a surprising reversal of expectations. Those very conditions and events that might seem likely to overcome the Christian—poverty, disease, calumny, and death itself—are turned to the believer's advantage. "For if we be right-minded (Ἂν γὰρ νήφωμεν), we are the greatest possible gainers by these things, as neither from the contrary to these shall we gain any advantage. But consider; does any one affront you and war against you? Does he not thereby set you upon your guard, and

53. Ibid.
54. Ibid., 405–6.
55. Ibid., 406.

give you an opportunity of growing into God's likeness (τοῦ γενέσθαι ὅμοιον τῷ Θεῷ)?"[56]

The key, Chrysostom argues, is to understand and embrace the reality communicated through baptism. For in baptism there are clearly "two mortifyings" and "two deaths": "the one is done by Christ in baptism, and the other it is our duty to effect by earnestness afterwards." "For that our former sins were buried, came of His gift. But the remaining death to sin after baptism must be the work of our own earnestness, however much we find God here also giving us help." The power present in baptism is efficacious for sins committed before baptism and "also secures against subsequent ones." In like manner, our "contribution" to our baptism was our faith that our sins would be "obliterated" in the water of baptism, and a continuing life of faith and sinlessness after baptism.[57] Just as one who is dead can no longer sin, "lying as a dead body, so must he that has come up from baptism, since he has died there once for all, remain ever dead to sin."

To do so, however, requires both that Christians remember, understand, and embrace what has occurred in their baptism and that they train themselves to live wisely after baptism has taken place. For Christ has come, Chrysostom reminds his audience, "not to destroy our nature, but to set our free choice aright (οὐ γὰρ τὴν φύσιν ἦλθεν ἀνελεῖν, ἀλλὰ τὴν προαίρεσιν διορθῶσαι). Then to show that it is not through any force or necessity that we are held down by iniquity, but willingly," Paul urges us not to allow sin to "reign" over us.[58]

Yes, it is possible for one who possesses "a mortal body not to sin." How so? Because of "the abundancy of Christ's grace." Sin reigns, "not from any power of its own, but from your listlessness." The problem is not with the body itself, which Chrysostom views as "indifferent between vice and virtue," much like a weapon of war that can be wielded effectively or ineffectively. "For the fault is not laid to the suit of armor, but to those that use it to an ill end. And this one may say of the flesh too, which becomes this or that owing to the mind's decision (τὴν τῆς ψυχῆς γνώμην), not owing to its own nature."[59] If, for example, one's eye slips and "is curious after the beauty of another," the eye has become an instrument of a faulty mind, "the thought which commands it." A "noble spirit" must itself be "acquainted . . . with the ways of the warfare" inherently part of life in the present time. A commander stands ready to aid the Christian soldier, but the soldier in turn must cultivate

56. Ibid., 407.
57. Ibid., 408, Homily 11.
58. Ibid., 410.
59. Ibid., 410–11.

the "purpose of mind" (προαιρέσεως) to handle well the armor and arms the commander supplies.[60]

A dramatic change has occurred in the Christian's life through baptism. Before baptism "our body . . . was an easy prey for the assaults of sin," precisely because we were ruled by a "great swarm of passions," the result of the death that Adam's sin introduced into human history. Thus, it was far from easy to run the "race of virtue." We had neither the Holy Spirit to assist us "nor any baptism of power to mortify." "But as some horse that does not answer the rein, it ran indeed, but made frequent slips, the Law meanwhile announcing what was to be done and what not, yet not conveying into those in the race anything over and above exhortation by means of words." After the coming of Christ, though, running the race well has become much easier, "in that the assistance we had given us was greater." Now, after Christ's coming, the law does not only exhort us, "but grace too which also remitted our former sins (ἀλλὰ καὶ χάρις ἡ καὶ τὰ πρότερα ἀφεῖσα)" also "secures us against future ones (καὶ πρὸς τὰ μέλλοντα ἀσφαλιζομένη)"[61] Indeed, grace not only holds out the promise of crowns for faithful believers, but it has actually "crowned them first, and then led them to the contest."[62]

Grace does not coerce us, however. On the one hand, "You were neither forced nor pressed, but you came of your own accord, with willing mind." On the other hand, "that you may learn that it came not of your own willing temper only, but the whole of it of God's grace also," after Paul writes "you obeyed from the heart" (Rom. 6:17), he adds "that form of doctrine which was delivered you." Once again Chrysostom's synergistic viewpoint is apparent. "For the obedience from the heart shows the free will. But the being delivered, hints the assistance from God."[63]

Of course, many will wonder how Chrysostom interprets Paul's words in Romans 9. Chrysostom himself must have felt that his preceding exegesis would stand or fall on his ability to make sense of Paul's argument in Romans 9, and it is interesting to note that Chrysostom's homily on Romans 9 contains no practical exhortation, a highly unusual omission for St. John.[64] Chrysostom provides a particularly interesting interpretation of Romans 9:11–13. "For the children being not yet born, neither having done any good or evil, that the purpose of God according to elec-

60. Ibid., 411.
61. Ibid.
62. Ibid.
63. Ibid., 412.
64. Ibid., 471, Homily 16. Cf. PG 60.564D. Chrysostom himself comments that he must bring his "discourse to a conclusion here, without saying anything to you on the more immediately practical points, as I generally do, lest I should make a fresh indistinctness in your memories by saying so much."

tion might stand, not of works, but of him that calls, it was said to her, the elder shall serve the younger. As it is written, Jacob have I loved, but Esau have I hated." "What," Chrysostom asks, "was the cause then why one was loved and the other hated? Why was it that one served, the other was served?" Chrysostom's answer? "It was because one was wicked, and the other good."[65] God's "intent" in electing Jacob and in rejecting Esau was to manifest the wonder and extent of God's foreknowledge. "Because He does not wait, as a human being does, to discern from the issue of their acts the one who is good and the one who is not, but even before these He knows who is wicked and who is not."[66]

Paul's principal aim at this point in the overall structure of Romans is "to show by all that he said that only God knows who are worthy, and no man whatever knows. . . . God only knows for a certainty who deserve a crown, and who punishment and vengeance."[67] Surprisingly, many people who by all appearances would be "esteemed good," God rejects. In like manner, God ends up justifying many people whom one would think should be rejected. How so? God understands the faith and character of people in a manner that is impossible for us to comprehend. By all appearances, one would expect it would be Esau who would receive God's approbation and blessing. After all, he was the firstborn. "Yet," Chrysostom comments, "this was not the only thing required, but the character too, which fact contributes no common amount of practical instruction for us."[68] God possesses a knowledge of Esau—even before his birth takes place—that forms the basis for his rejection of Esau and his election of Jacob. That is to say, God recognizes a "virtue of soul" in Jacob that Esau lacks. Hence, God's election of Jacob "was a sign of foreknowledge, that they were chosen from the very birth."[69]

God, unlike mere humans, "knows how to assay the soul, knows which is worthy of being saved." Thus, Chrysostom argues, human beings are called by Paul to acknowledge the "incomprehensibleness of the election." If election was left up to human decision and opinion, we would constantly make the wrong choice. Chrysostom points us to the example of St. Matthew. How many living in Matthew's day would have recognized him as appropriate material for apostleship? Many others seemed to have greater qualities, at least according to appearances. "But he that knows things undeclared," Chrysostom states, "and is able to assay the mind's aptitude, knew the pearl though lying in the

65. Ibid., 464, Homily 16.
66. Ibid., 464–65. My own translation.
67. Ibid., 465.
68. Ibid.
69. Ibid., 466.

mire, and after passing by others, and being pleased with the beauty of this, he elected it, and by adding to the noble born free-will (καὶ τῇ τῆς προαιρέσεως εὐγενείᾳ) grace from himself (τὴν παρ᾽ ἑαυτοῦ προσθεὶς χάριν), he made it approved."[70]

Here we have the classic Chrysostomic synergism. Matthew's soul, though covered with mire and dust, possesses a beauty that God recognizes and supplies with the needed grace to respond fully in faith. Only God, though, possessed the profound knowledge to recognize the reality of the situation. The same principle, Chrysostom is convinced, manifests itself often in daily life. Those who break horses frequently see qualities in a wild horse that others with a less trained eye would overlook. Those who cut and polish gems will frequently select stones that for all appearances possess little worth. The critical point is that God does not judge by appearances but looks beneath the surface to judge the interior state of human beings.

Therefore, Chrysostom insists, the importance of Paul's words in Romans 9:20: "No, but, O man, who are you that reply against God?" Those who question God's election—an election based on God's foreknowledge—are guilty of "unseasonable inquisitiveness and excessive curiosity (τὴν πολλὴν πολυπραγμούνην) . . ."[71] "For our business is to obey what God does, not to be curious even if we do not know the reason of them." This is the point of Paul's famous illustration of the potter and the clay. Paul, Chrysostom contends, "does not mean to do away with free-will" with this illustration. Instead, Paul is warning his readers against foolishly "calling God to account" for God's decisions. "For in respect of calling God to account, we ought to be as little disposed to it as the clay is. For we ought to abstain not from gainsaying or questioning only, but even from speaking or thinking of it at all, and to become like that lifeless matter, which follows the potter's hands, and lets itself be drawn about anywhere he may please."[72]

Chrysostom warns against stretching Paul's illustration beyond its proper boundaries and is particularly concerned that readers will understand Paul to be advocating a kind of monergism in which God coerces or violates the human will. "Do not suppose," Chrysostom writes, "that this is said by Paul as an account of the creation, nor as implying a necessity over the will . . . for if here he were speaking about the will, and those who are good and those not so, God will be himself the maker of these, and humankind will be free from all responsibility."[73] No, Chrysostom

70. Ibid.
71. Ibid., 467.
72. Ibid.
73. Ibid., 468.

insists, "there is nothing else then which he here wishes to do, save to persuade the hearer to yield entirely to God, and at no time to call him into account for anything whatever."[74] We are to submit to the mystery of God's decisions, not because an unconditional election would be mysterious and incomprehensible, but because God's foreknowledge of the character of human beings is incomprehensible. It would be "monstrous" to imagine that because the same lump is made of the same "substance," there is also an identity of "dispositions." The "honor and the dishonor of the things made of the lump depends" not on the potter, but "upon the use made by those that handle them," that is, on the free choice exercised by the clay itself. To move beyond this understanding of Paul's illustration, Chrysostom believes, is to undercut fatally its fundamental meaning and purpose.

Yes, Chrysostom acknowledges, Paul does write that God has prepared vessels for glory and vessels for destruction, but this preparation "does not mean that all is God's doing. Since if this were so, there were nothing to hinder all persons from being saved." That is, if all were simply left up to the will of God alone, God would save everyone. The fact that all are not saved does not demonstrate God's sovereign election but the reality of free will. "Because when he says, 'it is not of him that wills, nor of him that runs,' he does not deprive us of free will, but shows that all is not one's own, for that it requires grace from above. For it is binding on us to will, and also to run: but to confide not in our own labors, but in the love of God toward humanity."[75] Why? The fundamental principle of salvation is that we are saved by faith, not by the works of the law.

74. Ibid.
75. Ibid., 469.

4

AUGUSTINE

Pamela Bright

Introduction

The Letter of Paul to the Romans, insofar as one can understand its literal content, poses a question like this: whether the Gospel of our Lord Jesus Christ came to the Jews alone because of their merits through the works of the law, or whether the justification of faith that is in Christ Jesus came to all nations, without any preceding merits for works. In this last instance, people would believe not because they were just, but justified through belief; they would then begin to live justly. This then is what the apostle intended to teach: that the grace of the Gospel of our Lord Jesus Christ came to all people. He thereby shows why one calls this "grace," for it was given freely, and not as a repayment of a debt of righteousness.[1]

This is Augustine's introduction to his commentary on the Epistle to the Romans, upon which he embarked about a year before his consecration to the episcopacy. Our understanding of Augustine's interpretation

---

1. Paula Fredriksen Landes, *Unfinished Commentary on the Epistle to the Romans* I.1, Texts and Translations 23, Early Christian Literature, series 6, ed. Robert L. Wilken and William R. Schoedel (Chico, CA: Scholars Press, 1982), 53.

of Romans may have been different if he had advanced beyond the first seven verses of chapter 1 of the epistle, or better still if, as with *De doctrina christiana,* he had taken up the work shelved thirty years previously and had completed the commentary. It would have been a boon to have a late commentary on Romans in which we would examine how his thought on the great epistle had finally matured. But this is empty dreaming. What we have is forty-three years of pastoral exhortation, of fierce debate, of spiritual reflection, and of intense theological creativity through which to sift in an attempt to discover the different phases of Augustine's encounter with the Epistle to the Romans.

About four years before his death in 430, as the fabric of Roman North African society was unraveling under the Vandal invasion, Augustine set about a highly unusual composition—his *Retractationes.* He did not choose to write a later version of the *Confessions* to pinpoint significant moments of his ministry as priest and bishop stretching over four decades; rather, he chose to write a series of reflections "with juridical severity"[2] on his literary production in its chronological order. The difficult task of assessing the impact of the Epistle to the Romans on the thought of Augustine may be guided by Augustine's own words at the beginning of the *Retractationes:*

> Let those therefore who are going to read this book not imitate me when I err, but rather when I progress toward the better. For perhaps, one who reads my works in the order in which they were written will find out how I progressed while writing. In order that this be possible, I shall take care, insofar as I can in this work, to acquaint him with this matter.[3]

This is the methodological approach of one of the most distinguished modern interpreters of the biblical thought of Augustine, Anne-Marie La Bonnardière. For over four decades she pursued many of the aspects of Augustine's exegesis,[4] but there were human limits even for this indefatigable scholar. La Bonnardière did not attempt an analysis of the Epistle to the Romans in the Augustinian corpus, but the present essay

2. Sr. Mary Inez Bogan, *St. Augustine: Retractations* (Washington, DC: Catholic University of America, 1968), 3.

3. Ibid., 5.

4. "Deuteronomy," "Joshua," "Judges," "Ruth," "Samuel," "Kings," "Chronicles," "Edras," "Tobit," "Judith," "Esther," "Macabees," "Jeremiah," "Proverbs," "Wisdom," "Minor Prophets," "Thessalonians," "Titus," "Philemon," "Galatians," in Anne-Marie La Bonnardière, *Biblia Augustiniana* (Paris: Études augustiniennes, 1960–1975). See Charles Kannengiesser, "A Select Bibliography (1945–1995)," in *Augustine and the Bible*, vol. 2, *The Bible through the Ages*, ed. Charles Kannengiesser and Pamela Bright (Notre Dame, IN: University of Notre Dame Press, 1999), 319–42. Note subsection "Paul," 336–38.

will follow her guidance—not in the detail of her scholarship, not in the vast erudition that was foundational to such an enterprise,[5] but, at least in the structuring of the present essay, the emphasis will be on the chronological rather than thematic analysis of the Epistle to the Romans in the thought of Augustine.

A chronological frame emphasizes the importance of the contextualization of Augustine's thought. The complexity—even the deliberate paradoxical nature of his style—militates against a simplistic systematization (even if his stature has encouraged mini-industries of such). An analysis of Augustine's interpretation of Paul's Epistle to the Romans is notoriously difficult. One has to resist the temptation to put the focus exclusively on the famous passages of chapters 7 and 9. This would result in a somewhat abstract and unbalanced presentation of Augustine's thought. The emphasis on contextual analysis is not to avoid precise exegetical concerns, but rather to insist on two things: first, the need for careful attention to different aspects of the epistle that informed his thought at different stages of his life and in different literary works, and second, the need to reflect upon which concerns remained central to his thought, which were abandoned, and which new insights transformed his thought over the years.

Meeting Paul—Again: The Early Writings

Augustine would have been introduced to Paul in the Manichean phase of his life, so it is not surprising that some of the earliest citations from the apostle, as Augustine familiarly speaks of Paul, are in his anti-Manichean writings begun in Rome, as he made his way from Milan back to Africa. Four of these anti-Manichean writings date from 388 to 392: *De moribus ecclesiae catholicae* and *De moribus Manichaeorum, On the Catholic and Manichaean Ways of Life* (begun in Rome in 388, and completed in Thagaste, 389–90),[6] *De Duabus Animabus contra Manichaeos* (391), and *Acta seu disputatio contra Fortunatum Manichaeum* (392).[7] At the beginning of *De moribus ecclesiae catholicae* (I.1) Augustine points out that his intention is to answer "the ignorant and profane attacks which the Manicheans make on the Law, which

5. One can only hope for a renewed initiative at such a level.

6. See John Kevin Coyle, "Augustin et le Manichéisme," in *Mani et le manichéisme*, ed. Marie-Anne Vannier, *Connaissance de Pères de L'Église Éditions Nouvelle Cité* 83 (2001), 45–55.

7. *Augustin: The Writings against the Manichaeans, and against the Donatists*, Nicene and Post Nicene Fathers (hereafter cited as NPNF), vol. 4, first series, ed. Philip Schaff (Peabody, MA: Hendrickson, 1995 [1887]).

is called the Old Testament."[8] The citation of Paul is not intensive, but it is worth noting that almost the first scriptural citations are taken from the Epistle to the Romans. In the context of an argument of the evidence of the goodness and love of God throughout both testaments, Augustine quotes Romans: "We know that all things issue in good to them that love God" followed by "Who then shall separate us from the love of Christ?" (Rom. 8:28, 35). Perhaps more significant for later developments of his thought in the *Confessions* (Books X and XIII) is Augustine's quotation of Romans 12:2: "Be not conformed to this world" (XIII 22.32). However, at this earlier stage of his writing, Augustine combined Romans 12:2 with Ecclesiastes 1:2–3—"Vanity of the vain"—as Augustine's text read:

> . . . the man, then, who is temperate in such mortal and transient things has his rule of life confirmed by both Testaments, that he should love none of these things, nor think them desirable for their own sakes, but should use them as far as it is required for the purposes and duties of life, with the moderation of an employer, instead of the ardour of a lover. (*De moribus Ecclesiae Catholicae* 21.39)[9]

The immediate context for the citation of Romans 12:2 is the scriptural condemnation of seeking for popular renown and of inquisitiveness—a condemnation which will be echoed more elaborately in his discussion of the concupiscences in *Confessions* X. The development of these same themes in Book X of the *Confessions* is joined to the analysis of the vulnerability of the will and the strength of the concupisences (1 John 2:16; *Conf.* X, 30.41–41.66). This immediately follows the famous saying: "Give what you command and command what you will" (*Conf.* X 29.40), which so shocked Pelagius and was a catalyst for his collision with Augustine.[10] The same text from Romans is taken up again (in Book XIII 21.30, 31) where in his commentary on the six days of creation, Augustine reflects on the need for a lifelong resistance to being "conformed to this world," and a lifelong journey of being re-formed in Christ. Augustine's citation of Romans 12:2 in the anti-Manichean work begun in Rome in 388, and then cited again in a similar context in a work some ten years later, is a witness to his enduring reflection on certain biblical insights throughout his pastoral ministry. *De duabus animabus contra Manichaeos* (*On the Two Souls, against the Manichaeans*)

8. "Of the Morals of the Catholic Church," in NPNF 4, trans. Richard Stothert, 39–63.

9. Ibid., 52.

10. Henry Chadwick, *St. Augustine: Confessions* (Oxford: Oxford University Press, 1991; reprint 1998). See footnote 27, on page 202.

(391) was critically reviewed by Augustine in his *Retractationes* (I 14)[11] because of the ambiguities in his treatment of sin and free will. On the other hand, in the disputation against Fortunatus, Augustine directly counters the arguments of the Manichean dualism by referring to the Pauline teaching of the action of grace upon the "old man." *Acta seu disputatio contra Fortunatum Manichaeum* (*The Acts or Disputation against Fortunatus the Manichaean*) records a fascinating moment, a Manichee and a Christian quoting the Epistle to the Romans. Fortunatus quotes Romans 7:23–25: "I see another law in my members, warring against the law of my mind. . . . Who will deliver me from this body of death unless it be the grace of God through our Lord Jesus Christ?" Augustine counters with Romans 5:19:

> The same apostle whom you also have cited says: "As through the disobedience of the one the many were constituted sinners; so also through the obedience of the one the many are constituted righteous" . . . as long as we bear the image of the earthly man that is, as long as we live according to the flesh, which is also called the old man, we have the necessity of our habit, so that we may not do what we will. But when the grace of God has breathed the divine love into us and has made us subject to his will to us it is said . . . "the grace of God has made me free from the law of sin and death." (22)[12]

Apart from these anti-Manichean works, the earlier writings are notable for the comparatively scanty references to the Pauline Epistles, in spite of "seizing Paul" as early as 386/7 in *De Academicis* (2.2.5).[13] *De libero arbitrio* (*On Free Will*) (387–88) takes up the anti-Manichean theme of the origin of evil and its relation to free will. But these important anti-Manichean themes did not immediately engage him in questions relevant to the Epistle to the Romans. That Paul was distant from his mind in dealing with this question is attested to by his defensive tone in the *Retractationes* some thirty-five years later: ". . . because in these books I have said many things in defense of free choice which the purpose of the disputation required" (8.3). Yet the challenge of the Epistle to the Romans was not to remain dormant.

Except for the completion of the studies *De dialectica* (387) and *De musica* (388–90), in settling back in Africa Augustine gave up a proposed set of commentaries on the liberal arts. It is in *De musica* that we have a foretaste of the crucial questions of grace and free will. The sixth book of *De musica* is a witness to the first engagement for Augustine with

11. Rom. 7:18. Bogan, *Retractations*, 10.14, 102.
12. Trans. A. H. Newman, NPNF 4, 121.
13. See reference in *Confessions* VII 21.27.

the great Pauline questions of the "old self" and the "new self." In his study "Augustine's Interpretation of Romans (A.D. 394–396)," William Babcock suggests: "Now, almost suddenly, Augustine seems to have discovered that the human will is not entirely at its own disposal, that the dispositions of the self are not fully under the self's control."[14] However, on the whole, the first years of his return to Africa were marked by what turned out to be the utopian dream of a life of holy leisure, devoted to prayerful retreat and edifying conversation in the embryonic monastic-like community (*servi Dei*) at his hometown of Thagaste. These hopes were to be proved ephemeral as his responsibilities deepened in the wake of his ordination.

The references to the Letter to the Romans remain sparse, or rather, they remain unfocused, in the writings of the beginning of the period that he devoted to the intense study of the scriptures immediately following his ordination. Augustine turned to commentaries on the Psalms and then to the Gospels.[15] This is hardly surprising. His prayer life was filled with the Psalms, and the daily focus of his life as a preacher would be the commentary of the Gospels. There are two significant exceptions to this lack of consistent attention to the great themes of Romans. The first is in relation to the presence (even the omnipresence) of the Donatists in the church of Africa. The second point of contact with Romans is a result of his participation in biblical discussion groups with the clergy in Hippo and Carthage in the years following his ordination.

As a young man Augustine had been distanced from the turbulence of the religious-political life of the African province, but in the early nineties of the fourth century he was swept into the vortex of what is properly African Christianity. Now, as a member of the clergy, he was an active participant in the revitalizing of Catholic institutions and spiritual life under his friend Aurelius, bishop of Carthage. In these circumstances Augustine began to wrestle with the ecclesiological and biblical questions proper to the Donatist controversy. These tended to focus on questions like the interpretation of scripture in relation to the holiness of the church and membership of the church; questions like who were the "wheat" and who were the "weeds" of the church, and when were they to be "separated" (Matt. 13:24–30) can be found in the documentation and the polemical writings of Optatus against the great Donatist bishop Parmenian, who had died around the time

---

14. William Babcock, "Augustine's Interpretation of Romans (A. D. 394–396)," *Augustinian Studies* 5 (1974), 58. See citation of Rom. 7:24–25 in *De musica* 6.5.14 and 6.11.33.

15. *Enarrationes in Psalmos*, 392, and *De sermone domine in monte*, 394. See Frederick van Fleteren, *Augustine through the Ages*, ed. Allan D. Fitzgerald (Grand Rapids: Eerdmans, 1999), 771.

of Augustine's ordination. Again, there was no special relevance of Romans in this particular ecclesial context. But there was an unexpected contact with the thought of Paul at this stage, and it was one that, many years later, would throw light on the mature thought of Augustine in relation to the Letter to the Romans. It was Augustine's encounter with the thought of Tyconius, a leading Donatist intellectual and author of an important lost commentary on the Book of Revelation as well as the *Liber regularum* (*LR*), *The Book of Rules*,[16] the first sustained treatise on biblical exegesis in the early church. Augustine was both puzzled and intrigued by the arguments of this African theologian and exegete. The third rule of Tyconius, significantly titled *De promissis et lege,* begins:

> Divine authority has it that no one can ever be justified by works of the law. By the same authority it is absolutely certain that there has always been some who do the law and are justified. (*LR* III.1)[17]

Tyconius continues this line of argumentation in citing texts from Romans and Galatians (Rom. 5:20; Gal. 4:24; 3:7; 4:28; 3:12; Rom. 4:13–15; Gal. 3:17–18, 21: Rom. 3:31; Gal. 3:10, 19, 11; Rom. 7:7–8, 5; Rom. 7:14–23; 8:7–9; Gal. 5:18). This substantial sampling of Pauline texts is quoted within the first quarter of Rule III alone. Whereas Galatians and Romans share equal prominence in Tyconius's treatment of the topic announced in the third rule (together with numerous citations of Corinthians and other books of the Old and New Testaments), the major questions of the Epistle to the Romans that would engage Augustine until the end of his life are cited in this Donatist text: Romans 3:20: *quia non iustificabitur ex lege omnis caro in conspectu eius* (for no flesh shall be justified in his sight by keeping the law); Romans 6:14: *Peccatum vestri non dominabitur, non enim estis sub lege* (Sin shall have no dominion over you since you are not under the law); Romans 5:20: *Lex autem subintravit ut multiplicaretur peccatum* (The law came to multiply sin); Romans 4:13–15: *Non enim per legem promissio est Abrahae aut semini eius ut heres esset mundi, sed per iustitiam fidei . . . lex enim iram operatur* (For the promise to Abraham and his descendants that they would inherit the world, comes not through the law but through the righteous of faith . . . for the law works wrath). Tyconius also pays careful attention to Romans 7:14–23 and Romans 8:7–9.

16. F. C. Burkitt, *The Book of Rules of Tyconius* (Cambridge: Cambridge University Press, 1894; reprint 1967); William Babcock, *Tyconius: The Book of Rules* (Atlanta: Scholars Press, 1989), introduction and notes; Pamela Bright, *The Book of Rules of Tyconius: Its Purpose and Inner Logic,* Christianity and Judaism in Antiquity, vol. 2 (Notre Dame, IN: University of Notre Dame Press, 1988).

17. Babcock, *Tyconius,* 21.

Chapter 9 of the Epistle to the Romans, dealing with the election of Jacob over Esau, is a major question in the Tyconian text, being directly related to Tyconius's teaching on what he calls the "bipartite" nature of the church. According to Tyconius, the pattern of praise and blame (for example, the same city, Jerusalem, is praised and blamed throughout the prophetic literature) is a ruling principle in scripture, a mystic principle structured into the text by its author, the Holy Spirit:[18] "making faith the price of truth, the Spirit produced an account marked by mysteries" (*LR* IV). This "mystery" of the same subject being alternatively "praised and blamed" by the Spirit alerts the reader of scripture to the fact that the church is a mixture, a mysterious intermingling of "two peoples," "two societies," or more exactly, a "bipartite" community of sinners and saints. For Tyconius, the true Christians, the "pilgrims" in the existing world, would be known only at the judgment.[19] In line with this refusal of the notion of the church as the unambiguous locus of holiness, the "spotless" bride of Donatist ecclesiology, Tyconius refused a simple dichotomy of Jacob and Esau as types of this bipartite community. In commenting on the mystery of predestination (which he links to God's foreknowledge), he claims that Jacob, in an inner ambiguity, is himself not only a type of the predestined but also a type of the "bipartite" church. Jacob, the patriarch, reveals that there is a mysterious "doubleness" within him.

A question raised by scholars[20] is whether the encounter with Tyconius just before his episcopal ordination had a significant impact on Augustine's understanding of the Epistle to the Romans. Certainly a distinctly Carthaginian voice commenting with magisterial ease on intricate questions of the Epistle to the Romans was something for Augustine and his circle to take into account. Without underrating the importance of other Catholic commentators, like Victorinus, "Ambrosiaster," and Jerome for the resurgent Catholic church in Africa, here was a home-grown professional exegete who could not be ignored.[21] Scholars have

18. Charles Kannengiesser, "Augustine and Tyconius: A Conflict of Christian Hermeneutics in Roman Africa," in *Augustine and the Bible*, ed. Kannengiesser and Bright, 149–77.

19. See William H. C. Frend, "Augustine and Orosius: On the End of the Ancient World," *Augustinian Studies* 20 (1989). See section on Tyconius, 11–14. Augustine, *De Baptismo contra Donatistas*, I 16.25, NPNF 4, 422.

20. Babcock, "Augustine's Interpretation of Romans," 55–73; Paula Fredriksen, "Beyond Body/Soul Dichotomy: Augustine's Answer to Mani, Plotinus and Julian," 239–40 (see Babcock's response, 254–55); in William Babcock, *Paul and the Legacies of Paul* (Dallas: Southern Methodist University Press, 1998).

21. See "Letter 41: From Alypius and Augustine to Aurelius," in Augustine, *Letters*, vol. 1, trans. Wilfrid Parsons (Washington, DC: Catholic University of America Press, 1951), 179.

traced the impact of Tyconian thought through Augustine's writings for the next thirty years,[22] but I would argue that it is not in the questions about grace and law raised by the Epistle to the Romans that the impact of Tyconian thought had the most direct and enduring impact on Augustine's thought. The Tyconian influence is to be found in questions relating to the nature of the church as a pilgrim community of saints and sinners—for Tyconius the church is "bipartite," whereas Augustine prefers to speak of a "mixed" community (*De doctrina christiana* III 32.45). In other words, it is more specifically in questions of ecclesiology that one can find the unlikely combination of the Donatist layman Tyconius and the Catholic bishop Augustine ranged against hard-line Donatists like Parmenian, Petilian, and Cresconius. For Tyconius it was always the mystery of evil (2 Thess. 2:7)[23]—"the internal warfare" (*de bello intestino*)[24]—manifesting its presence within the very community of the baptized that was the focus of attention. On the other hand, for Augustine, especially in the early years of his conversion, and indeed throughout his life, it was another "internal warfare" that galvanized him, that of the "internal warfare" of the interior psyche, within the recesses of the will itself. It was the awareness of *that* "clear and present danger" that was to focus Augustine's attention and continued to draw him ever more deeply toward Paul and the Epistle to the Romans.

In later life, at the time when he was writing the *Retractationes*, Augustine included a detailed summary of all seven rules of *The Book of Rules* in Book III of the *De doctrina christiana* (*DDC* III 30–37). The relevance of Augustine's summary of the *Book of Rules*, especially of Rule III (*DDC* 33.46) with regard to his mature understanding of Romans will be considered at the conclusion of the present study. One comment of Augustine's is of special significance in relation to the impact of Tyconius's thought on Augustine's own interpretation of Romans, especially with regard to grace and election: ". . . the want of clear views originated, or at least aggravated, the Pelagian heresy." The implication is that his own early views were unclear, but so were those of Tyconius's—these were "good, but incomplete" (*DDC* III 33.46).

The second point of contact with the thought of Augustine with respect to the Epistle to the Romans at this early stage is the work entitled *De diversis quaestionibus octaginta tribus* (*The Eighty-three Questions*) (388–97).[25] As

---

22. See the study on Tyconius in Charles Kannengiesser, *A Handbook of Patristic Exegesis* (Leiden: Brill, 2003), chap. 11.

23. Bright, *Book of Rules*. See the discussion on the mystery of evil "in the midst," 49–51 and 66–69.

24. A lost book of Tyconius.

25. See W. Geerlings, "Augustine," in *Dictionary of Early Christian Literature*, ed. Siegmar Döpp and Wilhelm Geerlings (New York: Crossroad, 2000), 66.

Augustine himself remarks in the *Retractationes,* it was not designed as a book but rather originated in a collection of discussions. *The Eighty-three Questions*[26] provides us with a montage of snapshots of the kind of dense conversations in educated church circles about problems in scripture and church teaching. Basically the same interchange was continued through correspondence, notably with Simplicianus, his former mentor in Milan. In *The Eighty-three Questions,* the Epistle to the Romans is treated in qq. 66–68 (q. 66: Rom. 7:1–8, 11; q. 67: Rom. 8:18–24; q. 68: Rom. 9:20).

> Among the things which we have written, there is also a work of a dif-fuse nature which, nonetheless, is thought of as a single book, and its title is *Eighty-Three Different Questions*. However, the questions had been scattered through many leaves of paper, because, from the very begin-ning of my conversion and after our return to Africa, the questions were dictated, without any order having been preserved by me, in response to the brothers who were ever asking me things when they would see me unoccupied. When I became bishop, I ordered that the questions be gathered together and made up into a single book, and that numbers be added so that anyone could easily find what he wanted to read. (*Retrac-tationes* I. 26)[27]

Question 68 is especially significant, because, in commenting on Romans 9:20, Augustine speaks of an *occultissimus meritus,* a "most hidden merit" of souls, a comment that witnesses to Augustine's interior debate over questions of faith and works at this early stage. But important as these reflections are for understanding significant moments in the development of Augustine's thought on Romans, there is no evidence of the epistle's capturing his full attention in the years immediately following his ordination to the priesthood. *The Eighty-three Questions* underlines the unfocused nature of the engagement with the text of Romans,[28] necessarily so, because of the range of his pastoral activities and his own tentativeness with regard to the exegesis of scripture. He himself regarded the period as a kind of apprenticeship to the full as-

26. St. Augustine, *Eighty-three Different Questions,* trans. David L. Mosher, The Fathers of the Church (Washington, DC: Catholic University of America Press, 2002).

27. Ibid., 2.

28. This does not imply that Augustine was not praying and reflecting on the Epistles of Paul at this stage of his life. Mosher includes a comment of Bardy on this very point: "There is . . . a certain order in the sequence of the *Questions.* If it is not clear that the author has expressly desired this order, circumstances have in some way imposed it on him. For the first portion of his residence in Africa was filled with the Manichaean con-troversy. With the priesthood, Holy Scripture assumed more and more a place in his life. Finally, the letters of Saint Paul became, for a time, the daily food of his spirituality. In their apparent disorder, the *Questions* trace approximately these steps" (11).

sumption of his pastoral duties. But this was about to change. Romans was poised to take center stage in the year and a half that preceded his consecration as bishop in 396.

Romans in Focus

A dramatic shift in Augustine's attention to Paul and specifically to the Epistle to the Romans occurred in the middle of the decade. The full explanation for this shift may well lie hidden in the many layers of Augustine's self-awareness. What we do have from this period 394 to 396 is a series of studies focused on Romans. Augustine notes the immediate circumstances of the writing of the *Propositions on Romans:*

> While I was still a priest, we who were in Carthage at the same time happened to read the Epistle to the Romans and, after I, to the best of my ability, replied to certain questions asked me by some of my brethren, they wanted my reply put into writing rather than merely spoken. When I yielded to this, another book was added to my previous works. (*Retractationes* 22)

In fact it was the first of four works devoted to the Pauline Epistles at this period. (1) *Expositio quarundam propositionum ex epistula apostoli ad Romanos, An Explanation of Certain Passages from the Epistle of the Apostle to the Romans* or *Propositions on Romans;* (2) *Expositio epistulae ad Galatas liber unus, One Book: An Explanation of the Epistle to the Galatians;* and (3) *Epistulae ad Romanos incoata expositio, liber unus, One Book, An Unfinished Explanation of the Epistle to the Romans,*[29] were written between 394 and 395. The fourth of these writings is the justly famous *De diversis quaestionibus ad Simplicianum* (396).[30] Twenty-seventh in the *Retractationes,* this work stands at the beginning of Book II and thus marks the beginning of the official record of the works penned by Augustine as bishop.

It is in these books that he develops more fully the fourfold pattern, tracing its outlines both in the history of salvation and in the spiritual life of the individual: *ante legem,* "before the law"; *sub lege,* "under the law"; *sub gratia,* "under grace"; *in pace,* "in peace." This pattern first appeared in *The Eighty-three Questions* (qq. 66–68) and then again in the *Propositions on Romans* (13–18; 36–65). In these works (and guided

29. Paula Fredriksen Landes, "Augustine on Romans: Propositions from the Epistle to the Romans," in Landes, *Unfinished Commentary on the Epistle to the Romans.*

30. John H. S. Burleigh, *Augustine: Earlier Writings,* Library of Christian Classics 6 (Philadephia: Westminster Press, n.d.).

by his later comments in the *Retractationes*), we can see a kind of elaborate maneuvering between issues about grace and free will, especially between stage 2 "under the law" and stage 3 "under grace," but this is no theological chess game. For Augustine, this is *the* existential issue, defining our adhering or nonadhering to God: How (against the Manichees) to maintain the sovereignty of free will? How (in the face of biblical revelation and his own experience) to acknowledge the sovereignty of God's grace? It is in Augustine's carefully framed responses to Simplicianus that these issues are newly illumined, and a perspective opened that is decisive.

An earlier demarcation[31] between Romans 7:25a "under law" and Romans 7:25b "under grace" is now nuanced in *Ad Simplicianum*.[32] The first of the two books of *Ad Simplicianum* (the second was devoted to the Book of Kings) was concentrated on the Epistle to the Romans, chapters 7 and 9. The first question concerned Romans 7:7 ("What shall we say then? Is the law sin? by no means") to verses 24 to 25 ("Who will deliver me from the body of death? The grace of God through Jesus Christ our Lord").

The second question of *Ad Simplicianum* dealt with Romans 9:10–29, concerning the election of Jacob over Esau (Rom. 9:11–13). James Wetzel makes this claim:

> In striking contrast to the rest of the work, the second part of Book I, on Romans 9:10–29, sets off a veritable revolution in his theology. In retrospect Augustine considered his reply there to have inaugurated the view of grace that he ended up defending against Pelagian critics decades later.[33]

Even "under grace," the will is insufficient to will the good. Grace alone is all-sufficient. Neither merit nor faith itself can move us toward God—all is gift, all is grace. In the double citation of Romans 7:22–25 and 1 Corinthians 4:7 (*quid habet quod non accepit?* "What have you that you have not received?") all becomes the effect of divine favor, not its cause,[34] *not* of "most hidden merits" suggested two years before (*Eighty-three Questions* 68), *not* of the merit of our faith response *prima merita fidei*

---

31. Babcock, "Augustine's Interpretation of Romans," 60–61. See Rom. 7:25a, b from *De Musica*, 6; *Eighty-three Questions*, 66; and *Propositions on Romans*, 45–46.

32. See discussion of the "crisis" in Goulven Madec, *Le Dieu d'Augustin* (Paris: Les Éditions du Cerf, 1998). See also Gaetano Lettieri, *L'Altro Agostino* (Morcelliana: Brescia, 2001).

33. James Wetzel, *Augustine through the Ages*, 798. See *De praedestinatione sanctorum ad Prosperum et Hilarium primus* 4.9, 428–29.

34. Ibid.

(*Prop ad Romans* 62), but within the mystery of the sovereign mercy and justice, "the most hidden equity," of God (*Ad Simpl* I q.2.16).

In the *Retractationes*, Augustine notes that the questions raised by these verses continue to be the focus of years of laborious clarification concerning questions of grace and free will.[35] Once again there is the question of human merit. Was it the merit of Jacob's foreseen faith (*exp. prop. Rm.* 60)? In *Retr.* 2.1 Augustine admits that his only exegetical struggle is still with free will and grace. Even faith is not to be boasted of (1 Cor. 4:7).

Babcock sums up this first series of encounters with the Epistle to the Romans:

> It is to this encounter (the encounter with Paul's own text) that we owe the double problem which Augustine's thought has fathered on Western theology: how is God's grace, understood in sheer grace operating without regard to merit and transforming the human will from the evil to the good, to be rendered compatible either with God's justice or with man's freedom?[36]

There is no way to overestimate the problem of this convoluted legacy, but what is equally important is to track the lines of how Augustine himself struggled with these issues in the decades that followed the "Copernican shift"[37] in acknowledging the all-sufficiency of grace in the economy of salvation.

The First Masterworks

The properly "restless" genius of Augustine resisted any temptation to make him a man of a single book, even one so profound as the Letter to the Romans. The next five years saw him embarking on the masterworks of his early maturity as theologian and biblical expert—*De doctrina christiana*, the *Confessions*, and *The Literal Interpretation of Genesis*. However, the great theological works of his maturity tend to reinforce the argument that for Augustine, the Epistle to the Romans was a constant companion of his intellectual and spiritual journey. The long process of thought during the ten years since his conversion is telescoped in the following passages from Book VII of the *Confessions:*

35. *Retractations*, 119–20. "Long afterwards, to be sure, I thought—and this is more probable—that these words ('under law' and 'under grace') could also refer to the spiritual man."

36. Babcock, "Augustine's Interpretation of Romans," 74.

37. See the argument of Lettieri, *L'Altro Agostino*.

With avid intensity I seized the sacred writings of your Spirit and especially the apostle Paul. Where at one time I used to think he had contradicted himself and the text of his words disagreed with the testimonies of the law and the prophets, the problems simply vanished. The holy oracles now presented to me a simple face, and I learnt to "rejoice with trembling" (Ps. 11; 70). I began reading and found that all the truth I had read in the Platonists was stated here together with the commendation of your grace, so that he who sees should "not boast as if he had not received" both what he sees and also the power to see. "For what has he that he has not received?" (I Cor. 4:7). . . . Even if a man "delights in God's law in the inner man," what will he do with "the other law in his members fighting against the law of his mind and bringing him into captivity under the law of sin, which is in his members?" (Rom. 7: 22, 23). . . . What will wretched man do? "Who will deliver him from this body of death" except your grace through Jesus Christ our Lord?" (Rom. 7: 24, 25). (*Confessions* VII 21. 27)[38]

The beginning of Augustine's episcopate had been marked by the impact of his new insight into the Epistle to the Romans. In the passage just quoted, we see again the welding together of Romans 7:24–25 and 1 Corinthians 4:7 from *Ad Simplicianum*. In the narrative of Book VIII, Augustine, reflecting on his spiritual state of stupor (*Conf.* VIII 5, 11) speaks of the split between "two wills"—"one old, and the other new, one carnal, the other spiritual"—constantly citing the verses of chapter 7 of Romans (17, 22, 24, and 25). Later in the same book, carefully refuting the Manichees (*Conf.* VIII, 8.9–11.24) he speaks of a will, half-wounded:

. . . the self which willed to serve was identical with the self which was unwilling. It was I. I was neither wholly willing nor wholly unwilling. So I was in conflict with myself. The dissociation came about against my will. Yet this was not a manifestation of the nature of an alien mind but the punishment suffered in my own mind. And so it was "not I" that brought this about "but sin which dwelt in me (Rom 7:17, 20), sin resulting from the punishment of a more freely chosen sin, because I was a son of Adam. (*Conf.* VIII, 10, 22)

The strong insistence on the woundedness of nature "in Adam" is a prelude to the themes developed in the Pelagian debates, but these are to be balanced by the importance of the elaboration of the theme of the renewal of our nature in Christ. Indeed, it the renewal in Christ that is the climax of the *Confessions*. Again, Augustine turns to the Epistle to the Romans, specifically to Romans 12:2. Earlier in the chapter, I had pointed to the significance of this verse for Augustine in his first writing

38. Chadwick, *Augustine,* 130.

against the Manichees in 388–89. In the *Confessions*, it is cited in his commentary on the fifth day of creation (*Conf.* XIII 21, 21–22, 32): "Be not conformed to this world." The immediate context is the woundedness revealed by the power of the concupiscences (cf. *De moribus catholicae* 21. 39 and *Conf.* X, 30, 41). The all-sufficiency of grace bestowed by Christ, Mediator and Physician, is underlined once more: "Be not conformed to this world" but "be renewed in the newness of your mind" (Rom. 12:2). Augustine then begins the climax of his commentary on the six days, our "renewal" in the image of God (*Conf.* XIII 22.32). Throughout the *Confessions*, Augustine weaves a delicate web between the two themes from Genesis: chapter 1, the spiritual reformation of our humanity, and chapters 2 and 3, our fallenness in Adam. To challenge his readers further, Augustine layers in further intricacies by framing these reflections on Genesis within his ever deepening understanding of Paul.

Two works, the *Confessions*, at the beginning of his episcopacy, and *The Letter and the Spirit (De Sp. Litt.)*, written just at the beginning of the Pelagian controversy, close to two decades later, witness to the continuing tension between the total insufficiency of the wounded self and the all-sufficiency of God's grace. However, as Augustine explores the human being in time in Book XI of the *Confessions*, the paradoxical "tension," the existential angst, is transformed into hope—"distension" into "extension" toward Christ (*Conf.* XI 26.33; 30.40).

The second half of Book XII of the *Confessions* is a remarkable treatise on hermeneutics, set in his commentary on the first day of creation. Augustine puts forward a renewed understanding of the principles of interpretation by insisting that the exegete forswear his (or her) own self-sufficiency as an interpreter of scripture. Anyone who claims that they have the one true opinion—rather than acknowledge that there are "diverse, yet true, opinions"—is a liar, to put it succinctly (*Conf.* XII, 25.34). Augustine proceeds to elaborate a theology of conversation, exegesis in a community of discourse. This ecclesial vision is founded, not upon self-sufficiency, but on self-*in*sufficiency. The distinction between the hermeneutical vision in *De doctrina christiana* and that of the *Confessions* is marked by continuities and discontinuities, which can partly be explained by the differences in genre and purpose, but the contrast in tone and insight between the first part of *De doctrina* (discontinued at the question of multiplicity of meanings in scripture in Book III 25.35) and the *Confessions* has drawn considerable speculation. A recent work by Gaetano Lettieri, entitled "The Other Augustine," relates this shift directly to the impact of Augustine's change of mind after *Ad Simplicianum*, written just prior to the *Confessions*.[39] *L'Altro Agostino* is the

39. Lettieri, *L'Altro Agostino*.

"other Augustine" of *DDC*-B (from III 25.36), written at the end of his life, and based on the grace of predestination as first perceived in *Ad Simplicianum* I, 2. The perspective of the "other Augustine" is found in Books XI–XII of the *Confessions*, a *retractatio* of the Platonizing onto-theology in *DDC*-A. The new "Christian Doctrine" (*DDC*-B) is written on the level of biblical hermeneutics with the notion of predestination in mind. In *De catechizandis rudibus* and in *De sancta virginitate*, this new perspective is developed on the level of ethics. Central is the no-tion of the *mirabilis omnipotentia Dei*—hence, the trinitarian paradox, the cosmological and anthropological paradox, the christological and eschatological paradox of the great works of his maturity.

Lettieri claims that *The Spirit and the Letter* has a "revolutionary significance, capable of putting on fire the new hermeneutics of grace elaborated by *Ad Simplicianum* I,2 and in *Confessions.*"[40] Central is the *topos*, at once rhetorical and juridical, concerning the relationship between *intentio* (the author's will) and the *scriptum* in scripture. Au-gustine had noted since the *Confessions* that the *intentio* remains alive and active in scripture, being its *spiritus*, the only true interpreter of the *littera*, God's Word. He insists now on that auto-interpretation due to the self-sufficiency of divine grace in the revelatory process of scripture. The fight against Pelagius has not yet really started—Augustine's insistence is not polemical; it is fundamental for him. In the controversy itself, he will apply the principle of that self-sufficiency of divine grace on the full scale of spiritual experience; hence, his exegesis of Romans 5:5 (*De Sp. Litt.* 33.59), and Romans 13:1 (*De Sp. Litt.* 31.59).

The Pelagian Debate

Central to Pelagius's teaching is the Christianized idea of *paidea*, redemption as a historical process of salutary education.[41] Pelagius's concern was "to bring to light the power and makeup of human nature" (*Epistola ad Demetriadem* 2, written in 313–14). In his *Expositiones XIII epistolorum Pauli* (405), Pelagius, in reference to Romans 5:12, speaks of Adam's sin as a model and a prototype. There is no provision for original sin.

> The universal habit of sinning (*exp.* Rom 7:23; Gal 4:4) led, because of God's saving care of us, to the Mosaic law as a reminder of the natural law and finally to the gospel, which goes beyond the Mosaic law. . . . In Pelagius's

---

40. Ibid., 307.
41. J. Stüben, "Pelagius," in *Dictionary of Early Christian Literature*, 473.

view then, grace resides in the area of exchange between natural endowment, environment, and a providence that strengthens human beings with helps given to all but does not determine their actions.[42]

In the study of the history of the reception of Romans, R. Morgan noted: "The centrality of Romans for Augustine's theology is clearest in his initial response to Pelagius, *De Spiritu et Littera* (412), which argues that God's help in effecting righteousness consists, not in the gift of the law (the letter), but in our will being aided and uplifted by the Spirit (cf. Rom. 7:6). This focus on human incapacity, based on Romans 7 and explained by a doctrine of original sin drawn from Romans 5 (v. 19, if not v. 12), is rather remote from Paul's concern; but it yielded a profound reading of the epistle and informed subsequent theological anthropology."[43]

There were two phases in Augustine's struggle against Pelagianism. The first was from 411 to 418, that is, from the condemnation of Caelestius, the disciple of Pelagius in Carthage, in 411, to the condemnation of Pelagius himself by Innocent I in Rome in 417, with his rehabilitation under Zosimus, followed by the final condemnation in 418. Augustine's writing in the first stage included *De peccatorum meritis et remissione et de baptismo parvulorum ad Marcellinum* (411–12); *De spiritu et littera* (in 412 and *ep.* 145), the Pauline contrast of law and grace; *De natura et gratia* (413–17); *De gratia Christi et de peccato originali* (418), written after the synod of Carthage. The second stage, which absorbed much of Augustine's attention till his death, began with the redoubtable Julian of Eclanum on the one hand and a movement led by John Cassian (so-called, or miscalled, semi-Pelagianism) on the other. In his writing against Julian, *Contra duas epistulas Pelagianorum* (420–21), Augustine criticizes Julian's teaching on the five *laudes* (*creaturae, nuptiarum, legis, liberi arbitrii, sanctorum*). His works against the so-called semi-Pelagians include *De gratia et libero arbitrio* (426–27), to the monks in Hadrumetum (for the monks, the problem of unmerited grace; for Augustine, grace and freedom); *De praedestinatione sanctorum liber ad Prosperum et Hilarium primus* (428–29), the beginning of faith is due to the unmerited election of God; and *De dono perseverantiae liber ad Prosperum et Hilarium secundus* (428–29), which argues that not only the initial grace but perseverance in it is a gracious gift of God. W. Geerlings sums up the difference between Pelagius and Augustine: for the former "grace is given in order that human beings may more easily do what is

---

42. Ibid.
43. R. Morgan, "The Letter to the Romans," in *Dictionary of Biblical Interpretation* (Nashville: Abingdon Press, 1999), 413.

good" (*ad facilius faciendum*); for the latter "grace is given that human beings may be able to do it at all" (*ad faciendum*).[44]

In his study "Augustine, the Bible and the Pelagians," Gerald Bonner notes:

> The message of I Cor 4: 7 wholly altered Augustine's outlook and revealed to him that faith, no less than works, is the gift of God. In the *Praedestinatione sanctorum*, one of his last writings, composed in 429, Augustine commented on his earlier view: "I had not sufficiently inquired, nor had I then found, what election by grace might be, about which the same Apostle says, 'There is a remnant, chosen by grace' (Rom 11:5), which is not grace, if any merits precede it; for what is given, not by grace, but according to what is due, is a reward for merits rather than a gift."[45]

In Retrospect

At the outset of the present study we asked which concerns remained central, which were abandoned, and which new insights informed his thought on Romans over the long years of his ministry. One of the best places to explore these questions is the "handbook" he wrote at the request of a certain Laurentius. In the *Enchiridion*, written at the beginning of the last decade of his life (421 or 423), there are two sections that are of particular interest for the present study. The first, following immediately on the fall of the angels, speaks of that promise where a restored part of humanity "should fill up the gap which the rebellion and fall of the devils had left in the company of the angels" (*Enchiridion* 29).[46] This leads Augustine to the question of whether this salvation is through merit of good works, or through the free determination of their free will, or by the grace of God. It is no surprise to read Augustine's careful refutation of being restored to the eternal kingdom through the merit of their own works or by the free determination of will. Both suggestions merit a "God forbid!" Not even the merit of their own faith is to be arrogated by such. Not even the freedom of the will—"this very liberty of good action"—is to be boasted of. "For it is God who works in you both to will and to do for his own good pleasure" (Phil. 2:13 NKJV). "So, then, it is not of him who wills, nor of him who runs, but of God who shows mercy" (Rom. 9:16 NKJV). It

44. Geerlings, "Augustine," 70.
45. Gerald Bonner, "Augustine, the Bible and the Pelagians," in *Augustine and the Bible*, ed. Kannengiesser and Bright, 236.
46. *Enchiridion*, in NPNF 3, trans. J. F. Shaw, 247.

is in this context that Augustine speaks of our true freedom, in terms redolent of his commentary on the sixth day of creation in Book XIII of the *Confessions*.

> We shall be made truly free, when God fashions us, that is, forms and creates us anew, but not as men—for he has already done that—but as good men, which his grace is now doing, that we may be a new creation in Christ Jesus, according as it is said: "Create in me a clean heart, O God" (Ps 51:10). For good has already created his heart, so far as the physical structure of the human heart is concerned; but the psalmist prays for the renewal of the life which still lingers in his heart. (31)[47]

The second section that holds special interest for the present study is a recapitulation of the four stages of the spiritual life, the fourfold pattern appearing as early as the *Eighty-three Questions*, some three decades earlier. It is worth quoting at some length to see how carefully he rephrases his earlier understanding of the four stages, particularly stage 3. Of special note is that, throughout the passage, "grace" is now identified with the action of the Holy Spirit. "For without the gift of God, that is, without the Holy Spirit, through whom love is spread abroad in our hearts, the law can command, but it cannot assist; and moreover, it makes man a transgressor, for he can no longer excuse himself on the plea of ignorance" (*Enchiridion* 117).[48] Augustine then continues:

> When sunk in the darkest depths of ignorance, man lives according to the flesh, undisturbed by any struggle or reason or conscience, this is his first state. Afterwards, when through the law has come the knowledge of sin, and the Spirit of God has not yet interposed his aid, man, striving to live according to the law, is thwarted in his efforts and falls into conscious sin, and so, being overcome by sin, becomes sin's slave . . . and thus the effect produced by the knowledge of the commandment is this, that sin works in man in all manner of concupiscence, and he is involved in the additional guilt of wilful transgression, and that is fulfilled which is written: "The law entered that the offense might abound" (Rom. 5:20). This is man's second state. But if God has regard to him, and inspires him with faith in God's help, and the Spirit of God begins to work in him, then the mightier power of love strives against the power of the flesh; and although there is still in man's own nature a power that fights against him (for his disease is not completely cured), yet he lives the life of the just by faith, and lives in righteousness so far as he does not yield to evil lust, and conquers it by the love of holiness. This is the third state of the

47. Ibid., 248.
48. Ibid., 275.

man of good hope; and he who by steadfast piety advances in this course, shall at last attain to peace, that peace which after this life is over, shall be perfected in the repose of the spirit, and finally the resurrection of the body. (*Enchiridion* 118)[49]

There is another late work that is often overlooked when one searches for evidence of the final maturing of Augustine's thought on Romans. This is the second part of the *De doctrina christiana* (*DDC*-B). The fact that it *is* one of his last works is often neglected. In this respect it is illuminating to see how passionately Augustine contests the views of Tyconius, whom he had encountered over thirty years before. In his summarizing of Rule III *De promissis et legis* of the *Book of Rules*, we read very little of the argument of Tyconius. Instead we read in considerable detail what Tyconius *should* have written if he had foreseen the Pelagian controversy. Throughout his critical summary or commentary on Tyconius, it is important to note that it is first and foremost Augustine's own stance that is revealed in his strictures against the long-dead Donatist author. First, Augustine contests the title, *The Promises and the Law*, and suggests instead that the title of his own book *The Spirit and the Letter* would have been more appropriate, or that the Rule should have been called "Grace and the Law" (*De gratia et mandato*). Augustine claims that Rule III is "a great question in itself, rather than a rule to be applied to the solution of other questions," and adds that "the want of clear views originated or at least aggravated the Pelagian heresy" (*DDC* III 33.46). Augustine then notes the particular deficiencies of Rule III. First, on the question of faith and works, Tyconius sees works as given by God as a reward of faith—but that faith was one's own! Countering this inadequate theology of grace, Augustine quotes Paul: ". . . love and faith from God the Father and the Lord Jesus Christ" (Eph. 6:23). Here Augustine admits that it was another text of Paul's (1 Cor. 9:19) that had made him very watchful in this matter, and he goes on to cite Romans 12:3, which points to faith itself as a gift of him who has "dealt to every man the measure of faith," and adds Philippians 1:29, "to you is given on behalf of Christ, not only to believe in Him, but also to suffer for his sake."

The epitome of *Book of Rules* of Tyconius toward the second part of Book III of *De doctrina christiana* is a rare instance in the early church of one author's work presented as an epitome in the work of another author (especially in recommending exegetical insights of a schismatic). Augustine's summarizing commentary was a mixed blessing for the Donatist writer. Rule III was particularly hard hit. Unlike the Monza

49. Ibid.

Epitome[50] of Tyconius's book, the Augustinian epitome neglected every Pauline citation of the original and deliberately moves the focus of the argumentation to the issues of the third decade of the fifth century. But Tyconius's loss is our gain. Rather than giving a summary of a problematics of the faction-riven church of the late fourth century, Augustine carefully recapitulates the Pauline themes that he had been wrestling with for a lifetime.

Conclusion

Augustine is a man of the Bible, but not the man of a single book of the Bible. It is clear that even in the most significant citations of Romans that frame and direct his understanding, issues engage him rather than minutiae of exegesis. Does this mean (to indulge in mixed metaphors) that he prefers a broad brush to a probing instrument? No, his capacity to focus on and intensely scrutinize the details of the text is remarkable. But this propensity to be galvanized by the profound questions of human existence tends, paradoxically, to make the specific genre of the scriptural commentary alien to the maturing of his genius as a scriptural commentator. On this point it may be argued that the great commentary on Genesis *De genesi ad litteram* was the crowning of his career as an exegete (401–15). But here one has to ask if this, too, was not issue-driven. On the one hand, it was the question of the proper exercise of *literal* exegesis, and on the other, it was the great anthropological questions that he had already been wrestling with a quarter of a century. Six or seven years before he began his work on this commentary, Augustine had written not a full continuous commentary, but a remarkably detailed set of notes on Romans. Then, in what seems to be short shrift, he produced a commentary on Galatians and began his commentary on Romans, dropping the project at verse 7 of the first chapter, as we noted at the outset of the present study. It is noteworthy that it was a particular issue that diverted his attention—the sin against the Holy Spirit (Matt. 12:32). Following on the heels of these tasks, Augustine immerses himself in the two-pronged issues raised by Simplicianus. It is here, in conversation with his former mentor, rather than in the more conventional genre of the commentary, that Augustine takes his place among the great expositors of the Epistle to the Romans.

50. See Burkitt, *Book of Rules*, 89–98; Pamela Bright, "The Preponderating Influence of Augustine: A Study of the Epitomes of the Book of Rules of the Donatist Tyconius," in *Augustine and the Bible*, ed. Kannengiesser and Bright, 109–28; Pierre Cazier, "Cassien auteur présumé de l'épitome des Règles de Tyconius," *Revue de études Augustiniennes* 21, nos. 1–2 (1975–76).

Is this insistence on the importance of issues a displacement of the centrality of scripture in Augustine's thought? Not at all. He is not a man of abstract thought. He is a man of conversation. He cannot be himself alone. He must surround himself with friends, with the stimulus of conversation. Above all his conversation is with scripture. Scripture is the firmament toward which his eye is always directed (*Conf.* XIII 15.18). It is the song toward which his ear ever strains. It is the image-world that permeates every aspect of his communication, and over the decades of his ministry, scripture gradually becomes inextricably enmeshed with the style and the content of his writing. He is in constant interaction with scripture. Scripture breaks open, like broken bread, and nourishes his thought.

In one of his many studies on Augustine, Henry Chadwick, while noting the continuing presence of Plotinus and Porphyry in the *Confessions*, insists on Augustine's "profounder engagement with Paul":

> Augustine became persuaded that the inner moral conflict described in Romans 7 was not just a personified portrait of man not yet under grace, but a self-portrait of Paul with a divided mind uncommonly like his own.[51]

I suspect that in heaven Augustine will not be found with the Epistle to the Romans tucked under his arm. More likely he will be found arm in arm with Paul, in deep conversation.

---

51. Chadwick, *Augustine*, 67–68.

5

THOMAS AQUINAS

Steven Boguslawski

Introduction

Thomas Aquinas's way of reading Romans 9–11 not only corrects and develops the received tradition, but also sustains a positive theology of Judaism by a deft interweaving of key theological "controlling concepts" and careful exposition of the Pauline text. Such an assertion violates contemporary sensibilities of exegetes who purport to maintain clear boundaries between theology and exegesis. Were we to begin with that premise (I might add, a quite faulty one), we would be impeded from understanding Aquinas or any premodern commentator of the sacred page. As one of my professors of New Testament taught me long ago, "there is no such thing as a presuppositionless exegesis." To claim that such a methodology exists is philosophically naive. Aquinas was neither philosophically naive nor theologically unsophisticated, so we should expect that philosophical concepts and theological tenets guide his exegesis of the literal meaning of a text. Romans 9–11 is no exception, especially in his treatment of the Jews and their role in salvation history.

To date, no study has located Thomas's understanding of the role of the Jews within the theological framework of predestination and election, and no contemporary studies analyze the connection between *Summa Theologiae* (*ST*) Ia.23 and *Commentary on Romans* (*CRO*) 9–11 on the role of Jews.[1] Study of select texts from Thomas's *ST, Commentary on the Sentences* (*Sent.*), and his *CRO* demonstrates what the theological significance is for Aquinas. For Thomas, the role of the Jewish people may be understood only within the larger theological context of divine providence and the doctrines of predestination and election.

For our purposes in this chapter, it is crucial to understand that Aquinas does not envision a discontinuity between systematic determinations of a given topic and a biblical commentary wherein the same subject matter arises. According to Thomas, there is a unity of theological and exegetical inquiry because the object under consideration, *sacra doctrina*,[2] is one and the same. The implication of this assertion is that any exegetical "science" or investigative methodology must be subalternated to the integrity of this sacred doctrine.

Indeed, this position was developed more fully by the Renaissance Thomist commentator Thomas de Vio Cardinal Cajetan (1469–1534). For him, *sacra doctrina* represents something quite comprehensive, namely all knowledge taught us by God's grace. He enunciates the principle that theology should remain a single science—enjoying a single formal light, to use his expression. He therefore considers the whole matter of our being taught by God as something prior to the establishment of distinct theological disciplines or crafts. More recently, the same point finds support in Edward Farley's book *Theologia*,[3] which provides a historical explanation of the disintegration of theological unity. The current brief study consciously seeks to illustrate this unified theological enterprise as typical of Thomas's exegesis of Romans 9–11.

---

1. In fact, apart from Garrigou-Lagrange's work on predestination fifty years ago, little has been written on the topic of predestination and election in Aquinas in contemporary studies. Representative studies that treat of predestination in Thomas include Lee H. Yearley, "St. Thomas Aquinas on Providence and Predestination," *Anglican Theological Review* 49 (1967), 409–23; Charles Partee, "Predestination in Aquinas and Calvin," *Reformed Review* 32 (1978), 14–22; J. J. Macintosh, "Aquinas and Ockham on Time, Predestination, and the Unexpected Examination," *Franciscan Studies* 55 (1998), 181–220; and Thomas M. Tomasic, "Natural Moral Law and Predestination in St. Thomas Aquinas: An Incurable Contradiction?" in *The Medieval Tradition of Natural Law*, ed. Harold J. Johnson (Kalamazoo, MI: Medieval Institute Publications, 1987), 179–89. A more comprehensive analysis of Aquinas's perspective of the Jews entitled *Aquinas' Commentary on Romans 9–11* will be published by Paulist Press and the Stimulus Foundation. I wish to thank the publisher of Paulist Press, Rev. Lawrence Boadt, CSP, and the foundation for permission to use that research in this project.

2. See *ST* Ia.1.1.; especially apt is his concluding remark: "It was therefore necessary that, besides philosophical science built up by reason, there should be a sacred science learned through revelation."

3. Edward Farley, *Theologia* (Philadelphia: Fortress Press, 1983), especially 29–48.

Provisionally, I wish to characterize Aquinas's exegesis as a "herme-neutical helix" because of the interplay of exegesis, systematic consider-ations (and other subalternated sciences), subjective experience (namely, Thomas's own experience, especially as it pertains to the Jewish people), and the understanding granted by the Holy Spirit.

Thomas's methodological approach to the sacred page is both simple and ambitious. For him, textual commentary must eventually yield to personal appropriation of the biblical text, lest the scriptural witness remain restricted to a specific exegetical, historically conditioned meth-odology and become, in the last analysis, a dead word. On the other hand, he knew that he must avoid systematic constructs that unduly constrain scriptural expression through an enforced conformity to theological articulations of doctrinal certitudes. Of course, personal experience and the light granted by God shape the interpretive lens. Aquinas knew that "scientific" presuppositions can blunt the power of the biblical text to confront, convert, and conform the reader. Con-versely, he knew that the commentary tradition (especially patristic and other authorities) and systematic formulations temper a subjectivist threat to privatize the meaning of the text and isolate the individual believer in a solitary world of discourse. (I contend that the synthetic understanding sought in the "hermeneutical helix" has both intel-lectual and experiential components but enjoys a single formal light in pursuit of the *sacra doctrina*.) We should recall that Thomas was first of all a Dominican friar, and that he began his career as Master of Theology precisely as a *Magister in sacra pagina* in 1256 in Paris. Both these factors are relevant insofar as the Order of Friars Preach-ers was given papal approbation by Honorius III for the "salvation of souls" through preaching—salvation for congregants and preachers alike. Secondly, Master of the Sacred Page is the "most ancient des-ignation for the medieval theologian"[4]—the sacred text is where one began, so to speak.

The fundamental unity of theological discourse is attested in Aquinas by a nearly seamless movement between "biblical text" and "theological text." Consequently, there should be little surprise that substantial agree-ment exists between Aquinas's *CRO*, (where the Pauline text exercises control) the *ST* (where the theological plan and doctrine exercise control), or his *Sent* (where the Lombard exercises control). In fact, this material correlation (if not borrowing) is exemplified in *ST* Ia.23 and *CRO* on the doctrine of predestination, as well as *I Sent.* d.41 and *CRO* on the doctrine of divine election, especially with reference to chapters 9–11

4. James A. Weisheipl, *Friar Thomas d'Aquino: His Life, Thought, and Works* (Garden City, NY: Doubleday, 1974), 111.

of Romans.[5] These passages from *Sent.* and *ST* (in particular) contain controlling concepts or hermeneutical keys that govern Thomas's exegesis and inform his teaching concerning the ongoing role of the Jewish people in salvation history. Therefore, the more comprehensive and systematic determinations of *ST* and *Sent.* provide the broader conceptual framework for Thomas's comments on these three chapters of his scriptural commentary and contextualize his discussion of the relationship between Jews and Gentiles. Those chapters and that relationship shall serve as a test of my theory. First, we shall attend to the general contribution that *ST* Ia.23 makes to Aquinas's use of the doctrine of predestination in *CRO*. Afterward, we will undertake a similar analysis of the doctrine of election in *I Sent.* and in *CRO*. Finally, we must delineate the distinctiveness of Aquinas's use of these doctrines in his treatment of Romans in general, and the Jews in particular.

Predestination in Aquinas's *ST* and *CRO*

Thomas wrote *ST* and the first edition of *CRO* contemporaneously, and, not surprisingly, there is a variety of ways in which *ST* and *CRO* agree. In the *prima pars* Thomas locates his discussion of predestination within an analysis of God's knowledge and will, specifically under the aspect of God's providence (Ia.22.1–4).[6] In Ia.23.resp. he explicitly states that "everything falls under his Providence, [and] also that the function of Providence is to arrange things to an end." (Interestingly, Romans informs Aquinas's argument, since he adduces Romans 8:30 in the *sed contra* of q. 23). God's will orders the individual to an end that is above the natural capacities of the rational creature: the end that is God himself. A similar care to establish the broader context of predestination within divine providence surfaces in *CRO* §§699ff. ". . . because as it is said in Prov 8.17: I love the ones loving me; to love is to will the

5. Since the *prima pars* was written between 1266 and November 1268, it is possible that there is a material borrowing from *ST* in *CRO*. Weisheipl delineates five "heterogeneous pieces" that make up Aquinas's *Expositio et lectura super Epistolas Pauli Apostoli*, the first of which is the edited text written or dictated by Thomas (*expositio*) "covering Romans to I Corinthians 7:9," and furthermore that ". . . Thomas did not lecture on Paul at Naples, but rather at Paris during his second regency" (Weisheipl, *Friar Thomas d'Aquino*, 373). This chronology is important when considering Aquinas's perspective of the Jews in Romans, because his regency follows the bitter Christian-Jewish disputes that resulted in the confiscation and public burning of Talmud in Paris in 1242. More to the point, it permits us to compare *CRO* in the form edited by Thomas himself with the *prima pars* completed earlier in 1268.

6. See also *I Sent.* d.39.2.

good for the beloved; however for God *to will is to work*. For all things whatever he wished, he did, as it is said in Ps 135.6."[7] Immediately, in *CRO* §700, Aquinas attributes predestination to "God's eternal will . . . who first predestined believers from eternity; secondly he calls them in time; thirdly he sanctifies . . . so that the purpose may be referred to predestination, which according to Augustine is the purpose of the one having pity, Eph 1.11: Ones predestined according to his purpose."[8]

From the outset of his commentary, even the definition of predestination that Thomas utilizes in *CRO* mirrors that found in *ST* Ia.23.1: to predestine is to send. In *CRO* §43 he writes: "Indeed destination is taken in two ways. Sometimes on behalf of a mission: for the ones who are sent for something are said [to be] destined." Thomas's second definition derives from the first: ". . . to predestine is nothing other than to dispose from the heart beforehand what is to be done concerning a certain thing."[9]

Additionally, Thomas is careful to note that predestination is not to be equated with the natural dispositions of a thing's constitution,[10] but properly said only of those creatures that are rational and ordered to the things that are above nature.[11] Of further significance in *ST* and *CRO* is the concern to place predestination within God as an immanent activity that has its effect in the object of his activity, namely, individual human beings. This can also be applied by extension to corporate entities (such as Israel) by the use of the hermeneutics often employed by Thomas.

Another element found in both texts involves the temporal aspect of an individual's salvation. We have seen above that in *CRO* §700 Thomas explains how God predestines the believer from eternity but calls and sanctifies the individual in time. In *ST* Ia.23.a.2, Thomas writes: ". . . predestination is like the plan, existing in God's mind, for the ordering of some persons to salvation. The carrying out of this is passively as it were in the persons predestined, though actively in God. When considered executively in this sense, predestination is spoken of as a 'calling' and

7. . . . [Q]uis, ut dicitur Prov. VIII.17: Ego diligentes me diligo; diligere est bonum velle dilecto; Dei autem velle est operari. Omnia enim quaecumque voluit fecit, ut in Ps CXXXIV.6 dicitur [emphasis mine].

8. . . . qui primo fideles ab aeterno praedestinavit; secundo ex tempore vocat; tertio sanctificat . . . ut propositum referatur ad praedestinationem, quae, secundum Augustinum, est propositum miserendi, Eph I.11: Praedestinati secundum propositum eius.

9. Destinatio autem dupliciter sumitur. Quandoque pro missione: dicuntur enim destinati qui ad aliquid mittuntur. . . . [S]ecunda significatio a prima derivari videtur. . . . Secundum hoc igitur praedestinare nihil aliud est quam ante in corde disponere quid sit de re aliqua faciendum.

10. See, for example, §45: ". . . sicut non dicimus proprie quod homo est praedestinatus habere manus. . . ."

11. See §45.

a 'glorifying,' thus St. Paul says, whom he predestinated, them also he called and glorified."[12]

Another textual congruence is evidenced regarding the concept of reprobation. In the *sed contra* of *ST* Ia.23.3, Thomas cites Malachi 1:2–3 ("Jacob I loved, but Esau I hated"); this is a verse that receives extensive treatment in the Romans commentary. In *ST* Ia.23.3 and in *CRO* §764, Thomas carefully distinguishes between those whom God ordains to be saved and those whom he permits to fall away from grace: "[A]s predestination includes the will to confer grace and glory, so reprobation includes the will to permit someone to fall into fault and to inflict the penalty of damnation in consequence."[13] ". . . [A]s predestination is the preparation for glory, so reprobation is the preparation of punishment."[14]

Furthermore, in ad 2 he explains that rejection and punishment derive from one's free decision and cites Hosea 13:9 ("Your destruction is from yourself, O Israel . . .") as scriptural warrant. The same text is employed in *CRO* §764.

The clearest example of the common use of the hermeneutical tools of predestination and election occurs in *CRO* §763 and *ST* Ia.23. In the former, Thomas reprises the argument advanced in Ia.23.4.resp., which defines predestination, election, and love, as well as the order of these in God and in us. The texts of *ST* and *CRO*, respectively, read:

> The predestination of some to eternal salvation means that God wills their salvation. This is where special and chosen loving come in. Special because God wills this blessing of eternal salvation to some . . . for . . . loving is willing a person good, chosen loving (*electio*) because he wills this to some and not to others for, . . . some he rejects. Election and dilection operate (*ordinatur*) differently in us and in God. When we love things our will does not cause them to be good; it is because they are good already that we are roused to love them; therefore we choose someone to love, and our choice precedes our loving. With God the converse is true. For when he chooses to love another and thereby wills him good, his will is the cause of the other being singled out and so endowed. Clearly, then, the notion of God's special loving precedes that of his choosing, and that of his choosing that of his predestining. Therefore all the predestined are picked loves (*electi et dilecti*). . . . However election and love are ordered differently in God and in man. For in man election precedes love, for the will of man is moved to loving from the good which he considers in the

---

12. The themes of *vocatio Dei* and the glorification of persons so elected, recur throughout *CRO* 10 and 11. See below.

13. Ia.23.3.resp.

14. §764.

thing loved, by reason of which he chooses this thing before another, and is the cause of every good which is in the creature. And in this manner, the good by reason of which one creature is preferred to another through the mode of election follows upon the will of God, for the good of that man, which pertains to the notion of love. Whence it is not on account of a good he may choose in a man that God loves him, but more from the fact that he loves him, he prefers him to others by electing him.[15]

Finally, Ia.23.5 asks whether foreknowledge of merits is the cause of predestination. This concern is substantially echoed in several sections of *CRO*, most of which occur within chapters 9–11. Indeed, the argument advanced in the third objection, citing Romans 9:14, is substantially reproduced in §773:

> For it is manifest that distributive justice has a place in the things which are owed from what is due; consider (for example), if some merit a wage, so that greater wages may be given to those laboring more. However it does not have a place in the things which one gives freely and merci-fully. . . . Since therefore all people on account of the sin of the first parents are born liable to damnation, God through his grace liberates them, by mercy only he frees [them]. And thus to certain ones whom he frees he is merciful; to certain ones he is just, whom he does not free; he is wicked to neither however. And in this manner the Apostle solves the question through the authority which ascribes everything to divine mercy.[16]

15. Electio autem et dilectio aliter ordinantur in Deo et in homine. In homine enim electio praecedit dilectionem. Voluntas enim hominis movetur ad amandum ex bono quod in re amata considerat, ratione cuius ipsam praeelegit alteri et praeelectae suum amorem impendit. Sed voluntas Dei est causa omnis boni quod est in creatura. Et ideo bonum per quod una creatura praefertur alteri per modum electionis, consequitur voluntatem Dei, quae est de bono illius, quae pertinet ad rationem dilectionis. Unde non propter bonum quod in homine eligat Deus eum diligit, sed potius eo quod ipsum diligit, praefert eum aliis eligendo. (§763)

Reginald Garrigou-Lagrange (*Predestination* [London: B. Herder, 1950 (1939)], 78) states the general principle succinctly: ". . . no created being would be better than another unless it were loved more by God [I. 20.3]. St. Thomas makes [predilection] the keystone of his treatise on predestination."

16. Manifestum est enim quod iustitia distributiva locum habet in his quae debentur ex debito, puta si aliqui meruerunt mercedem, ut plus laborantibus maior merces donetur. Non autem habet locum in his quae sponte et misericorditer aliquis dat. . . .

Cum igitur omnes homines propter peccatum primi parentis nascantur damnationi obnoxii, quos Deus per gratiam suam liberat, sola misericordia liberat. Et sic quibusdam est misericors, quos liberat, quibusdam autem iustus, quos non liberat, neutris autem iniquus.

Et ideo Apostolus quaestionem solvit per auctoritatem, quae omnia divinae miseri-cordiae adscribit.

Thomas had provided the rationale for *CRO* §773 earlier, in Ia.23.5 .ad 3:

> God wills to manifest his goodness in men, in those whom he predestines in the manner of mercy by sparing them, in those whom he reprobates in the manner of justice by punishing them. This provides a key to the problem why God chooses some and rejects others; it is offered by St. Paul, What if God, desiring to show his wrath . . . and to make known the riches of his glory for the vessels of mercy, which he hath prepared beforehand for glory. . . . Why does he choose some to glory while others he rejects? His so willing is the sole ground. . . . We cannot complain if God prepares unequal lots for equals. This would be repugnant to divine justice as such were the effect of predestination a due to be rendered, not a favor. He who grants by grace can give freely as he wills, be it more be it less, without prejudice to justice, provided he deprives no one of what is owing. In the householder's words of the parable, Take what is thine and go thy way. Is it not lawful for me to do what I will with my own?[17]

Indeed, several common components emerge in comparing these texts: concern to locate election within the ambit of divine mercy and, correlatively, reprobation within divine justice; the assertion that divine volition orders all things and persons providentially; the exempla employed to illustrate the principle; and most importantly (because the effect of predestination is granted gratuitously, not from an owed debt), the denial of the infringement of justice. Divine mercy and providence account for the election of certain individuals and the reprobation of others; as we shall see, they also account for the hardening of some for the benefit of others considered corporately. In all this, God does not act unjustly: a determination that finds extensive treatment in *CRO* §§766–74.

For Thomas the certitude of predestination (a.6) finds scriptural expression in Romans 8:29, regarding which ". . . the Gloss comments [that] Predestination is the foreknowledge of and the preparation for God's benefits, whereby those who are liberated most certainly are."[18] Foreknowledge and a certain eternal causality with respect to the benefits of salvation are ascribed to God in *CRO* §702 also; again, the material congruence is striking. Aquinas uses the core of this argument to deal with the impugnment of divine justice in Romans 9:14, an issue that

---

17. Also in this article, Thomas refutes theological positions taken by Origen and Pelagius; the former claimed that souls were allotted bodies on the basis of preexisting merit, the latter that the impetus for doing well begins with the human person and the consummation from God. In each case preexisting merit elicits divine election. Thomas cites Rom. 9:11–12 to refute the former and 2 Cor. 3:5 to refute the latter. Again, each of these concerns is replicated in *CRO* §§758 and 767, as well as §§771 and 772.

18. *sed contra.*

is raised by Paul himself. That is, on the conceptual level, by making remote the causality of God, he preserves God from taint of injustice. For, although divine providence is certain, it also functions through contingent causes "according to the condition of the proximate causes providentially appointed them" (Ia23.6.resp.). Therefore, predestination considered as an effect in individuals does not obliterate human free will from which it contingently issues. In brief, God's knowledge and will do not dispense with contingent causality in the material world nor in the exercise of free will.[19] At the same time, God owes nothing to creatures, and divine predestination is prior to the enactment of free choice and the graces that enable it. As with *ST*, so too in the manner of argumentation in *CRO*, Thomas moves from primary to secondary causality and the role of human willing.

Most important in Ia23.6, however, is the principle expressed in ad 1, a principle that is at the heart of *CRO* chapters 9–11. Thomas writes:

> A person may wear the crown on two titles, from divine predestination, and thus no one loses it, and from the merit of grace, for what we merit is in a sense ours, and thus we can lose it by subsequent mortal sin. Another, who is substituted in his place, gains the lost crown. *God does not allow some to fall without raising others in their place* according to the text in Job. He will shatter mighty men without number, and set others to stand in their stead. Accordingly human beings took the place of the fallen angels, *and Gentiles that of the Jews*. (emphasis mine)

Thomas, commenting on Romans 11:11 in *CRO* §879, writes:

> Therefore he says, moving the question, have they stumbled such that they fall? This can be understood in a two-fold way. By one mode, thus: Did God permit them to stumble solely such that they fall, that is, for no other use from that following afterward, except only wishing them to fall? That indeed would be against the divine goodness, which is such that . . . he would never permit anything evil to be done except for the sake of the good which he elicits from the evil. Wherefore also in Job 34.24 it is said: He will crush the many and innumerable men, and he

---

19. "Precisely as transcendent universal cause of the being and activity of creatures, God's providential governance of the universe makes our free activity possible. . . . God's causality embraces and empowers the diverse sorts of causality in the universe by making it possible for each created agent to act according to its nature; determined, physical agents acting necessarily according to pre-established patterns, and intelligent, deliberative human and angelic agents acting freely. . . . In his goodness, God shares the dignity of being a real cause with creaturely agents." J. Augustine DiNoia, O.P., "Providence," in *The Encyclopedia of Catholic Doctrine*, ed. Russell Shaw (Huntington, IN: Our Sunday Visitor, 1997), 548.

will make others to stand for them. And Rev 2.11: Hold fast to what you have, lest another should take your crown, because namely God permits certain ones to fall thus, so that the fall of some may be the occasion of the salvation of others.[20]

The material correspondence between *ST* Ia.23.6.ad 3 and §879 is apparent. How it is that the Gentiles may be said to "take the place of the Jews" without necessitating a supersessionist stance vis-à-vis the Jews, we shall see in the later analysis of Romans 9–11.

The seventh and eighth articles of Ia.23 also cite Romans 8:28 and 11:29, respectively. The number of the predestined is fixed, "not only by reason of his knowledge . . . but also by reason of his own defining decision and choice."[21] This concern substantially appears in *CRO* §§915ff, where Thomas discusses what constitutes the "fullness of the Gentiles" (*plenitudo Gentium intraret*), as well as the salvation of "all Israel" (*omnis Israel salvus fiet*). The identity of the predestined is determined and foreknown by God, and those reprobated are such for the benefit of the elect—a tenet that is applicable to Jews and Gentiles alike.

What these passages demonstrate, at the very least, is the consistency of Thomas's thought on predestination and election between the writing of the *prima pars* in 1268 and the *CRO expositio* of 1272. These texts, especially *ST* Ia.23.1–7, also elucidate Thomas's Romans commentary. The fuller theology of predestination in *ST* contextualizes Thomas's understanding of the status and role of the Jewish people. The phenomenon of textual congruity demonstrated in these fundamental principles of predestination will be evidenced similarly in Thomas's understanding of the doctrine of election in *I Sent.* and *CRO*.

Election in Aquinas's I Sent. and CRO

The doctrine of election is closely allied to Thomas's understanding of predestination.[22] This association should not surprise us in *CRO*

---

20. Quod potest dupliciter intelligi. Uno modo sic: numquid Deus permisit eos offendere solum ut caderent, id est propter nullam aliam utilitatem inde consequentem, sed solum volens eos cadere? Quod quidem esset contra bonitatem divinam . . . quod numquam permitteret aliquid mali fieri nisi propter bonum, quo ex malo elicit, unde et Iob XXXIV.24 dicitur: Conteret multos et innumerabiles, et stare faciet alios pro eis. Apoc. II.11 dicitur: Tene quod habes, ne alius accipiat coronam tuam, quia scilicet Deus aliquos sic permittit cadere, ut quorumdam casus sit aliorum salutis occasio.

21. Ia.23.7.resp.

22. Est autem . . . considerandum, quod tria posuit in Deo pertinentia ad sanctos, videlicet electionem per quam intelligitur predestinatio, et dilectio. Que quidem realiter sunt idem in Deo, sed differunt ratione. (§763)

insofar as Paul links the two concepts in Romans 8:29–33. However, we must ask whether the doctrine of election warrants the prominence given it by Aquinas in *CRO*.[23] Is Aquinas's consideration of election, with reference to the Jews, simply dictated by the Pauline text, or (as with predestination) does the topic enjoy a certain prominence in Aquinas's thought independent of his *lectio continua* on Romans?

Although Paul rarely uses election (ἐκλογή) and its cognate forms, significantly, more than half of the Pauline uses occur in Romans (8:33; 9:11; 11:5; 11:7; 11:28, and 16:13). In these texts, we see that the purpose (κατὰ πρόθεσιν) of God is manifest in predestination (προορίζω, 8.29; 8.30) and, "so that his purpose might remain" steadfast, in accordance with divine election (κατ᾽ ἐκλογήν, 9.11). Indeed, election serves to bracket chapters 9–11, commencing with 9:11 and culminating in 11:28. The "purpose of God" is explained by predestination and election as associated concepts, which receive greater specificity in the intervening material. "[T]he Latin terms *predestinatio* and *predestinare* include the election idea, but go further by pointing to a foreordination, thus referring primarily to God's foreordaining our salvation (ἡ κατ᾽ ἐκλογὴν πρόθεσις)."[24] All Israel remains beloved κατὰ . . . τὴν ἐκλογήν on account of their fathers, despite the hardening which has come upon a portion of it (11:28).[25] Nevertheless, there is also an elect part of Israel (ἡ . . . ἐκλογή, 11:7), identifiable with a remnant (λεμμα) according to the election of grace (κατ᾽ ἐκλογὴν χάριτος, 11:5). Corporate Israel is elect; a faithful remnant is elect; individuals are elect (see 16:13 in addition to 9:11). Paul (in the non-Pauline Pastoral Epistles) endures for the sake of the elect (2 Tim. 2:10) and is a servant apostle κατὰ πίστιν ἐκλεκτῶν θεοῦ (Titus 1:1). God's activity of choosing bestows a titular status to those selected. In all of this, there seems to be a certain elasticity in Paul's application of the term ἐκλογή.

In Romans 8:33 Paul explicitly asserts that no one may lay a charge against or condemn God's elect. Furthermore, he states that elect Israel

23. Aquinas's use of "elect/election" occurs in eighteen paragraphs within chapters 9–11 and within five additional paragraphs in the remainder of the letter. By contrast, Paul uses "election" 4 times in Rom. 9–11, specifically 9:11; 11:5; 11:7; and 11:28. He speaks of the "elect" in 8:33 and 16:13.

24. Erich Dinkler, "The Historical and the Eschatological Israel in Romans Chapters 9–11: A Contribution to the Problem of Predestination and Individual Responsibility," *Journal of Religion* 33 (1956), 120.

25. See *ST* I.21.4.ad 4, where Thomas writes that "God's justice and mercy appear both in the conversion of the Jews and of the Gentiles. But an aspect of justice appears in the conversion of the Jews which is not seen in the conversion of the Gentiles; inasmuch as the Jews were saved on account of the promises made to the fathers." In *CRO* Aquinas does not identify the "beloved Jews" specifically as converts.

perdures beloved by God (ἀγαπητοί)[26] while being ("according to the gospel") simultaneously enemies (ἐχθροί) for the sake of the Gentiles (11:28): ". . . for the gifts and the call of God are irrevocable" (11:29). Yet how can all of these claims be true? And what is Thomas's position on Paul's plotline, especially with reference to the doctrine of Israel's irrevocable election?

As we shall see, Thomas teaches in *CRO* that God pre-elects Jacob over Esau, not because the former was holy but so that he might become holy; Aquinas explicitly states that ". . . this is the proposition of predestination, concerning which it is said: Predestined according to his purpose."[27] Some preliminary questions must be asked: does Thomas's understanding of election in *CRO* replicate or refine certain aspects of predestination? And, regarding election, are there material borrowings from or substantial correspondence with works prior to or contemporaneous with *CRO*?

It should not surprise us that the subsidiary theme of election appears in tandem with Aquinas's understanding of predestination in *CRO*, since they are linked by Paul. That Thomas has observed the linkage in Romans is not wholly attributable to his careful reading of the apostle, however. Indeed, the two theological concepts are intertwined from the beginning of Thomas's teaching career in Paris: in his first and third commentaries on the *Libri Sententiarum*[28] (as well as in *ST* Ia.23.4, as we have seen above).[29] The interrelation is made explicit in *I Sent*. d.41.1.2.[30] In *distinctio* 41, Thomas defines election as a "certain segregation," which in one mode is eternal, [and] by another mode temporal. For if it may be understood according to which the proposition is of God himself, thus it is eternal, because from eternity he willed to segregate the good from the evil in glory. But if it may be understood accordingly as it is in the execution of a work, thus it is temporal, just as when someone is segregated from original or actual fault in grace, or from common

---

26. See also 1 Thess. 1:4, wherein Paul addresses the brothers as "beloved by God" and immediately acknowledges their election (εἰδότες . . . τὴν ἐκλογὴν ὑμῶν). Also cf. Col. 3:12: "ὡς ἐκλεκτοὶ τοῦ θεοῦ ἅγιοι καὶ ἠγαπημένοι."

27. Hoc autem est propositum praedestinationis, de quo ibidem dicitur: Praedestinati secundum propositum eius. (§759)

28. See *I Sent*. d.40.1.ad 4. ("Quod sit praedestinatio. . . .") and especially d.41.aa.1,2. The four books of *Sent*. were completed between 1252 and 1256, prior to Thomas's first lectures on Paul in Italy.

29. Cf., *I Sent*. d.41.1.2.ad 1 for the order of election and predestination, and *III Sent*. d.32.2. resp., which specifies *dilectio amicitiae* as the cause of election. Aspects of these two *distinctiones* are seen in *ST* Ia.23.4 (e.g., compare ad 3 with d.32.resp.) and are substantially developed in *CRO*.

30. There is no article exclusively dedicated to the question of election in *ST*, although it enjoys a certain prominence in Ia.23.4. Therefore, I have chosen Thomas's earlier discrete treatment of the subject in *I Sent*. for analysis and comparison with *CRO*.

status in a prelate's office, and so on concerning the other things that, by divine gift, are especially conferred to certain ones.[31]

Predestination adds something to the concept of election, "just as providence adds [something] above [the concept of] a disposition."[32] Aquinas succinctly defines election as "the divine ordination itself, by which certain ones are preferred to others for the attaining of beatitude."[33] Predestination, additionally, signifies the preparation of the goods of grace and the goods of glory for the elect by means of which they are conformed to that end. These basic theological distinctions and definitions, culled from the I and III *Sentences,* recur not only in *ST,* but also in *CRO* with specific application to Jews and Gentiles alike. For example, commenting on Romans 9:24, Thomas writes: "After the Apostle shows that the grace of God is given to people from divine election, through which people are called to grace, here he shows that the aforementioned election or call belongs not only to the Jews (such that they may be able to boast on account of that which is said in Dt 4.37: I loved your fathers and chose their seed after them) but also to the Peoples."[34]

Those who are predestined, called, justified, and glorified (Rom. 8:30) have a certain assurance rooted in God's election. Paul

> shows that no accusation is able to be injurious to the saints of God: and this by reason of divine election. For he who chooses a certain one, in virtue of this is seen to approve him. However the saints were chosen by God. Eph 1.4: He chose us in himself before the constitution of the world, so that we should be holy. Nevertheless he who accuses, reproves him whom he accuses. However the accusation of someone has no force against the approbation of God. And for that reason he says who shall accuse, namely efficaciously, against the elect of God, that is against the ones God chooses so that they may be holy? Whence it is said Rev 12.10: The accuser of our brothers is cast out.[35]

31. *I Sent.* d.41.1.2.resp.

32. Ibid.

33. Ibid. Thomas uses Dionysisus's comparison of divine goodness and the sun found in *I Sent.* d.41.1.ad 2 in *ST* Ia.23.4.obj.1. In ad 2, however, he writes: "Speaking more precisely . . . of the sharing of this or that good, then God does not grant without choice (*non absque electione*), for some blessings he gives to some and not to others. Hence there is choice (*electio*) of those he brings together in grace and glory."

34. Postquam Apostolus ostendit quod Dei gratia datur hominibus ex divina electione, per quam homines ad gratiam vocantur, hic ostendit quod praedicta election sive vocatio non solum pertinet ad Iudaeos ut ipsi poterant gloriari, propter hoc quod dicitur Deut. IV.37: Dilexi patres tuos et eligi semen eorum post eos sed etiam ad Gentes. (§796)

35. . . .[O]stendit quod nulla accusatio possit esse sanctis Dei nociva: et hoc ratione divinae electionis. Qui enim aliquem elegit, ex hoc ipso eum approbare videtur. Sancti autem sunt electi a Deo. Eph I.4: Elegit nos in ipso ante mundi constitutionem, ut essemus sancti. Qui autem accusat, improbat eum quem accusat. Non autem valet alicuius

Thomas proposes Paul as an example of God's elect from the outset of *CRO*, a status that is signified by his name[36] and by his task, which is distinct from that of the other disciples.[37] A more explicit argument is advanced by Thomas regarding Paul's status as a Jew, chosen and predestined by God, who instantiates God's fidelity to his people:

> Then, when he says Far be it, etc., he solves the question showing that God did not reject totally the people of the Jews. And this is what he says Far be it, such that the people of the Jews be rejected totally by God. And this indeed, first, he proves as far as his own person, saying For I too, who am living in the faith of Christ, am an Israelite, namely with the people; 2 Cor 11.22: They are Israelites and so am I.[38]

For Jews and Gentiles alike, Aquinas makes it eminently clear that election is from the grace of God, not from preceding works.[39] God is the agent whose purpose (i.e., considered as an end or final cause) is to manifest in them the "abundance of his goodness" by means of election and compassion; God recalls the elect from evil, draws them toward justice, and ultimately, leads them to glory.[40] Indeed, being children of God derives from election, as does the dignity of the Jews.[41]

---

accusatio contra Dei approbationem. Et ideo dicit quis accusabit, scilicet efficaciter, adversus electos, id est adversus quos Deus elegit ut sint sancti? Unde dicitur Apoc XII.10: Proiectus est accusator fratrum nostrorum. (§716)

36. ". . . insofar as it is from the Hebrew, it is the same as 'wonderful' or 'elect' (*mirabilis vel electus*). . . . And these indeed fit him. In fact he was elect with respect to grace (*electus . . . fuit quantum ad gratiam*), hence Acts 9.15: This one is to me as a vessel of election" (§17; also see §64).

37. "Set apart . . . either through conversion from unbelievers . . . or . . . whether set apart by election (*segregatus per electionem*) from the other disciples, accordingly Acts 13.2: Set apart for me Saul and Barnabas, etc." (§23).

38. Deinde, cum dicit, Absit, etc., solvit quaestionem ostendens quod Deus non totaliter reppulerat populum Iudaeorum. Et hoc est quod dicit Absit, ut scilicet populus Iudaeorum sit totaliter a Deo repulsus. Et hoc quidem, primo, probat quantum ad personam suam, dicens: Nam et ego, qui in fide Christi existens, Israëlitae sum, scilicet gente; II Cor XI.22: Israëlitae sunt et ego. (§861)

39. See §796. But in §735 the *origin of grace* derives from the "sole election of God," not from any merit from "preceding works."

40. Finis enim electionis et miserationis bonorum est, ut manifestet in eis abundantiam bonitatis suae, revocando eos a malo, et ad iustitiam eos trahendo, et finaliter eos perducendo in gloriam. (§794)

41. Postquam posuit dignitatem Iudaeorum, ostendit quod ista dignitas non pertineat ad eos qui processerunt ex antiquis patribus carnaliter sed ad spirituale semen quod est a Deo electum. Et primo ostendit, quod huiusmodi dignitas proveniat ex electione divina; secundo ostendit, quod hac electio pertinet communiter et ad Iudaeos et ad Gentiles. (§748)

The seeming ambiguity evidenced in Aquinas's doctrine of predestination is similarly apparent in his doctrine of election. The election of some from among the Jews and of some from among the Gentiles (as opposed to others) is attributable to the "absolute will of God."[42] Divine *predilectio* results in the election of particular individuals.[43] Since neither one mode of divine activity nor one creature could manifest adequately the divine goodness, God's mercy is manifest in those freed by his grace, and God's justice, likewise, is manifest in those whom he punishes for sin, i.e., reprobates. As Thomas writes:

> However the excellence of such things is from the divine goodness which is not able to exist neither by one mode nor to be manifested sufficiently in one creature. And for this reason he produced diverse creatures, in whom by diverse modes it is manifested. However, especially in rational creatures (in whom his justice is manifested as far as those whom he punishes for their merits), certainly his mercy is in those whom he frees by his grace. And in this manner so that both would be manifested in people, he freed some mercifully, but not all.[44]

The application of these principles is most complex regarding the Jews. Thomas, following Paul, must articulate a resolution that preserves the elect status of corporate Israel (on the one hand), while simultaneously seeing the distillation of a remnant and the incorporation of some Gentiles (on the other hand) as not being a betrayal of the divine promise — or, worse yet, seeing God as the perpetrator of a grave injustice. How may each assertion be true? For example, in §863

---

42. "[O]n what account he may wish to have mercy on this one and that one or to harden him . . . is not able to be assigned except the absolute (*simplex Dei voluntas*) will of God."

Thomas continues illustrating the principle from the builder's craft, selecting equal stones for varying locations in a wall; "[B]ut why one may place these stones in the summit and those at the base has not a certain reason, except that the craftsman willed it" (§788).

43. Cf. §763, as above. Garrigou-Lagrange (*Predostination*, 80) posits that "Thomas expresses what is the foundation for the principle of predilection, in the fine distinction he draws between the antecedent will, which is the principle of sufficient grace, and the consequent will, which is the principle of efficacious grace. On this point he says: 'Whatever God simply wills takes place; although what he wills antecedently may not take place' [cf., I.19.6.ad 1]." This distinction becomes particularly relevant to Rom. 11:26. See below.

44. Tanta est autem divinae bonitatis excellentia, quod non potest nec uno modo nec in una creatura sufficienter manifestari. Et ideo diversas creaturas condidit, in quibus diversimode manifestatur, praecipue autem in creaturis rationalibus, in quibus eius iustitiam manifestatur quantum ad illos quos pro eorum meritis punit, misericordia vero in illis quos ex sua gratia liberat. Et ideo ut utrumque in hominibus manifestaretur, quosdam misericorditer liberavit, sed non omnes. (§792)

we read: "Therefore first he says: Not only am I not rejected, but God did not reject his people, the whole [people], which he foreknew, that is, predestined. Above 8.8: The ones whom he foreknew, these he also predestined. Ps 93.14: The Lord will not reject his people. That the Apostle here expounds as far as concerns the ones predestined."[45] But previously, in §802, he commented:

> It was said because Hosea spoke for the Gentiles, Isaiah cries out, that is, he speaks openly for the conversion of Israel. Isa 58.1: Cry out do not cease, as though your voice [be] a trumpet. However in this first authority firstly, he posits the paucity of those converted from out of Israel, saying Though the number of the sons of Israel shall be as the sand of the sea, that is, innumerable in advance of the multitude. Gen 22.17: I shall multiply your seed . . . etc. 3 Kgs 4.20: Judah and Israel are innumerable as the sand of the sea.—A remnant shall be saved, that is, not all, nor the major part, but a certain few who are left from the fall of others. . . . Below 11.5: The remnant, according to the election of grace, were saved.[46]

Thus, in §802 the predestination of Israel reduces to the predestination of a remnant, but later in §863, Thomas asserts that the whole people shall be saved. Can these competing claims be reconciled simply by appeal to God's antecedent and consequent will in predestinating and electing?[47]

For Aquinas, God loves the elect more because he wills more good for them, and these chosen are taken from among Jews and Gentiles alike. Divine election effectively relativizes the status of Jew and Gentile, making them equal in their present call, justification, and glorification. At the same time, however, Thomas preserves the Jews' dignity and their

45. Dicit ergo primo: Non solum ego non sum repulsus sed Deus non reppulit plebem suam, totam, quam prescivit, id est praedestinavit, supra VIII.8: Quos praescivit, hos et praedestinavit. Ps XCIII.14: Non repellet Dominus plebem suam. Quod Apostolus hic exponit quantum ad praedestinatos.

46. Dictum est quod Oseam loquitur pro Gentibus, Isaias clamat, id est aperte loquitur pro conversione Israel. Is LVIII.1: Clama, ne cesses, quasi tuba vocem tuam.

In hac autem prima auctoritate, primo, ponit paucitatem conversorum ex Israel, dicens si fuerit numerus filiorum Israël tamquam arena maris, id est innumerabiles prae multitudine. Gen. XXII.17: Multiplicabo semen tuum velut arenam que est etc. III Reg IV.20: Iuda et Israël innumerabiles quasi arena maris. Reliquiae salvae fient, id est non omnes, nec maior pars, sed aliqui pauci qui relinquenter ex excidio aliorum. . . . Infra XI.5: Reliquiae secundum electionem gratiae salvae factae sunt. (§802)

47. Thomas's commentary in §932 seems to imply this distinction: . . . ut omnium misereatur, id est ut in omni genere hominum sua misericordia locum habeat . . . quod quidem non est extendum ad daemones . . . nec etiam quantum ad omnes homines sigillatim, sed ad omnia genera hominum. Fit enim hoc distributio pro generibus singulorum et non pro singulis generum.

privileged status, not only historically, but as essential to the outworking of election in time. The gift of God and the call are temporal.

> Because it must be said that the gift here is taken for a promise which is made in accordance with the foreknowledge and predestination of God. However, the call is taken for election, because on account of the certitude of both, what God promises, now by a certain mode he calls. Nevertheless also the very gift of God is temporal and the call temporal; it is not made void through a change of God as though of one repenting, but through the change of man, who rejects the grace of God.[48]

The status of corporate Israel, the role of the remnant, and the election of the individuals are integrally preserved. Since this is so, there is a necessity and a responsibility incumbent upon the Christian church to preserve the role of the Jews in the temporal outworking of salvation history. Thomas accomplishes this objective theologically by attributing that temporal process to God's eternal predestinating will and election; these principles are the hermeneutical key to understanding *CRO* chapters 9–11. Election is a "certain segregation" seen in the separation of Israel from the nations and the isolation of a remnant from among the Jews and the Gentiles. The former establishes the fundamental prerogative of Israel, which the distillation of the remnant does not abrogate. If there is a seeming ambiguity in Aquinas's exposition, it is one that reflects the enactment of divine providence among Jews and Gentiles alike—a temporal tension that Paul himself recognizes. We see, in particular, this dynamic tension in *CRO* chapters 9 and 11.

Since Aquinas has a consistent understanding of the historical nature of divine activity, and the principles of predestination and election are equally applicable in Paul's or Thomas's own day, I argue that Aquinas's exegesis in *CRO* concerning the role of the Jews is uniquely tied to these theological concepts. However, some scholars hold the position that Thomas simply inherits and transmits an Augustinian interpretation concerning the relationship between the Jews and Gentiles. Were I to demonstrate that this is not the case, it would require us to investigate Augustine's *Propositions from the Epistle to the Romans* and his *Unfinished Commentary on the Epistle to the Romans* to compare the topics of predestination, election, and the role of the Jews in order to demonstrate

---

48. Sed dicendum est quod donum hic accipitur pro promissione, quae fit secundum Dei praescientiam vel praedestinationem. Vocatio autem hic accipitur pro electione, quia propter certitudinem utriusque, quod Deus promittit, iam quodammodo dat et quos elegit, iam quodammodo vocat. Et tamen ipsum temporale Dei donum et temporalis vocatio, non irritatur per mutationem Dei quasi poenitentis sed propter mutationem hominis, qui gratiam Dei abiicit. (§926)

that Aquinas's exegesis is not simply derivative. From a comparison of
Aquinas's hermeneutics with those of Augustine, I could demonstrate
that Thomas does not merely transmit the received Augustinian tradition
but frames the Jew-Gentile problem in a unique manner. Additionally, it
would become apparent that to characterize Aquinas simply as a supersessionist, that is, one who puts eschatological Israel, the church, in
opposition to empirical Israel, the Jewish people, would be incorrect.

Conclusion

Aquinas does not view Paul's Letter to the Romans through the hermeneutical prism of forensic justification; he sees Romans 9–11 as the
material center of the letter. He utilizes the controlling concept of divine
providence and, particularly, the theological categories of predestination
and election to delineate the relationship between Jew and Gentile, as
well as the ongoing role of the Jews in salvation history.[50]

The student of Thomas must resist modernizing him in order to respond to the challenge of contemporary Jewish-Christian dialogue or
our own prevailing Zeitgeist in academe. This is particularly true when
analyzing Thomas's biblical commentaries in general and especially his
Commentary on the Romans. To modernize Aquinas would mean that
we are twice removed from Paul's resolution of the Jew-Gentile and
Jewish-Christian/Gentile-Christian problem.

Aquinas defends the corporate soteriological status of the Jews
throughout his commentary. He repeatedly asserts that "Salvation" after
all, "is from the Jews" (John 4:22). Also, we have seen briefly that in *CRO*
(as well as in other Thomistic texts) predestination and the ancillary
doctrine of election account for the ongoing role and status of the Jews
as a privileged, temporal manifestation of God's eternal will. God's election of the Jews and the call of the Gentiles retain a temporal tension or
ambiguity, which Paul recognized and which he struggled to articulate
in corporate and individual aspects. Thomas preserved the inherent
ambiguity of the apostle and sought to provide an explicit theological
rationale for the soteriological interdependence of Jews and Gentiles
and, by implication, of his Jewish and Christian contemporaries.

---

50. For contemporary commentators utilizing a similar hermeneutical key, cf. G. B.
Caird, "Predestination—Romans IX–XI," *Expository Times* 68 (1957), 324–27; Ragnard
Bring, "Paul and the Old Testament: A Study of the Ideas of Election, Faith and Law in
Paul, with Special Reference to Romans 9:30–10:13," *Studia Teologica* (1971), 25–28; and,
C. K. Barrett, "Romans 9:30–10:21: Fall and Responsibility of Israel," in *Essays on Paul*
(London: SPCK, 1982), 132.

Although chapters 9–11 of *CRO* were the chief concern of this brief study, references to the role of the Jews elsewhere in the commentary could be cited extensively to supplement the primary texts under consideration. The task, methodologically considered, has been primarily one of internal description, i.e., discerning the controlling concepts that he employs in order to define the passage under consideration in Romans 9–11, and assessing his use of authoritative references that serve to explicate its meaning (especially John 4:22). By so doing, we witness Aquinas's pursuit of the *sacra doctrina* through scriptural commentary and systematic theological sciences.

In my estimation, *CRO* represents a significant resource for the development of a reading of Romans that sustains a positive theological appraisal of the Jewish people. Contemporary reappraisals of medieval anti-Judaism frequently reproach Thomas for an allegedly negative, supersessionistic view of the Jews; these critics selectively interpret Aquinas's writings, largely ignoring his most sustained treatment of Jew-Gentile relations found in *CRO* 9–11. Analysis of these chapters in his commentary, in tandem with other Thomistic texts, demonstrates that Thomas is not anti-Jewish; he simply remains faithful to the plotline established by Paul.

In Aquinas we discover (or rediscover) a significant voice that should be heard in the contemporary exegetical debate about hermeneutics in general and Romans in particular. Thomas's hermeneutical keys to understanding Romans 9–11 are readily applicable to the contemporary Jewish-Christian dialogue: it is God who predestines and elects; it is God who grants Jew and Gentile their privileged status; it is God who saves "all Israel" once the "fullness of the Gentiles" has entered into salvation; and it is God to whom the synagogue and the church—and their theologians—are accountable.

6

MARTIN LUTHER

Timothy George

In the first volume of his vast *History of Dogma*, Adolf von Harnack
described the writings of St. Paul as the conscience of the church, and
declared that the critical epochs in the development of Christian doctrine
could be explained as a series of Pauline reactions.

> One might write a history of dogma as a history of the Pauline reactions
> in the church, and in doing so would touch on all the turning points of the
> history. Marcion after the Apostolic Fathers; Irenaeus, Clement and Origen
> after the Apologists; Augustine after the Fathers of the Greek Church; the
> great Reformers of the Middle Ages from Agobard to Wessel in the bosom
> of the medieval Church; Luther after the Scholastics; Jansenism after the
> Council of Trent; everywhere it has been Paul, in these men, who produced
> the Reformation. Paulinism has proved to be a ferment in the history of
> dogma, a basis it has never been.[1]

Harnack wrote these words, of course, before yet another Pauline
reaction had set in, this one brought about by Karl Barth's discovery
of the strange new world within the Bible, a theocentric revolution following a century and a half of neo-Protestant efforts to smooth over the

---

1. Adolf von Harnack, *History of Dogma*, trans. Neil Buchanan (Boston: Little, Brown,
1901): 1:136.

rough edges of Paul's radical notions about sin, grace, faith, election, and judgment. The fact that Harnack himself saw only a ferment, not a basis, in this recurrent Paulinism perhaps says more about Harnack than it does about the writings of the apostle borne out of due time. It reflects Harnack's own captivity to the historicizing and relativizing, and indeed the de-dogmatizing, of the Christian faith, an impetus stemming from Schleiermacher's elevation of religious self-consciousness, rather than divine self-revelation, as the starting point for theological reflection. There is very little of Paul in Harnack's "das Wesen des Christentums"!

It is not surprising, of course, that Martin Luther should rank among the foremost exponents of a Pauline renaissance in Christian theology, or indeed that his name should be forever linked with Paul's letter to the Romans as a pivotal intersection in that doctrinal trajectory. Following his courageous stand at Worms and his productive solitude in the Wartburg, Luther prepared for publication the first edition of his translation of the New Testament in German, which appeared in 1522. In addition to writing a general introduction to the entire New Testament, Luther also provided separate prefaces to the individual books he had translated. In his *Preface to the Epistle of St. Paul to the Romans*, Luther said this: "This Epistle is really the chief part of the New Testament, and is truly the purest Gospel. It is worthy not only that every Christian should know it word for word, by heart, but also that he should occupy himself with it every day, as the daily bread of the soul. We can never read it or ponder over it too much; for the more we deal with it, the more precious it becomes and the better it tastes."[2]

This was not hyperbole! Luther's high estimation of Romans had been hard won through his own intense struggle with the issues Paul raises in this *Hauptbriefe,* issues that had pursued Luther in his torturous quest to find a gracious God. It was in fact Luther's succinct summary of Romans in his 1522 preface that was to become so well known and to have such great influence on figures from Tyndale and Wesley to Spurgeon and Robert Murray McCheyne. Luther's famous preface was a manifesto of Reformation theology, reflecting as it does the reformer's mature thought at the end of the indulgence controversy and his final break with Rome.

However, Luther's decisive grappling with Paul and Romans had taken place some seven years earlier, in a series of lectures he had given in Wittenberg. For nearly 400 years these Romans lectures were lost to history. Their rediscovery in the early twentieth century was a major

2. Martin Luther, *Luther's Works,* vol. 35, *Word and Sacrament,* ed. E. Theodore Bachmann (Philadelphia: Fortress Press, 1960), 365.

event in Reformation studies, comparable to the discovery of the Dead Sea Scrolls in biblical studies. Though I shall come back to the Romans preface several times in this essay, I want to focus on the earlier and much longer *Lectures on Romans* of 1515–16. We shall examine first the mystery of the missing manuscript, then how Luther approached his task as a teacher of Holy Scripture, the sources and traditions with which he worked, and finally how the Romans lectures fit into his developing theology as a reformer of the church.

The Mystery of the Missing Manuscript

Almost from the time of his entrance into the Augustinian monastery at Erfurt in 1505, Luther had been recognized as a promising teacher, both within his order and in the larger university setting. Early on he had lectured on Aristotle's *Ethics,* and, in 1509 (the year of Calvin's birth), he was appointed *Sententiarius,* which made him eligible to lecture on the first two books of Peter Lombard's *Books of Sentences,* the standard medieval textbook in theology. Apart from his trip to Rome in 1510, it is hard to pinpoint Luther's chronology during these early years, but we know from his later testimony that he was deeply concerned (perhaps *obsessed* would be a better word) with the holiness and justice of God, the sacrament of penance, and his own desperate inadequacy to obtain salvific solace from it, with issues of predestination and grace, all reinforced by bouts of dread and fear, the famous *Anfechtungen,* so that even the rustling of a dry leaf would bring on the torments of hell, referring to a verse in Leviticus 26:36. (Luther will return to the image of the windblown leaf in his *Lectures on Romans.*)[3] In the course of Luther's spiritual depressions, Johann von Staupitz, his superior, confessor, and mentor, directed him to proceed to complete the requirements for his doctorate in theology. On October 18, 1512, the degree was solemnly conferred. He was appointed for life *lectura in Biblia* at the University of Wittenberg, succeeding Staupitz himself.

In the winter of 1512, Luther began preparation for his first course of biblical lectures at Wittenberg, the *Dictata super Psalterium,* which he actually presented over the course of two years, from the summer semester of 1513 until the end of the winter semester of 1515. He next took up Paul's Letter to the Romans, which he pursued for three semesters beginning at Easter in 1515 and concluding in early September of 1516. This constituted ninety class hours in all, as Luther followed

3. *Luther: Lectures on Romans,* ed. Wilhelm Pauck, Library of Christian Classics, vol. 5 (Philadelphia: Westminster Press, 1961), 283. Hereafter, *Romans.*

this sequence in his lectures: first semester, 1:1–3:4; second semester, 3:5–8:39; third semester, 9:1–16:27. After Romans, he continued his academic lectures in Paul, first with Galatians and then Hebrews (regarded then as Pauline). Then, after this long exegetical sojourn in Paul, he returned to the Psalms, publishing a second commentary in 1519–20: *Operationes in Psalmos*. This second visit to the Psalms was cut short at Psalm 22, as Luther was caught up in the crisis leading to his excommunication.

Why did Luther never publish his *Lectures on Romans*? There are at least two possible reasons for this. In the first place, it is likely that Luther never regarded his *Lectures on Romans* as a definitive, publishable exposition of this Pauline epistle. In a letter of December 16, 1515, Luther referred to his first Psalms lectures as trifles, quite worthy of being destroyed.[4] While he never made any comparable statement about his Romans commentary, as far as we know, even after he became a reformer Luther was usually reticent about promoting his published writings, the one notable exception being his larger commentary on Galatians (1535), which he referred to in the most endearing terms as "my Katie von Bora." When Luther first lectured on Romans, his reformational theology was still fluid, with new ideas bursting from almost every page. Later on, he was happy for his followers to learn their Reformation theology from his Galatians work, the Schmalkald Articles, the two Catechisms, and the Augsburg Confession, rather than from the unfinished and uneven comments of the young Luther of Romans, who at the time believed in purgatory and still defended celibacy and monasticism.

There is a second, more practical, reason why the Romans lectures were never published in Luther's lifetime. In 1518 Philipp Melanchthon was brought from Tübingen to Wittenberg to become professor of Greek and New Testament. Romans was assigned to Melanchthon and he offered at least five lecture courses on it during his long tenure as Luther's beloved associate and successor. Within the university faculty, Luther himself gravitated more and more to the Old Testament, offering lectures on Genesis, Deuteronomy, Isaiah, the Minor Prophets, and Wisdom Literature. When specific questions about Romans were directed to Luther in later years, he usually referred them to Melanchthon. However, Romans continued to have a formative influence in Luther's theology and preaching, as we have seen from the high praise he lavished on Romans in his 1522 *Preface*. There are also more than thirty extant

---

4. Pauck's translation is based on the critical edition of Luther's *Römerbriefvorlesung* by Johannes Ficker, published as vol. 56 in the Weimer edition of Luther's works. A complete translation of the Romans lectures is also provided in vol. 25 of the American edition of Luther's works. Hereafter, *LW* 25.

Luther sermons from various texts in Romans, and a major portion of Luther's *De Servo Arbitrio* against Erasmus (1525), particularly part 6, is a reworking of predestinarian arguments first put forth by Luther a decade earlier in his *Lectures on Romans*.

Now to the mystery of the missing manuscript. The fact that Luther's *Romans* was not read for some 400 years is the result of what James Atkinson has called one of the "freaks of historical accident."[5] After his death in 1546, the manuscript of Luther's *Lectures on Romans* passed into the possession of his son Dr. Paul Luther, who was a court physician to the Elector of Saxony. In 1582, perhaps at Paul's behest, the document was bound in red leather and stamped in gold with the electoral coat of arms. In 1587, the theologian John Wiegand referred to Luther's early writings and said, "I have held his own autographs in my hands and looked at them with admiration."[6] Later historians were aware of the Romans manuscript but assumed that it had been lost. In fact, Luther's grandchildren (Paul's sons) had sold all of their grandfather's manuscripts and books to Joachim Frederick, Margrave of Brandenburg, about the year 1594. This entire library, including Luther's Romans manuscript, was later incorporated into the Royal Library of Berlin. In this way, Luther's *Lectures on Romans* was consigned to the anonymity of the archives. The oldest catalog of the library, from 1688, lists Luther's Romans manuscript, and it is also referred to again in 1846 when it was put on display in celebration of the three hundredth anniversary of Luther's death. In 1905 the librarian noted his surprise that no Luther scholar had ever come to study this original work of the Reformer.

Meanwhile, down in Rome, a copy of this very manuscript had indeed been discovered in the Vatican Library and used extensively in the hostile researches of the Dominican scholar and Luther iconoclast Heinrich Denifle. In his learned attack against the Reformation, *Luther and Lutheranism* (1904), Denifle cited the Romans lectures as evidence of Luther's ignorance and misinterpretation, as he saw it, of the medieval Catholic tradition. In the *Confessionsstreit* that ensued, Protestant scholars renewed their search to find the original autograph of the copy Denifle had found in the Vatican Library.

The story of this copy is itself fascinating. That copy in fact had been made by Johannes Aurifaber, one of the scribes who had taken down much of Luther's *Table Talk*. It had been bought by Ulrich Fugger, a later

5. James Atkinson, *Luther and the Birth of Protestantism* (Atlanta: John Knox Press, 1981), 108. Much of the material in the following paragraphs is based on Pauck's introduction to his translation of the Romans lectures, which in turn follows the account of Johannes Ficker in his introduction to the critical edition in *WA* 56.

6. Ibid.

descendant of the great German banking house that had been involved in the original indulgence controversy. He in turn had bequeathed this copy of *Romans* to the Palatine Library at Heidelberg. Then, during the Thirty Years War, it fell into the hands of the Catholic sovereign of Bavaria, Maximilian I, who presented it, along with the rest of the library of which it was a part, to Pope Gregory XV. Thus it had made its way from the Neckar to the Tiber. In 1899, Pope Leo XIII opened the Vatican Libraries to the scholarly world, and Denifle, hound of heresy that he was, discovered this long-lost copy and made it the centerpiece of his polemical attack against the Reformation.

Meanwhile, on the Protestant side, Johannes Ficker, a paleographer and historian from Strasbourg, renewed his efforts to locate the Luther original. This eventually led him to the Royal Library in Berlin, where the true treasure had lain dormant for those several centuries. Ficker hurriedly published a critical edition of his great find in 1908. It was still thirty years later, in 1938, when Ficker brought out the definitive edition of Luther's Romans lectures, published as volume 56 of the *Weimar Ausgabe*.

The discovery and publication of these long-lost lectures inaugurated a new era in Reformation scholarship. We cannot begin to unravel the threads of this vast literature, but we do well to note three interrelated questions to which numerous scholars have looked again to the Romans manuscript for answers. First, is Luther, and the Reformation in general, to be understood as essentially medieval or modern? This was the great debate between Ernst Troeltsch and Karl Holl. Troeltsch argued that Luther, and Calvin too in a different way, belonged far more to the ethos and mind-set of the preceding Middle Ages than to the ensuing era of modernity. The real cultural and theological break, Troeltsch believed, came with the Enlightenment, not at the Reformation. By contrast, Karl Holl, the doyen of the "Luther renaissance," believed that Luther had provided the basis for the Protestant transformation of Christian culture through the personal actualization of moral and religious union with God. Holl was building on the insights of Albrecht Ritschl in the nineteenth century. His reading of Luther was much in sync with the reigning liberal theology of German *Kulturprotestantismus*, which dominated Reformation studies in the early twentieth century.

The second question is closely related to the first: Was Luther the first liberal or the last conservative? Hegel had describe Luther as a figure of epochal significance, the all-illuminating sun, which follows that daybreak at the end of the Middle Ages.[7] This image came to dominate the

---

7. H. Glockner, ed., *Georg Wilhelm Friedrich Hegel, Sämthiche Werke* (Stuttgart-Bad Constatt, 1956–57): 11:519.

heroic view of Luther as the champion of freedom and conscience, the lonely liberator of the human spirit. To a great extent, this is the view of Luther that remains in both mainline and evangelical Protestantism today. Karl Barth and other theologians in his circle read Luther differently. Luther was the theologian who recovered a biblical view of the living God by listening afresh to the Word of God—not least in Romans! Perhaps the best exposition of this perspective on Luther is Phillip S. Watson's justly famous *Let God be God!* (London: Epworth, 1947).

And, finally, the third question: Was the young Luther a precocious Protestant or a constructive Catholic? This issue became entwined in the emerging ecumenical movement as Protestant enthusiasts wanted to claim Luther for the "home team" as early as possible and so tended to push back the date of his "Reformation breakthrough" to as early as 1511 or 1512. (Ebeling is a good example here.) On the other hand, Catholic scholars in the school of Josef Lortz had strangely fallen in love with the young Luther and so wanted to keep him a Catholic as long as possible. The lectures on Romans became a major battleground for these competing schools of interpretation.

Luther at the Lectern

Before seeing how some of these issues play out in the lectures themselves, we should briefly look over the shoulder of Luther the teacher. What was his methodology? What were his sources and style?

We know that Luther's lectures took place on Monday and Friday at 6:00 in the morning. As far as we know, they were the first university lectures on the Bible delivered in the German tongue. John Oldecop of Hildesheim, who later became a bitter enemy of Luther, registered at the University of Wittenberg just as Luther began his course on Romans at Easter in 1515. "The students liked to hear him for no one like him had been heard there who translated so boldly every Latin word," he reported.[8] Another student from this same time has left us the following portrait of Luther at the lectern:

> He was a man of middle stature, with a voice which combined sharpness and softness; it was soft in tone; sharp in the enunciation of syllables, words, and sentences. He spoke neither too quickly nor too slowly, but at an even pace, without hesitation very clearly, and in such fitting order that each part flowed naturally out of what went before. . . . His lectures never

8. Robert Herndon Fife, *Young Luther: The Intellectual and Religious Development of Martin Luther to 1518* (New York: Macmillan, 1928), 185.

contained anything that was not pithy or relevant. And, to say something about the spirit of the man: if even the fiercest enemies of the Gospel had been among his hearers, they would have confessed from the force of what they heard that they had witnessed, not a man, but a spirit, for he could not teach such amazing things from himself, but only from the influence of some good or evil spirit.[9]

It was difficult to be so inspiring at 6 a.m. even in 1515!

But what exactly were the students hearing from Luther? Already, in his first lectures on the Psalms, Luther had developed a style of lecturing that he continued to use with Romans. He had asked the local printer, Johann Grunenberg, to print the Vulgate text of Romans (from the 1509 Froben edition published at Basel) on a special sheet of paper with broad margins and a full centimeter between the lines. The text of Romans printed in this way took up twenty-eight sheets, with fourteen lines on each page. Luther followed closely the medieval exegetical tradition of glossing the text, writing in a small meticulous hand his own marginal comments in this special edition of the text prepared by Grunenberg. The students were provided with an identical copy of this text and copied down, word for word, Luther's carefully dictated comments. (We know this from several student copies of Luther's lectures that were discovered and published by Johannes Ficker in the *Weimar Ausgabe*.)

In developing his glosses on Romans, Luther drew on the tradition of Christian exegesis that had preceded him, making special use of five sources:

1. The *glossa ordinaria* of Strabo, a scholar associated with the school of Alcuin in the ninth century. Strabo had provided a word-by-word analysis of the biblical text, drawing on the patristic witnesses, including Ambrose, Augustine, Gregory the Great, Origen, Chrysostom, Jerome, the Venerable Bede, and others.
2. The *glossa interlinearis* of Anselm of Laon. A somewhat more expansive interpretation of the phrases of the biblical texts, with special emphasis on their spiritual meaning.
3. The *postillae perpetuae* of Nicholas of Lyra (d. 1340), a Franciscan theologian from Paris, whose commentary on scripture emphasized the literal or historical interpretation of the text. These three resources, Strabo, Anselm, and Lyra, had been made conveniently available in Froben's six-folio volumes of the Bible, an edition with which Luther was thoroughly familiar.

9. *Romans,* 1xi–xii.

4. Jacques Lefèvre d'Etaples, a French humanist scholar, whose translation and commentary on Paul's letters Luther had before him as he developed his lectures.

5. Erasmus. In his comments on the early chapters of Romans, Luther frequently referred to the Greek in Lorenzo Valla's Greek edition of the New Testament, as well as to Faber's Latin translation, which was based on the Greek. However, from chapter 9 onward, Luther had available, and frequently cited, Erasmus's newly published critical edition of the Greek New Testament.

Even in his glosses, Luther displayed a remarkable freedom in dealing with all of these sources. He appreciated Lyra's focus on the literal meaning of the text, but he did not hesitate to criticize his interpretation of Romans 1:17: "the righteousness of God is revealed from faith to faith." Lyra interpreted that phrase, in typical medieval fashion, to mean "from unformed faith to formed faith." Luther finds this distinction invidious, claiming that "there is only one faith, the same for the laity as the scholars—and that while there may be growth in saving faith, that 'growth does not make it more real but only gives it greater clarity.'"[10] As for Erasmus, while Luther was appreciative of his philological prowess, there was already a growing disdain for his inability to grasp the gravity of sin and the true dilemma of the human before God. "No one is a wise Christian just because he knows Greek and Hebrew," Luther noted. Between *Romans* and the *Bondage of the Will* ten years later, the theological chasm between Luther and Erasmus would grow deeper and wider.

In addition to his glossing of the text, Luther also prepared extensive expository notes, which were handwritten on 123 separate sheets of paper. These *scholia,* as this part of the commentary was called, constitute the bulk of the Romans manuscript. While Luther did not present most of this material to the students, it is precisely here that we can track most clearly his personal struggles with the text and his evolving theology of grace.

Initia Reformationis: **The Lure of Biblical Theology**

In popular Protestant lore, the beginnings of the Reformation are frequently equated with dramatic moments in the life of Luther: his famous "tower experience," when he grasped the true meaning of justification; the posting of the Ninety-five Theses on All Hallows Eve in

10. Ibid., 19.

1517; his debate with John Eck at Leipzig in 1519; his "here I stand" speech at Worms in 1521. Yet these later events are inexplicable apart from the exegetical labors that took place along a seven-year trajectory (1512–18) during which Luther developed what Heiko Oberman has called the "theological grammar" of the scriptures.[11] Could it be that Luther's reformatory revolution began not with a high drama of ecclesiastical confrontation, but with the petty faculty politics of curricular revision? With reference to Romans, this meant two things:

1. A hermeneutical shift toward a dynamic and Christocentric reading of scripture; and
2. The triumph of biblical theology over scholastic methods and assumptions.

Both Gerhard Ebeling and James S. Preus locate Luther's key hermeneutical shift in his first lectures on the Psalms in the years immediately preceding his Romans commentary. Ebeling argues that Luther's "new hermeneutics" involved his reducing of the traditional four senses of scripture to two: Christ himself as the literal sense, and faith in Christ as the moral or tropological sense. Justification by faith was deduced from the merging of these two senses—in other words, "faith became Jesus Christ tropologically understood, or what Jesus means *for me*" (*christus pro me*).[12] Preus presents Luther's hermeneutical shift somewhat differently: instead of seeing Christ speaking directly in the Psalms, eliciting personal faith from the believer, Luther "began to appreciate the Psalms as the witness of a historical person, David, who, like himself and other Christians, had to sustain his life by faith in God's Word and promise."[13] Reformation theology thus focused on the promise or the covenant (*pactum*) through which David heard the word of justification in his day, just as we do in ours as we listen to the Word of God in Holy Scripture. *Fides ex auditu:* Faith comes by hearing, as Luther says in his commentary on this phrase in Romans 10:17: "The Word is of such a character that unless it is received by hearing and by faith, none can grasp it." In the gloss on this text, Luther quotes several scriptural passages to prove the importance and prior-

---

11. Heiko A. Oberman, "Martin Luther contra Medieval Monasticism: A Friar in the Lion's Den," in Timothy Maschke, et al., eds., *Ad fontes Lutheris: Toward the Recovery of the Real Luther* (Milwaukee: Marquette University Press, 2001), 183–84.

12. Steven Ozment, *The Age of Reform* (New Haven: Yale University Press, 1980), 71. See also Gerhard Ebeling, "The Hermeneutics and the Early Luther," *Theology Today* 21 (1964): 34–46; James S. Preus, *From Shadow to Promise: Old Testament Interpretation from Augustine to the Young Luther* (Cambridge: Harvard University Press, 1964).

13. Preus, *From Shadow to Promise*, 226–28.

ity of hearing (Ezek. 7; Obad. 1; Ps. 16; 110; Isa. 1; Heb. 3). Luther's emphasis on hearing the Word of promise led him to exalt preaching above mere reading and study alone. As he would later say, the church is not a "pen house" but a "mouth house": Christ himself has not written anything, nor has he ordered anything to be written, but rather to be preached by word of mouth. Or, again, "the Word of God shall remain free, to be heard by everyone."[14]

It needs to be stated that Luther's hermenuetical revolution was carried out *within* the structures of the medieval exegetical tradition. Throughout his Romans lectures, Luther still makes use of the medieval *quadriga*. Even later, when he had abandoned its use as standard exegetical technique, he would sometimes revert to allegorical interpretations. Richard Muller has expressed well the basic Reformation hermeneutic: "Both Luther and Calvin strengthen the shift to the letter (increased by the emphasis on textual and philological study), but they then proceeded to find various figures and levels of meaning embedded in the letter itself."[15]

Running throughout the Romans lectures is a steady critique of scholastic theology—Aristotle, and "those fools, the pig theologians," as Luther unkindly referred to some of his predecessors and contemporaries. He speaks against the "quiddities" and "foolish opinions of the philosophers that befog us in metaphysics."[16] It is well known that Luther was well trained in Nominalist theology (the *via moderna* of the late Middle Ages), and, indeed, in some ways he continued to be Nominalist for the rest of his life. He could sometimes condemn his scholastic masters with faint praise. At the conclusion of his Romans series, in October 1516, Luther wrote to his friend Johannes Lang, who had just become the prior of the Augustinian convent in Erfurt (Luther's old stomping grounds). He wrote to Lang the following comment concerning Gabriel Biel, whose works they had both studied and commented on as students: "I know what Biel says and it is all good except when he deals with grace, love, hope, faith and virtue."[17]

Luther went on in this letter to accuse Biel of "pelagianizing" the gospel. Evidently, the students at Wittenberg were voting with their feet.

14. *LW* 39:22. See Timothy George, *Theology of the Reformers* (Nashville: Broadman and Holman, 1988), 91.

15. Richard Muller, *Biblical Interpretation in the Era of the Reformation* (Grand Rapids: Eerdmans, 1996), 12.

16. *Romans*, 236. See William S. Campbell, "Martin Luther and Paul's Epistle to the Romans," in *The Bible as Book: The Reformation*, ed. Orlaith Sullivan (London: The British Library and Oak Knoll Press, 2000), 103–14.

17. Ibid.

In May 1517, six months after he had completed the Romans course, Luther wrote: "Our theology and St. Augustine's is progressing well. Lombard's *Sentences* are disdained. No one can expect to have students if he does not lecture on the Bible and St. Augustine."[18] In the same year, Luther wrote his *Disputation against Scholastic Theology,* in which he said that it is wrong to think that one cannot become a theologian without Aristotle. The truth, he wrote, is that "one cannot become a theologian unless he becomes one without Aristotle, for Aristotle is to the study of theology as darkness is to light."[19] Long before the principle of *sola scriptura* had become a matter of public controversy at Leipzig, Luther was insisting that the true theologian would pay attention to God's way of speaking (*modus dicendi*) in Holy Scripture, where God defines his own terms not in the speculative grammar of scholastic theology, saturated as it was with the definitions of Aristotle, but rather in his direct address to the prophets and apostles, and through them, and by his Spirit, to us.

Romans and the Shape of Reformation Theology

Near the end of his life, in 1545, Luther looked back on his early work as a biblical theologian and the difficulty he had had in understanding Romans 1:17: "For in the Gospel is the righteousness of God revealed."

> I hated the expression "righteousness of God," for through the tradition and practice of all the doctors I had been taught to understand it philosophically, as the so-called "formal"—or, to use another word, "active"—righteousness through which God is just and punishes sinners and the unjust. But I could not love the righteous God, the God who punishes. I hated him. . . . I pondered incessantly, day and night, until I gave heed to the context of the words, namely: "for in the Gospel is the righteousness of God revealed, as it is written: the just shall live by faith." Then I began to understand the righteousness of God as a righteousness by which a just man lives as by a gift of God, that means by faith. I realized that it was to be understood this way: the righteousness of God is revealed through the Gospel, namely the so-called "passive" righteousness we receive, through which God justifies us by faith through grace and mercy. . . . Here I felt

18. Walther von Loewenich, *Martin Luther: Man and His Work* (Minneapolis: Augsburg, 1986), 103. See *LW* 48:42.19. James Atkinson, ed., *Luther: Early Theological Works* (Philadelphia: Westminster, 1962), 269–70.

19. Atkinson, *Luther,* 269–70.

that I was altogether born again and had entered paradise itself through open gates.[20]

The context of this autobiographical reflection makes it clear that this decisive shift occurred when Luther began his second exposition of the Psalms, that is, around 1518–19. However, many Reformation scholars, finding an evangelical understanding of the gospel in Luther's earlier writings, including Romans, have laid this late dating to an old man's faulty memory. Thus the sharp divide between "the young Luther" and "the mature Luther," between Luther the Augustinian monk, and Luther the Protestant Reformer.

Could it be, however, that we should distinguish two separate experiences of Luther: one, an initial evangelical awakening prompted by the counsels of Staupitz, dated perhaps prior to or even during his first lectures on the Psalms in 1513–14; the other, a theological discovery that led to a clear and different understanding of justification, dated around 1518 or 1519, that is, after the indulgences controversy and before the great treatises of 1520? If this interpretation is correct, then Luther's theology in the Romans lectures will be transitional: redolent of Reformation motifs, yet reflective of a mind and theology in process. This is indeed what we should expect from Luther's own testimony. "I did not learn my theology all at once," Luther later remarked, "but I followed where my temptations led me. It is not reading, nor writing, nor speculating that makes one a theologian. Nay, it is rather living, dying, and being damned that makes one a theologian."[21] Let us look briefly now at several central themes in the Romans lectures, each an indicator of Luther's developing theology. Let us see how Luther treats the themes of sin, God's righteousness, and humility.

The Concept of Sin

There is a great deal about sin in Romans, and Luther devotes many pages of his *scholia* to unpacking this neuralgic theme of medieval theology. At the very beginning of his *scholia* he said (in words which echo the first chapter of Jeremiah):

The chief purpose of this letter is to break down, to pluck up, and to destroy all wisdom and righteousness of the flesh. This includes all

20. WA 54:179–87; LW 34:336–37. For a balanced assessment of this famous and much discussed test, see Bernhard Lohse, *Martin Luther's Theology* (Minneapolis: Fortress Press, 1999), 85–95.
21. WA TR 1:146; WA 5:163.

works which in the eyes of people or even in our own eyes may be great works. No matter whether these works are done with a sincere heart and mind, this letter is to affirm and state and magnify sin, no matter how much someone insists that it does not exist, or that it was believed not to exist.[22]

How is it that Paul seeks to "magnify" sin, to "establish" sin in Romans? Luther's reading of the human situation disallowed the kind of watered-down, attenuated doctrine of original sin that had come to prevail in Nominalist soteriology of the late Middle Ages. For example, in his comments on Romans 5:12–14, Luther opposes those theologians who construe original sin as the mere *absence* of original righteousness. According to this teaching, original sin is privation; it is deprivation—that original standing Adam had enjoyed with God before the fall no longer obtains. The human will has been weakened, impaired. This is a serious breach that must be restored initially through sacrament of baptism (*gratia gratum faciens*). This initial healing must then be supplemented/ enhanced through the penitential-Eucharistic channels of sacramental grace (*gratia gratis data*).

But for Luther this schema is totally inadequate. Original sin is not merely the privation of quality in the will, indeed, not merely the loss of light in the intellect or of strength in the memory, but, in a word, the loss of all uprightness and of the power of all our faculties of body and soul and of the whole inner and outer man. Over and beyond this: proneness toward evil; the loathing of the good; the disdain for light and wisdom, but fondness for error and darkness; the avoidance and contempt of good works, but an eagerness for doing evil.[23]

Luther describes humans affected by sin as *incurvatus in se*, "curved in on themselves." This is so because, due to original sin, our nature is so curved in upon itself at its deepest levels that it not only bends the best gifts of God toward itself in order to enjoy them (as the moralists and hypocrites make evident), nay, rather "uses" God in order to obtain them, but it does not even know that, in this wicked, twisted, crooked way, it seeks everything, including God, only for itself. As the prophet Jeremiah says in Jeremiah 17:9: "The heart of man is crooked and inscrutable; who can know it?" That is, the heart is so curved in upon itself that no man, be he ever so holy, can know it (apart from a testing experience). As it says in Psalm 19:12: "Who can discern his errors? Clear thou me from my hidden faults!"[24]

22. *Romans*, 135.
23. Ibid., 167–68.
24. Ibid., 159.

Luther did not invent the *curvitas* image: it was a well-worn motif in the Augustinian tradition, signifying pride, self-seeking, and rebellion against God. But, as Anders Nygren noted, there is a significant difference in the way Augustine and Luther employ this image. While Augustine speaks of sinners as bent or crooked, curved and bowed down to the earth, Luther makes the self, not just earthly goods, the supreme object of this distorted curvature.[25] In other words, Luther deepens and radicalizes the Augustinian notion of sin as *amor sui*.

Luther's deepened doctrine of the radicality of sin anticipated by more than three centuries the deepest insights of modernity's two great prophets of atheism: Ludwig Feuerbach and Sigmund Freud. In his commentary on Romans 1:20, Luther anticipated Feuerbach's critique of religion when he observed that the root of all idolatry is human "worship [of] God not as he is but as they imagine and think him to be." They think of God as they wish him to be and measure him only in terms of the benefits they receive from him.[26] Thus religion itself, the very thing that is supposed to help us and connect us with the divine, becomes an expression of our very captivity, as we project onto God our own wishes and desires. Rather than "letting God be God," we turn him into "the God who looks like me."

Luther's insight here derives not only from his critique of external religious practice, but also from his own tortured quest to find a gracious God. In his struggles with penance and confession, he wrestled with Psalm 19:12, "Clear thou me from hidden faults" (ASV). Luther's problem was never whether his sins were large ones or small ones, but whether in fact he had confessed every single one. What about the sins he could not remember? What about the sins committed in his sleep? Luther anticipated Freud by recognizing a depth-dimension to the human person and by refusing to limit the effects of sin to the conscious mind alone. Such a radical reading of the human situation could only be answered with an even more radical reading of divine grace.

Justification by Faith

Alister McGrath, among others, has pointed to the Romans lectures as the locus of Luther's decisive break with the theology of justification

25. Anders Nygren, *Agape and Eros,* trans. Philip S. Watson (New York: Harper and Row, 1953), 713–15. See also the discussion in Gordon Rupp, *The Righteousness of God* (London: Hodder and Stoughton, 1953), 164–67.

26. *Romans,* 23–25.

in which he had been trained as a student of the *via moderna*. Elements of Luther's later view are present already in *Romans:*

(1) an emphasis on God's righteousness as *iustitia aliena;*
(2) the utter passivity of humans in their own justification;
(3) the abandonment of the idea (earlier embraced by Luther) that by doing one's best—*facere quod in se est*—one could prepare for the reception of grace.

In all our efforts to procure divine favor, Luther says, we are treating God "like a cobbler handles leather."[27] Such a strategy is not only futile, but blasphemous.

All the same, at this point in his theological trajectory, Luther was still working within the framework of medieval Augustinian soteriology. From the time of the Romans lectures in 1515–16 until his *Preface to Romans* in 1522, Luther abandoned a set of images and ideas inherited from the Augustinian tradition in favor of what he took to be a more purely Pauline approach. Luther later evaluated his definitive position on justification vis-à-vis Augustine thus: "Augustine got nearer to the meaning of Paul than all the Schoolmen but he did not reach Paul. In the beginning I devoured Augustine, but when the door into Paul swung open and I knew what justification by faith really was, then it was out with him."[28] Luther's new insight was that the imputation of Christ's alien righteousness was based, not on the gradual curing of sin, but rather on the complete victory of Christ on a cross. The once-for-allness of justification was emphasized: "If you believe, then you have it!" Nor is there any direct correlation between the state of justification and one's outward works, as Luther made clear in his sermon on the pharisee and the publican (1521): "And the Publican fulfills all the commandments of God on the spot. He was then and there made holy by grace alone. Who could have foreseen that, under this dirty fellow?"[29]

Luther's doctrine of justification by faith fell like a bombshell on the theological landscape of medieval Catholicism. It shattered the entire theology of merit and indeed the sacramental-penitential basis of the church itself. It is no wonder that the Dominican inquisitor of Cologne, Jacob Hochstraten, regarded it as blasphemy for Luther to describe the

27. Ibid., 33.
28. Quoted in Gordon Rupp, "Patterns of Salvation in the First Age of the Reformation," *Archiv für Reformationsgeschichte* 57 (1966): 52–66. See also David Maxwell, "Luther's Augustinian Understanding of Justification in the Lectures on Romans," *Logia: A Journal of Lutheran Theology* 5 (1996): 9–14.
29. *WA* 17:404.

union of the soul to Christ as a spiritual marriage based on faith alone. How could Christ be thus joined to a sinner? This was to make the soul "a prostitute and adulteress" and Christ himself "a pimp and a cowardly patron of her disgrace."[30] Hochstraten was rightly shocked at the import of Luther's message. But it is no less shocking than the statement of Paul upon which it was based: "God justifies the *ungodly.*"

But this does not mean that Luther had no place at all for good works in the Christian life. While we are in no way justified by works, works follow faith as its proper fruit. The fruit of justification is faith active in love. Such love is directed in the first instance not toward God in hope of attaining some merit toward salvation, but toward one's neighbor, for "the Christian lives not in himself, but in Christ and in his neighbor." In his 1522 *Preface*, Luther describes such faith as "a living, busy, active, mighty thing. . . . It is impossible for it not to be doing good works incessantly. It does not ask whether good works are to be done but before the question is asked, it has already done them, and is constantly doing them. Whoever does not do such works, however, is an unbeliever. . . . Thus it is impossible to separate works from faith, quite as impossible as to separate heat and light from fire."[31]

Humility

Throughout his *Lectures on Romans,* Luther seems very nearly to equate humility and faith. Humility is the predisposition required for the verdict of justification. "Therefore we must keep ourselves humble in all these respects, as if we were still bare, and look for the naked mercy of God that he may reckon us righteous and wise."[32] According to Ernst Bizer and others, it was precisely Luther's break with this *humilitas* theology that led to his mature doctrine of justification.

It would be a mistake, however, to regard Luther's all-pervasive emphasis on humility in Romans as a mere phase through which he passed. No, while his emphasis on humility was transformed by his deepened doctrine of justification, it remained a distinctive mark of his spirituality.

Luther's emphasis on humility in Romans is informed by his profound encounter with the mystical tradition. True, Luther has some quite negative comments about mysticism in his *Lectures on Romans.* For example, in commenting on Romans 5:2, he says, "Mystical rapture

---

30. Ozment, *Age of Reform,* 150.
31. *LW* 35:370–71.
32. *Romans,* 5.

is not a passageway to God."[33] But as the context shows, Luther refers here to that stream of Dionysian mysticism with its doctrine of inner darkness, its disparagement of the incarnation, and its illicit desire to hear and contemplate only the uncreated Word apart from the cross and the scriptures. However, just as he was beginning the Romans course, Luther became acquainted with another stream of mysticism, a tradition of mystical theology represented in Germany by the Dominican preacher Johannes Tauler. In fact, Luther published two editions of sermons from the German mystics (1516, 1518), the famous *Theologia Deutsch*, precisely in the same period that he was wrestling with Paul in Romans.

We can identify two themes in the *Lectures on Romans* that recur throughout Luther's lifelong teaching on humility. The first is the theme of self-abandonment (*Gelassenheit*). In commenting on Romans 8, Luther quotes the voice of the birds from the Song of Solomon (2:5), " I am sick with love." He then comments: "We must always take the word love to mean a cross and suffering. Without these the soul becomes languid and tepid. It ceases to long for him and does not thirst for him, the Living Fountain."[34] Here we see the visible roots of an emerging theology of the cross, an emphasis that will become prominent in Luther's Heidelberg Disputation of 1518. In explaining Paul's depiction of the "groanings" that mark the life of faith, Luther declares that the soul must "suffer or endure God" (*Gott leiden*). Like a field about to be tilled by a farmer, the soul must submit itself to the plow of experience; it must be broken and split open if it is ever to bring forth fruit. Luther will later resort to this theme especially in his letters of spiritual counsel and pastoral advice to individuals who have appealed to him for help in times of grief and personal crisis.

The ultimate form of self-abandonment, of course, is the willingness to be consigned to eternal damnation, a spiritual disposition that the mystics called *resignatio ad infernos*. This topic emerges in Luther's discussion of predestination in Romans 9–11. Here he declares that "to be blessed means to seek in everything God's will and His glory, and to want nothing for oneself, neither here nor in the life to come." Indeed, one of the marks of divine election is precisely the willingness to resign oneself to eternal damnation, as Christ himself did on the cross:

> But the true saints actually achieved this resignation, because their hearts overflow with love, and they do this without great distress. For they are so completely dedicated to God that nothing seems impossible for them

33. Ibid., 156.
34. Ibid., 255.

to do, not even the suffering of the pains of hell. And because of this very readiness, they escape from such a punishment. Indeed, they do not need to fear that they will be damned because they submit gladly and willingly to damnation for God's sake. But it is those who want to escape from damnation that will be damned.[35]

This paradoxical theology underscores the role of humility in the life of faith. Since God's electing grace was grounded on his eternal decree, there was no room for boasting or self-assertion. But Luther recognized that the gift of resignation to hell was dispensed to the elect briefly and sparingly, most often at the hour of death. More commonly, Luther's advice to those tormented by the question of election was, "Thank God for your torments!" It was characteristic of the elect, he said, not of the reprobate, to tremble at the hidden counsel of God. Beyond this, he urged a flat refutation of the devil and a contemplation of Christ. All these themes were present *in nuce* in the *Lectures on Romans* but would receive fuller exposition in Luther's classic answer to Erasmus in *The Bondage of the Will* (1525).

Luther's *Lectures on Romans* can be read with profit today as an example of one who sought to read scripture in the company of the whole people of God through the ages. It was never Luther's idea to start a new church, but ever to be a faithful and obedient servant of the one, holy, catholic, and apostolic church. That the theology which emerged from Luther's *Romans* eventually led to a decisive break with the Church of Rome remains a part of the tragic necessity of the Reformation. Luther would surely be pleased to know that recent advances in ecumenical theology have been based in large measure on a fresh engagement with the biblical text, especially with Paul's Epistle to the Romans. Jerome once said that when he read the letters of the apostle Paul he could hear thunder. That same thunder reverberates through the writings of Luther as well, for, as Karl Barth has said, "What else was Luther than a teacher of the Christian church whom one can hardly celebrate in any other way but to listen to him?"[36]

---

35. Ibid., 263.
36. Karl Barth, "Lutherfeier," *Theologische Existenz heute* 4 (1933): 11.

7

WILLIAM TYNDALE

Jeffrey P. Greenman

Introduction

William Tyndale (1494–1536) is justly famous as a leading figure in the English Reformation, as the first translator of the Bible into English from the original Hebrew and Greek, and as the first person to produce a printed version of the New Testament in English. As a reformer and martyr, translator and linguist, Tyndale is well known among church historians and biblical scholars. My purpose in what follows is to shed light on an aspect of Tyndale's work that is less widely recognized, namely, his contributions as an important Protestant thinker. As a theologian, Tyndale has received relatively little attention, and his thought continues to be overlooked. For instance, Tyndale is omitted from the recent *Oxford Companion to Christian Thought,* although lesser luminaries of theological history such as Don Cupitt and John A. T. Robinson are included, as is a most unusual figure, Charlotte von Kirschbaum, who was Karl Barth's secretary.[1] If I am successful in what follows, then scholars and students in historical, biblical, and theological disciplines alike will have reason to hold a more rounded picture of Tyndale's significance.[2]

---

1. Adrian Hastings, ed., *Oxford Companion to Christian Thought* (Oxford: Oxford University Press, 2000). On the other hand, we should note that Tyndale is included in the *Historical Handbook of Major Biblical Interpreters,* ed. Donald K. McKim (Downers Grove, IL: InterVarsity Press, 1998).

2. Compare the opinion of Tyndale's foremost modern biographer, David Daniell: "Tyndale as theologian, making a Reformation theology that was just becoming discernibly

"Many people have heard of Tyndale: very few have read him."[3] This observation by a leading Tyndale scholar applies not merely to Tyndale's historic translations themselves, but even more aptly to his theological writings. Tyndale is first and foremost an outstanding translator, but he is more than that, because any outstanding translator must exercise the careful judgments that can come only from being a skilled biblical theologian. In this essay, I will examine key texts in his constructive theology in order to demonstrate that the Epistle to the Romans was not merely Tyndale's personal favorite, but that engagement with Romans played a central role in his theology. Although Tyndale never wrote a commentary on Romans (his only biblical expositions dealt with 1 John and with Matthew 5–7, and none of his sermons has survived) his encounter with Romans was so profound that the book held a place for him unlike any other biblical book and provided the organizing center of his thought.[4]

In examining Tyndale's understanding of Romans, it is necessary to consider his debt to Luther, and specifically to Luther's 1522 *Preface to Romans*. Nevertheless, as this study will demonstrate, Tyndale distinguished his own views from those of Luther in several notable ways. Distinctive features of Tyndale's theology will become clear as we examine his reading of Romans as displayed in three major sources: *A Pathway into the Holy Scriptures*, *Prologue to Romans*, and his major theological work, *The Obedience of the Christian Man*.

A Pathway into the Holy Scriptures

Forbidden by law to translate the Bible into English without special permission, and opposed in his efforts to obtain such permission by the bishop of London, Cuthbert Tunstall, Tyndale left England in 1524 to pursue his project. Apparently he was in Wittenberg in that same year,

---

English when he was killed, has been at best neglected and at worst twisted out of shape" (*William Tyndale: A Biography* [New Haven: Yale University Press, 1994], 2).

3. David Daniell, ed., *Tyndale's New Testament* (New Haven: Yale University Press, 1989), vii.

4. Because there is not yet a full critical edition of Tyndale's writings, it is still necessary to rely upon the Parker Society edition. *The Obedience of a Christian Man*, his most substantial theological work, was published in 2000 as a Penguin Classics paperback, edited by David Daniell. A four-volume project undertaken by the Catholic University of America Press is publishing the *Independent Works of William Tyndale*. At the time of writing, only the third volume has appeared, *An Answer unto Sir Thomas More's Dialogue*, edited by Anne M. O'Donnell and Jared Wicks. David Daniell has edited modern spelling editions of Tyndale's translations as *Tyndale's New Testament* (New Haven and London: Yale University Press, 1989) and *Tyndale's Old Testament* (New Haven: Yale University Press, 1992).

and would eventually settle in Antwerp, but he began translation work in Cologne. Working from the Greek text made available by Erasmus, in Cologne during 1525 he published an English translation of a fragment of the New Testament (up to Matthew 22).[5] The Cologne edition begins with a fourteen-page prologue, whose chief importance, as Daniell has pointed out, is that it was the "first English Protestant tract, giving to English people Lutheran ideas in print for the first time."[6]

Tyndale's prologue does not merely contain Lutheran ideas, but actually is an adaptation of Luther's own preface to the 1522 German translation of the New Testament. Luther's explicit intention was to teach the proper way to approach the books of the New Testament, "by which a simple man can be brought back from the old notions to the right road." It also is the text wherein Luther notoriously declares the book of James to be an "epistle of straw" and declares which are the "best books" in the New Testament: "John's Gospel and St. Paul's Epistles, especially that to the Romans, and St. Peter's first epistle are the true kernel and marrow of all the books. They ought rightly to be the first books and it would be advisable for every Christian to read them first and most, and by daily reading, make them as familiar as his daily bread."[7] Despite the opportunity to endorse explicitly Luther's view, Tyndale offers no opinion on the book of James and makes no mention of Romans as the "kernel and marrow" of the New Testament.[8]

Adopting Luther's strategy for his own 1525 preface, Tyndale also presents a hermeneutical key to reading the New Testament. In so doing, Tyndale adopts Luther's definition of the gospel as the promises of God, cites *verbatim* the opening sections of Luther's preface, and follows Luther's lead in structuring the preface around an explanation of the biblical meaning of the terms *gospel* and *law,* as well as *faith* and *works.* What is remarkable about the 1525 prologue, and little known, is that the text of the first printed English-language New Testament began with an adaptation of Luther's guide to biblical interpretation. Tyndale's preface

5. William Tyndale, *The Beginning of the New Testament Translated by William Tyndale. 1525. Facsimile of the Unique Fragment of the Uncompleted Cologne Edition*, ed. A. W. Pollard (Oxford: Clarendon Press, 1926).

6. Daniell, *William Tyndale*, 111.

7. Martin Luther, *Works of Martin Luther*, vol. 6 (Philadelphia: Muhlenberg Press, 1932; reprint, Grand Rapids: Baker, 1982), 443.

8. In my view, Tyndale's silence on the status of Romans should not be taken as a theological disagreement with Luther's assessment, but more likely stems from the simple fact that Tyndale chooses not to draw at all upon the later sections of Luther's preface, where this comment appears. Tyndale draws primarily upon early sections of Luther's preface, and has left his source behind, so that he shapes the final segments of his own preface without making any reference to Luther's statement about Romans.

begins by following Luther quite strictly, but the preface quickly leaves Luther's text behind. According to one scholar with a mathematical bent, "one eighth of Tyndale's prologue consists of a good translation of roughly half of Luther's prologue."[9] More importantly, the remainder of what Daniell calls Tyndale's "first manifesto" moves *away* from Luther's theological approach. The prologue was revised and appeared in 1531 as an independent tract, *A Pathway into the Holy Scripture.*

Tyndale's writing style constantly weaves together biblical phrases with endless allusions and direct citations, making it both tedious and virtually impossible to decipher every reference to scripture. Tyndale's theological writings are rhetorically framed by a myriad of biblical idioms, patterns, and allusions. Page after page is densely filled with scripture. However, a general reliance upon biblical material cannot disguise the fact that his argument in *A Pathway* relies upon several key passages from Romans. The antiphonal structure of the text is fairly simple, with a recurring alternation of themes related to the meaning of the gospel and its relationship to law, with themes related to the relationship between nature and grace.

Tyndale cites Luther's statement that the term *gospel* (*euangelion*) "signifieth good, merry, glad and joyful tidings, that maketh a man's heart glad, and maketh him sing, dance, and leap for joy." Soon he turns to Romans 1:2 ("the gospel he promised beforehand through his prophets in the Holy Scriptures") to support the claim that God promised this gospel "in the Old Testament by the prophets." Tyndale alludes to John 1:17 to describe the law as "given by Moses: but grace and verity by Jesus Christ," which leads him to a critical claim: "The law (whose minister is Moses) was given to bring us unto the knowledge of ourselves, that we might thereby feel and perceive what we are, of nature. The law condemneth us and all our deeds; and is called of Paul (in 2 Cor. iii) the ministration of death." This statement begins the interweaving of the gospel-law dialectic with the nature-grace distinction that persists throughout the treatise. The law is seen here in typically Lutheran terms as that which drives the sinner to despair, because the law requires what fallen human nature cannot do. The law requires nothing less than "the deeds of an whole man" and a "perfect love, from the low bottom and ground of the heart." On the other hand, Tyndale states that the gospel is the "ministration of life" because it is the "ministration of the Spirit and of righteousness." Then comes this critical affirmation: "In the gospel, when we believe the promises, we receive the spirit of life; and are justified, in the blood of Christ, from all things whereof the law

---

9. L. J. Tinterud, "A Reappraisal of William Tyndale's Debt to Martin Luther," *Church History* 31 (1962): 24–45, at 26.

condemned us. And we receive love unto the law, and power to fulfill it, and grow therein daily."[10] That last sentence encapsulates the most important element in Tyndale's theology.

The first half of this statement is consistent with Luther, but the second half turns in other directions that resonate more with Melanchthon or Calvin. The concept of receiving from the Holy Spirit the capacity to love the law, and power to fulfill it, typifies Tyndale's own distinctive theological vision. We notice that ideas related to Romans 5:5 ("God has poured out his love into our hearts by the Holy Spirit" [NIV]) are given a central position. Tyndale develops the idea that gospel and law are inseparable, functioning in tandem. The law condemns those persons who do not believe the promises of the gospel, serves as the norm for condemning human "unperfectness," and creates an ongoing awareness of sin and unrighteousness, while the gospel promises keep a person from despair by bringing to bear the work of Christ and his cross, which "fulfilled for me that which I could not do." Our sins are not counted against us on account of Christ's death. Shortly thereafter Tyndale adds that "love only is the fulfilling of the law," a reference to Romans 13:10. Since his own translation of that verse merely says "love is the fulfilling of the law," we notice that in *A Pathway* he has added "only" at this juncture in his treatise in order to strengthen the claim to an exclusive fulfillment of law through love.

Tyndale continues by describing the human condition, stating that "by nature, through the fall of Adam, are we the children of wrath, heirs of the vengeance of God by birth" and so on, such that we are utterly condemned by the law. He uses the organic metaphor of fruitbearing to describe the effects of sin: an evil tree brings forth evil fruit. On the other hand, "by grace . . . we are plucked out of Adam, the ground of all evil, and grafted in Christ, the root of all goodness." This transformation changes our stance in relationship to law

> when the gospel is preached to us, openeth our hearts, and giveth us grace to believe, and putteth the Spirit of Christ in us; and we know him as our Father most merciful, and consent to the law, and love it inwardly in our heart, and desire to fulfill it, and sorrow because we cannot: which will (sin we of frailty never so much) is sufficient, till more strength be given us . . .[11]

Carl Trueman rightly observes: "the function of law and gospel in the life of the individual is determined by whether the person concerned is in

10. William Tyndale, "A Pathway into the Holy Scriptures," in *The Work of William Tyndale*, ed. G. E. Duffield (Appleford, U.K.: Sutton Courtenay Press, 1964), 2–23, at 7.
11. Tyndale, "A Pathway into the Holy Scriptures," 11.

the state of nature or grace. In the former, the Lutheran opposition holds good; in the latter, there is a considerable degree of mutuality."[12]

This is Tyndale's characteristic way of connecting soteriology with ethics. Less cryptically, Tyndale believes that regeneration—receiving by God's grace a new nature—is the work of the Spirit, whose activity in a believer's heart leads the person to take pleasure in obeying God's law. This understanding lays the groundwork for saying that believers are able to grow, with God's help, in their capacity for keeping the law. For Tyndale, there is such a thing as "a full righteousness," when "the law is fulfilled from the ground of the heart." Neither Peter nor Paul achieved this, he says, but they "sighed after it." At this point in his argument, Tyndale draws support from Romans 7. He interprets that chapter as proving that Paul had a "thirst" for such a "full righteousness" that consists in perfectly loving the law, when he consented to the law yet cried out, "O wretched man that I am! who shall deliver me from this body of death? I thank God—through Jesus Christ our Lord" (Rom. 7:24–25 NKJV).

This passage illustrates Tyndale's thesis about the inseparability of gospel and law, even for the regenerate. In his pursuit of perfect righteousness before the law, Paul discovers the law's condemnation of his sin, which turns him toward the gospel's promise of deliverance by Jesus Christ. The law has brought Paul to a knowledge of himself as a sinner, which is followed by the gospel announcement of a pardon for him because Christ has satisfied the law for him. This results in joy and praise, which in turn fuels a renewed desire for "full righteousness": "he henceforth is an hungered and athirst after more righteousness, that he might fulfill the law; and mourneth continually, commending his weakness unto God in the blood of our Saviour, Christ Jesus."[13] The key theological argument here is that Paul in Romans 7 exemplifies the broader principle that when a person is born again and receives the Spirit, "they begin to love again, and to consent to the law of God" and "desire to fulfill the law, even as a sick man desireth to be whole, and are an hungered and athirst after more righteousness, and after more strength, to fulfill the law perfectly."[14] With regard to the law, the Holy Spirit brings the "power in our members to do it, though imperfectly."[15]

At the same time, lest anyone think that Tyndale has abandoned the idea of justification *sola fide,* he says: "By faith we are saved only, in

---

12. Carl R. Trueman, "Pathway to Reformation: William Tyndale and the Importance of the Scriptures," in *A Pathway into the Holy Scripture,* eds. P. E. Satterthwaite and D. F. Wright (Grand Rapids: Eerdmans, 1994), 11–29, at 27.

13. Tyndale, "A Pathway into the Holy Scriptures," 13.

14. Ibid., 15.

15. Ibid., 19.

believing the promises." There is no hint here that any sort of combination of faith *and* works is necessary for salvation. Quite to the contrary, Tyndale keeps both faith and works from playing any role in the *ground* of our justification. Christ's death is the meritorious cause of our salvation; faith alone is the instrumental cause. There is a strong emphasis upon those good works which result from our justification, as the fruit of a renewed nature in Christ by the Spirit.

Trueman has shown that Tyndale's hermeneutical framework primarily is organized not around the categories of law and gospel, but rather by the concepts of nature and grace; in fact, "fallen nature and grace" function as "the basic categories of the Bible and human existence."[16] The approach to biblical interpretation offered by Tyndale emphasizes a concern for regeneration, actual righteousness, the activity of the Holy Spirit, and the believer's moral response to God's grace. These emphases show that Tyndale has begun with Luther's own preface to the New Testament, and drawn material from it, but actually shifted away from Luther's sharp opposition of gospel (as a "word of grace") and law (as a "word of destruction"), and moved in a theological direction that reflects the humanist strain of Reformation theology.[17] Tyndale's developing theology of gospel and law more closely resembles the approach of Philipp Melanchthon than the views of Luther himself. Whereas Luther never endorsed the so-called third use of the law, it is clear that Tyndale, along with Melanchthon, Calvin, and the mainstream Reformed tradition, upheld a "didactic use" of law for moral instruction and sanctification in the lives of believers. What is vital to see is that the preface to the first-ever English New Testament included a preface adapted from Luther and oriented to showing how justification by faith expresses the Spirit's regenerative work in fostering a love for the law.

Prologue to Romans (1526, 1534)

The complete 1526 New Testament and subsequent editions included prologues to most of the books. These are brief, often rather selective summaries of the books, patterned after Luther's prefaces, which usually offer some explanatory points of historical background or theological orientation to assist the reader. Of these prologues, by far the longest and most interesting is his *Prologue to Romans*, a document deeply indebted to Luther's own *Preface to Romans* in his 1522 German New

16. Trueman, "Pathway to Reformation," 24.
17. A. E. McGrath, "Humanist Elements in the Early Reformed Doctrine of Justification," *Archiv fur Reformationsgeschichte* 73 (1982): 5–20.

Testament, which had already become quite famous by the time Tyndale encountered it.

David Daniell's note in the critical edition of *Tyndale's New Testament* states that it "for the most part translates Luther's prologue. The last five paragraphs are Tyndale's."[18] However, we will see that Daniell's statement needs greater nuance. Tyndale begins with an exact quotation from Luther to the effect that "this epistle is the principal and most excellent part of the New Testament and most pure evangelion." But even in the first sentence, Tyndale quickly inserts his own comment: "and also is a light and a way unto the whole Scriptures." He echoes Luther again in saying that Romans "of itself is a bright light, and sufficient to give light unto all the scriptures." Toward the end of the prologue, Tyndale again paraphrases Luther when he says, "Paul's mind was to comprehend in this epistle all the whole learning of Christ's gospel, and to prepare an introduction unto all the old Testament. For without doubt, whosoever hath this epistle perfectly in his heart, the same hath the light and the effect of the Old Testament with him."[19] Remarks of this kind perhaps are not unexpected for a Reformer, in the wake of Luther's comments, but we need to ask: What is it about the teaching of Romans that illumines all of scripture? If Romans provides the hermeneutical key to unlocking the Old Testament, what specifically does Tyndale have in mind? And does Tyndale have in mind what Luther's preface had in mind?

Daniell's comment that Tyndale "for the most part" paraphrases Luther is potentially misleading, if it is taken to suggest that Tyndale has made only the usual sorts of semantic refinements or stylistic adjustments that any skilled translator normally makes. The differences upon a first reading might seem subtle or unimportant, given Tyndale's extensive citations from Luther, and the fact that Tyndale adopts Luther's outline by discussing key terms (such as sin, grace, and faith), then providing a short summary of each chapter. But more careful comparison of the two texts reveals that Tyndale has made numerous additions to Luther's text, that these additions are consistently focused theologically, and that they move Tyndale in a different theological direction from Luther.

Some examples of Tyndale's interjections will go a long way toward illuminating his particular reading of Romans. The first area to notice is Tyndale's ongoing intensification of the inwardness of genuine faith. Early on, Tyndale not only accepts, but extends, Luther's distinction between keeping the law "from the bottom of the heart" and "keeping

---

18. Tyndale, *Tyndale's New Testament*, 207.
19. William Tyndale, "A Prologue upon the Epistle of St Paul to the Romans," in *The Work of William Tyndale*, ed. G. E. Duffield, 119–46 (Appleford, U.K.: Sutton Courtenay Press, 1964), 144.

the law outwardly." Tyndale expands upon Luther's point by drawing out the reasoning with greater specificity and further explanations, particularly by emphasizing the importance of keeping the law "inwardly in the heart." On this point, Luther's text quotes from Romans 2:21 that "you teach others, but not yourself; and you yourself know not what you teach, and have never yet rightly understood the law." Tyndale uses Luther's text, and glosses this failure to understand the law by saying that they fail to see "how that it cannot be fulfilled and satisfied, but with an unfeigned love and affection; much less can it be fulfilled with outward deeds and works only."[20]

Tyndale repeatedly goes beyond Luther in emphasizing the inwardness of the law and the necessity of love for the law. On occasion Luther does speak of the necessity of love for the law. For Tyndale, however, this love for the law becomes the dominant concern. For instance, in another early passage, Luther had said: "To fulfill the law . . . is to do its works with pleasure and love, and to live a godly and good life of one's own accord, without the compulsion of the law." Notice how Tyndale amplifies Luther's text: "To fulfill the law is to do the work thereof, and whatever the law commands, with love, lust, and inward affection and delectation, and to live godly and well, freely, willingly and without compulsion of the law, even as though there were no law at all."[21] Tyndale intensifies the rhetoric of interiority. Not merely love, but "love, lust, and inward affection and delectation" are required.

Probably the most striking passage in the early segment of the preface comes when Tyndale inserts a long addition (nearly two full pages) to that section of Luther's text meant to explain what is meant by the term *sin*. The burden of Tyndale's argument is to show from a variety of New Testament texts that love for God is expressed in obedience to God's commandments. Predictably, he cites what he calls the first commandment: "Thy Lord God is one God; and thou shalt love thy Lord God with all thine heart, with all thy soul, and with all thy power, and with all thy might." Then Tyndale immediately comments: "And the whole cause why I sin against any inferior precept is, that this love is not in mine heart; for were this love written in mine heart, and were it full and perfect in my soul, it would keep mine heart from consenting unto any sin."[22]

The second area of Tyndale's difference with Luther lies in Tyndale's frequent injections of references to the work of the Holy Spirit. In a section dealing with the terms *flesh* and *spirit*, Luther says: ". . . you

20. Ibid., 122; cf. Luther, *Works of Martin Luther*, 448.
21. Ibid., 124; cf. Luther, *Works of Martin Luther*, 449.
22. Ibid., 127.

should learn to call him 'fleshly' who thinks, teaches, and talks a great deal about high spiritual matters, but without *grace.*" Tyndale's version of this statement is: "Call flesh therefore whatsoever we think or speak of God, of faith, of good works, and of spiritual matters, as long as we are without *the Spirit of God.* Call flesh also all works which are done without *grace,* and without the working of the *Spirit,* howsoever good, holy, and spiritual, they seem to be."[23] Tyndale accepts Luther's point about "flesh" being opposed to grace, but adds two references to the Holy Spirit in order to make the crucial point that grace is operative precisely by the Holy Spirit. This move is typical of Tyndale.

In another passage, with reference to Abraham's circumcision as an outward sign of faith, Luther states: ". . . all good works are only external signs which follow out of faith, and show, like good fruit, that a man is already inwardly righteous before God." Tyndale's adaptation of Luther says: ". . . even so are all other good works outward signs and outward fruits of faith *and of the Spirit;* which justify not a man, but shew a man is justified already before God, inwardly in the heart, through faith, and *through the Spirit* purchased by Christ's blood."[24] Here Tyndale adds two references to the Holy Spirit that are absent in Luther.

In both instances Tyndale extends Luther's point with a different (but not contradictory) theological emphasis. Tyndale agrees with Luther about works as a sign of faith but adds "and of the Holy Spirit." He also agrees that justification is through faith but adds "and through the Spirit purchased by Christ's blood." Tyndale's rationale here, I believe, is that he wants to safeguard the primacy of divine agency. The fruit of faith is not a human achievement, but the result of a work of God in and through the believer. As he states later, ". . . of a man's own strength is the law never fulfilled; we must have thereunto God's favour, and his Spirit, purchased by Christ's blood."[25] In addition, the person's faith is the instrumental cause of justification, but salvation is grounded upon the meritorious cause of Christ's blood mediated to the agent by the action of the Holy Spirit. As Tyndale continues on to say, "For we are justified, and receive the Spirit, for to do good works; neither were it otherwise possible to do good works, except we first had the Spirit." None of this is found in Luther's *Preface to Romans.* Tyndale adds almost two pages on these themes, with a particular concern to show "that good works spring of the Spirit."[26]

Tyndale's soteriology gives a prominent place to the Spirit. This passage draws together the themes of inwardness and the Spirit:

23. Ibid., 130; cf. Luther, *Works of Martin Luther*, 453.
24. Ibid., 133; cf. Luther, *Works of Martin Luther*, 455.
25. Ibid., 139.
26. Ibid., 135.

No man . . . can prevent [go before] the Spirit in doing good. The Spirit must come first, and wake him out of his sleep with the slumber of the law, and fear him, and show him his miserable estate and wretchedness; and make him abhor and hate himself, and to desire help; and then comfort him again with the sweet promises of God in Christ, and stir up faith in him to believe the promises. Then, when he believeth the promises, as God was merciful to promise, so is he true to fulfill them, and will give him the Spirit and strength, both to love the will of God, and to work thereafter.[27]

For Tyndale, to love the will of God is synonymous with loving the law of God, for the law reveals God's will, and this love is the result of the Spirit's action in the believer's heart. Whereas Luther said, "grace . . . makes the law dear to us, and then sin is no more there, and the law is no longer against us, but with us," we find Tyndale modifying this text, saying, "For grace, that is to say, God's favour, *bringeth us the Spirit*, and maketh us love the law."[28] I suggest that Tyndale understood the need for a theological explanation for how a sinner could possibly come to love the law, and that he felt Luther had failed to offer an adequate explanation in his 1522 preface to Romans.

What was needed, for Tyndale, was an articulation of the correlation between the believer's relationship to the law and working of the Holy Spirit as the agent of inner transformation. The Spirit engenders a faith that includes a capacity to respond from the heart with love for God's law. Tyndale's translation of Romans 3:31 as "But we rather maintain the law" is accompanied by a marginal gloss that says, "Faith maintaineth the law, because thereby we obtain power to love it and to keep it."[29]

Tyndale follows Luther's structure straight through Luther's summaries of the various chapters of Romans, and even adapts Luther's final section. But Tyndale does not stop there. He adds two concluding pages of his own, ones that reveal a great deal about his characteristic reading of Romans. He starts by saying, "The sum and whole cause of the writing of this epistle is, to prove that a man is justified by faith only; which proposition whoso denieth, to him is not only this epistle and all that Paul writeth, but also the whole scripture, so locked up, that he shall never understand it to his soul's health."[30] These final two pages indeed contain a crystal clear summary of the doctrine of justification *sola fide*, but Tyndale's own distinctive concern for loving the law is central and unmistakable.

27. Ibid., 134.
28. Ibid., 137.
29. Tyndale, *Tyndale's New Testament*, 228.
30. *Prologue to Romans*, 144.

For instance: ". . . Paul proves that the whole nature of man is so poisoned and corrupt, yea, and so dead, concerning godly living or godly thinking, that it is impossible for her to keep the law in the sight of God; that is to say, to love it, and of love and willingness to do it as naturally as a man eats or drinks, until he be quickened again and healed through faith."[31] The focus here is power of divine regeneration in the believer—a quickening and healing received through faith—that restores a capacity to love the law and a willingness to do it "naturally" (i.e., according to the new nature received from God).

Then, on the next page, Tyndale argues with regard to works: ". . . mine own works can never satisfy the law, or pay that I owe it: for I owe the law to love it with all mine heart, soul, power and might; which to pay I am never able, while I am compassed with flesh. No, I cannot once begin to love the law, except I be first sure by faith, that God loveth me and forgiveth me." What is striking here is the substitution of *law* for the place of *God* as the object of an all-encompassing love involving the believer's heart, soul, power, and might in the Great Commandment.

One cannot avoid the impression that Tyndale was moving deliberately to fend off any possibility that antinomianism could be deduced from justification by faith alone. The Lutheran movement was accused from its very earliest days of preaching license rather than true liberty. Tyndale must have known that and shapes his reading of Romans to counter that suggestion. Not only is he at pains to spell out the organic connection between faith and good works, so that authentic faith is never inert, but equally he is at pains to show that renewal by God's grace, received by faith alone, restores the believer's capacity to love. Love is at the heart of Tyndale's theology. He finds in Romans testimony to the human purpose as loving God and therefore doing God's law, and finds there that God's love is received in justifying faith. Assured of God's love, we then love God in response: we love his law, which for Tyndale is synonymous with loving his *will,* and as we have seen, loving his law is even synonymous with loving God himself.

The Obedience of a Christian Man (1528)

Tyndale's longest and most important theological treatise appeared in October 1528. According to Daniell, "if we had nothing else from Tyndale but his *Obedience,* he would still be of high significance for the time."[32] Perhaps this major document of the early English Reformation will re-

---

31. Ibid., 144.
32. Daniell, *William Tyndale,* 223.

ceive the renewed attention it deserves now that it has become readily accessible in the Penguin Classics series. A more complete study of the place of Romans in this treatise would include a discussion of his treatment of civil authorities (Romans 13), the church (especially in relation to Rom. 10:14, "How can they hear without a preacher"), and the sacraments as preaching Christ's promises (especially in relation to Romans 6). Our interest will be focused upon the prominence of Romans 15:4 in Tyndale's understanding of the function and value of scripture.

In the opening section of the treatise, a lengthy letter (twenty-two pages) to the reader, Tyndale includes a passionate argument for the necessity of translating the Bible into the vernacular. He says:

> The sermons which thou readest in the Acts of the Apostles and all that the apostles preached were no doubt preached in the mother tongue. Why then might they not be written in the mother tongue? As if one of us preach a good sermon why may it not be written? Saint Jerome also translated the Bible into his mother tongue. Why may not we also?[33]

The book comes exactly two years after Tunstall had copies of Tyndale's English New Testament gathered up and burned at St. Paul's in London. The opening section (twenty-seven pages) of *Obedience* provides ample insight not only into why Tyndale was so insistent upon his life's work as a translator, but also into Tyndale's understanding of the function and value of scripture.

The 1526 burning of his New Testament prompted Tyndale to claim on his very first page that being forbidden to read the scriptures, which he calls "the word of thy soul's health," was a persecution not only of Tyndale's readers, but of the Word of God itself. Tyndale urges his readers to identify themselves with those who are persecuted for the sake of what he calls "the true word of God," which is "ever hated of the world, neither was ever without persecution." He cites John 15 to characterize himself and his readers as those whom God has "chosen out of the world to serve Christ in the Spirit" and thereby become those whom the world hates. In the very next paragraph, on the opening page of the treatise, he begins by stating:

> Another comfort hast thou, that as the weak powers of the world defend the doctrine of the world so the mighty power of God defendeth the doctrine of God. Which thing thou shalt evidently perceive, if thou call to mind the wonderful deeds which God hath ever wrought for his word in extreme necessity since the world began beyond all man's reason. Which are written

---

33. William Tyndale, *The Obedience of a Christian Man*, ed. David Daniell (New York: Penguin Books, 2000), 19.

as saith Paul (Rom. 15) for our learning (and not for our deceiving) that
we through patience, and comfort of the scripture might have hope.[34]

This text from Romans 15:4 plays a central role in Tyndale's understanding of the function of scripture. Tyndale's own translation is: "Whatsoever things are written aforetime, are written for our learning, that we
through patience and comfort of the scripture, might have hope."[35] He
returns to that verse repeatedly in the opening section of *Obedience*. It
becomes the interpretative tool that enables Tyndale to relate biblical
narratives to the present difficulties of his readers. It opens up a warmly
pastoral reading of the texts. Tyndale discusses a long series of biblical
episodes, from both testaments, designed to show that "the nature of
God's word is to fight against hypocrites." For example:

> How wonderfully were the children of Israel locked in Egypt? In what
> tribulation, cumbrance and adversity were they in? The land also that was
> promised them, was far off and full of great cities walled with high walls
> up to the sky and inhabited with great giants. Yet God's truth brought
> them out of Egypt and planted them in the land of the giants. This was
> also written for our learning, for there is no power against God's neither
> any wisdom against God's wisdom, he is stronger and wiser than all his
> enemies.[36]

Next, Tyndale reviews a number of Old Testament miracles, including
the plagues and exodus, and directly associates these with God's faithful-
ness to his promises to Abraham, Isaac, and Jacob. Tyndale asserts: "This
is written for our learning. For verily he is a true God, and is our God as
well as theirs, and his promises are with us as well as with them, and he
is present with us as well as he was with them."[37] Tyndale's use of Romans
15:4 is designed to enable him to derive maximum pastoral benefit for a
minority faction under serious duress. He reminds his readers that "there
is no other way into the kingdom of life, than through persecution and
suffering of pain and of very death, after the example of Christ. Therefore
let us arm our souls with the comfort of the scriptures."

Another document by Tyndale, his prologue to Genesis, also discusses
the use of the scriptures. After citing 2 Timothy ("scripture is good to
teach") and Ephesians 6 ("the sword of the Spirit"), he turns to Romans
15:4, saying, "the ensamples that are in the scripture comfort us in all
our tribulations, and make us put our trust in God, and patiently to abide

---

34. Ibid., 4.
35. Tyndale, *Tyndale's New Testament*, 240.
36. *Obedience*, 5.
37. Ibid., 6.

his leisure."[38] He cites the same Romans text two more times in the next three pages. Tyndale's frequent rehearsal of the comfort and hope that flow from knowing and believing scripture suggests that Tyndale not only upheld scripture as a source of divine truth in written propositions, but that he championed the pastoral function of scripture when it is read, known, and applied directly to the individual soul. According to Donald Smeaton, Tyndale understood that "the primary role of Scripture was not polemical, however, but pastoral. Its proper use resulted in spiritual health and salvation. Pastorally, the scriptures, rightly understood, was the means of spiritual life."[39]

What we see here, unmistakably, is an emerging Protestant biblical piety. Romans 15:4 plays an integral part in his concept of authentic Christian spiritual experience: the soul is sustained by direct relationship to the Bible itself, wherein the entirety of scripture is held to be directly applicable to the individual as a source of comfort and hope. Roughly thirty years later, this same biblical text is used to enshrine liturgically the pastoral significance of scripture in the Anglican tradition through Thomas Cranmer's famous collect for the second Sunday in Advent: "Blessed Lord, who hast caused all holy Scripture to be written for our learning: Grant that we may in such wise hear them, read, mark, learn, and inwardly digest them, that by patience and comfort of thy holy Word, we may embrace and ever hold fast the blessed hope of everlasting life, which thou hast given us in our Saviour Jesus Christ. Amen."[40]

Conclusion

This study of Tyndale's understanding of Romans gives us reason to believe that if Tyndale had lived longer, he would have produced a series of commentaries and treatises that could have developed more fully a distinctive biblical theology for English Protestantism. My argument has been that Tyndale's handling of Romans, and of Luther's 1522 *Preface to Romans,* shows that Tyndale was a significant thinker with a large debt to Luther, but whose theology moves also in the direction of Melanchthon or Calvin, especially with regard to issues of gospel and law. Tyndale develops his own theological response to the challenges of

38. William Tyndale, *Doctrinal Treatises and Introductions to Different Portions of the Holy Scriptures,* ed. Henry Walter (Cambridge: Cambridge University Press, 1848), 389–99.

39. Donald Dean Smeaton, "William Tyndale on the Reformation of Pastoral Care," unpublished manuscript, 4.

40. There are many theological similarities between Tyndale and Cranmer that would be well worth exploring further.

antinomianism by explicating how not merely obeying the law, but loving the law, is an integral part of Christian identity and experience. This study also demonstrates that it is quite inaccurate to consider Tyndale's thought as nothing more than a rather uninteresting series of footnotes to Luther.[41] We have observed two characteristic dimensions of Tyndale's theology, both of which are forged in relationship with the teaching of the book of Romans. First, there is a distinctively Tyndalian emphasis, primarily drawn from Romans 5:5 and 13:10, concerning the work of the Holy Spirit in engendering a capacity to love the law and to obey God's will. Second, Tyndale's understanding of the function and pastoral value of scripture, shaped in relationship to Romans 15:4, articulated an emerging Protestant biblical piety. Tyndale's ways of developing these central features of his thought provide ample evidence of the centrality of Romans to his theology.[42]

---

41. Also *contra* Philip Edgcumbe Hughes, who held that "Tyndale can hardly be reckoned a religious thinker of any real importance. The ideas he puts forth are none of them his own, nor does he add anything of importance to their content." See Philip Hughes, *The Reformation in England* (London: Hollis, 1956), 1:138.

42. I am grateful to my colleague Tim Larsen for his comments and suggestions about an earlier draft of this essay.

8

JOHN CALVIN

David Demson

The purpose of this essay is to show that Calvin's exposition of Romans is organized around the theme of the mercy of God in Christ as the central meaning of the gospel. Given this focal concern, I will not address Calvin's expository methods. This task is carried out admirably by T. H. L. Parker in his book *Calvin's New Testament Commentaries*, and anything I would say on this point in an introduction would not be much more than a concise account of what Parker says.[1] Nor am I going to compare Calvin's *Commentary on Romans* with those of his contemporaries. Parker has analyzed this in his book *Commentaries on the Epistle to the Romans, 1532–1542*, in which he compares twelve commentaries on Romans from that period, Calvin's first edition of 1540 being one of them.[2] Nor will I try to place Calvin's *Commentary on Romans* in the history of commentaries on Romans, partly because that task will be fulfilled to some degree by the other chapters in this volume.

1. T. H. L. Parker, *Calvin's New Testament Commentaries* (London: SCM Press, 1971). Also see Hans W. Frei, *The Eclipse of Biblical Narrative: A Study in Eighteenth and Nineteenth Century Hermeneutics* (New Haven: Yale University Press, 1977), chap. 2.
2. T. H. L. Parker, *Commentaries on the Epistle to the Romans, 1532–1542* (Edinburgh: T & T Clark, 1986).

As we begin, a brief word about the history of the text of Calvin's *Commentary on Romans*. Calvin's first edition was published in 1540. It contains the lectures he gave on Romans in Geneva between the autumn of 1536 and Easter 1538. A second edition, with a few revisions, was published in 1551 in an edition of Calvin's commentaries on all the Epistles. A third edition was published in 1556; deletions from the first edition are few, the additions many. Basically, the 1556 edition is the 1540 edition with a considerable number of additions.[3]

I am using here the English translation of Ross Mackenzie, which appears in the series *Calvin's Commentaries*, edited by David W. and Thomas F. Torrance.[4] Referring to volume 77 of the *C.R.*, in this chapter I have altered the wording of the Mackenzie translation where I thought such a change better corresponded to the sense of Calvin's Latin. I did not make changes in order to make Calvin's statements more palatable to myself or anyone else.

Introduction

I begin with two statements that Calvin makes in the "Introduction" to his *Commentary on Romans*.

When we have gained a true understanding of this Epistle, we have a door opened to us to *all* the most profound treasures of Scripture.[5]

The main theme of the whole Epistle is that we are justified by faith . . . the human being's only righteousness is the mercy of God in Christ, when it is offered by the Gospel and received in faith."[6]

When these two statements are combined, we hear Calvin saying: God's mercy in Christ upon human beings is the content of the Gospels, according to Paul, and as such is the primary theme of all scripture. Justification by faith, then, is not just a doctrine, but rather the all-encompassing orientation of all Christian thought and action.

While Calvin's reading of Paul's account of justification by faith as the all-encompassing orientation of all Christian thought and action

---

3. Volume 77 of the *Corpus Reformatorum* prints the 1540 edition in roman type and includes the additions in italic type.

4. David W. Torrance and Thomas F. Torrance, eds., *Calvin's Commentaries* (Grand Rapids: Eerdmans, 1995); hereafter, *C.C.*

5. *C.C.*, 5; and G. Baum, E. Cunitz, and E. Reuss, eds., *Ioannis Calvini Opera Quae Supersunt Omnia*, vol. 49 (Brunsvigae, 1892), 1; hereafter *C.O.*

6. Ibid.

might seem only to echo Luther's reading, in fact Calvin finds a different emphasis in Paul's account of justification. Honoring God's mercy in all our doing and thinking is constitutive of the Christian life. Following the two passages cited above, Calvin makes this point negatively by speaking of sin as "dishonouring God."[7] To refuse God's mercy (in thought or act) is to dishonor God—this is ungodliness. And in his commentary on Romans 1:18 Calvin finds Paul connecting ungodliness with unrighteousness.[8] Unrighteousness occurs where humans transfer to themselves what belongs to God (righteousness). If ungodliness is dishonoring God, unrighteousness is the way or manner of such dishonoring—transferring to the self or to humans more generally what belongs to God. Thus, Calvin's reading of Paul's account of justification as the all-encompassing orientation of the Christian life may be put this way: every truly Christian thought or action is an *honoring* of the *mercy of God in Christ* upon human beings.

The purpose of this chapter, then, is to show how Calvin's exposition of Paul's Letter to the Romans finds this theme to be the focus of each of the topics Paul addresses. I will also show how Calvin fails to bring this off in one crucial instance. The topics are: knowledge of God, judgment, the law and the works of the law, original sin, and election.

Knowledge of God

What Calvin says about the knowledge of God was contested during much of the last century. In this chapter the circumscribed question is: does Calvin find Paul's account of the knowledge of God in his Letter to the Romans to be at one with what Calvin discerns to be the theme of the epistle? In other words, is it an honoring of the mercy of God in Christ? It surely is when Calvin paraphrases Paul as saying, "To search for wisdom apart from Christ means not simply to be foolish, but to be completely senseless,"[9] a statement Calvin makes in commenting on Romans 1:3. But in commenting on Romans 1:18ff, Calvin says, "although the structure of the world and the most splendid ordering of its [intercreaturely] relations ought to have induced the human to glorify God," none does.[10]

Could it be that the honoring of the mercy of God in Christ is not the sole pivot of all Christian thought? The notion of a source of the

7. *C.C.*, 5–6; *C.O.*,1–2.
8. *C.C.*, 30; *C.O.*, 22–23.
9. *C.C.*, 15; *C.O.*, 9.
10. *C.C.*, 29–30; *C.O.*, 22.

knowledge of God other than God's mercy in Christ is ameliorated, although not resolved, when Calvin, expanding on the quotation just cited, speaks of God mirroring himself in the world. So at least God is doing the revealing, and the human is not deducing her or his knowledge of God.

Calvin begins to resolve the tension in his comments on Romans 1:20, where alluding to Hebrews 11:3—and he supposes Paul wrote the Letter to the Hebrews—he says that only by faith does a human come to the knowledge of God as Creator.[11] Incidentally, when Calvin speaks in his Romans commentary of two kinds of knowledge of God, he means that there is a true knowledge of God and a confounded knowledge of God; not two types of true knowledge. Calvin, in his commentary on 1:20, cites two texts that bespeak true knowledge of God—John 17:2–3, "The Father has given the Son the power to give eternal life. And this is eternal life: *to know* the only true God and Jesus Christ whom [he has] sent," and Jeremiah 9:24, "Let those who boast boast in this: that they understand and know me, that I am the Lord, that I act with steadfast love, judgment, and righteousness in the earth, for in these things I delight."

The structure of the world and the splendid ordering of its intercreaturely relations are not the gospel, just as the promises to the patriarchs and prophets are not the gospel,[12] but the God of the gospel (i.e., the God who enacts mercy in Christ that is received by faith) mirrors himself in the promises to patriarchs and prophets and in the structure of the world, and in the splendid ordering of its intercreaturely relations. This mirroring is recognized only by faith, faith in the gospel, says Calvin, citing Hebrews. He who is the Light of the Gospel confirms himself by mirroring himself in the prophetic witnesses he called and in the structure of the world wrought through him and for him.

Calvin tells us that when the human creature in faith honors God the Creator, he honors the God who bestowed mercy upon him in Jesus Christ, who has mercifully made this known to him and mercifully confirms the scope of his mercy by mirroring himself in the structure of the world and its ordered intercreaturely relations. Calvin certainly finds in Paul a theology of nature, but one which observes Paul's and scripture's encompassing orientation of justification by faith; i.e., Christian thinking about God (here thinking about God the Creator) is an honoring of the mercy of God in Christ upon human beings received by faith.

11. *C.C.*, 32; *C.O.*, 24.
12. *C.C.*, 15; *C.O.*, 9.

Calvin does say in commenting on 1:21 that God manifests himself to all, pressing in upon all.[13] This does not mean that Calvin speaks of a universal and empty manifestation, for he goes on to say that no conception of God can be formed that does not take account of his attributes. God in mirroring himself in the structure and orderings of the world manifests himself in his attributes. And later he describes God's attributes in this way: God's mercy is known by God's bearing the perversity of his human creatures; God's righteousness in his punishing of the guilty and delivering the innocent.[14] God is not known apart from his revelation of himself in these attributes.

Calvin's exposition of Paul's account of our knowledge of God keeps hold of the notion that all genuine knowledge of God is an honoring of God's mercy in Christ upon human beings. Calvin retains in his comments about what Paul says concerning our knowledge of God what he discerns as the central theme of the whole letter. He does so awkwardly, because the text he is reading, Romans 1, is awkward due to the fact that the main axis or theme is constellated by a rush of many declarations.

Judgment

In his exposition of Romans 2:16, Calvin summarizes Paul's declarations about God's judgment.

> We need not be surprised that the Gospel is said to be the messenger and proclamation of the future judgment. If the fulfillment of the Gospel's promise is delayed until the full revelation of the kingdom, it must be necessarily connected with the final judgment. Christ cannot be preached without speaking of the resurrection of some and the destruction of others. Both of these refer to the Day of Judgment. . . . [when] the Lord will execute His judgment by Christ who has been appointed by the Father to be the Judge of the living and the dead. This judgment by Christ is always reckoned by the apostles among the chief articles of the Gospel.[15]

Paul's teaching about the judgment of Jews and Gentiles, according to Calvin, is an anticipation of the final judgment to be executed by Jesus Christ. On the way to that judgment, God in Christ draws near to

13. *C.C.*, 32; *C.O.*, 24.
14. Ibid.
15. *C.C.*, 49–50; *C.O.*, 39.

both Jews and Gentiles in mercy. Those who honor that mercy go into resurrection; those who do not go into destruction.

Commenting on 3:6, Calvin remarks, "although Paul's teaching [about judgment] extends to the ongoing government by God, it has precise reference to the final judgment, when a real renewal of right order will take place."[16] And he adds, "it is not that unrighteousness, as such, makes the righteousness of God clearer. Rather, the righteousness of God is made clear as God's goodness overcomes our wickedness in such a way as to give us a different direction."[17]

Calvin, by concentrating his explication of Paul's account of God's judgment of Jews and Gentiles upon the final judgment rendered by Jesus Christ upon all flesh, certainly finds that Paul's account of God's judgment focuses on what he has discerned to be the axis of the whole epistle. But his account of human beings living by God's mercy in Christ or not so living is rendered hollow by his treatment of Paul on election, where Calvin neglects Paul's emphasis on a *living* divine agency and a real human agency. (This point will be briefly developed at the end of this chapter.)

The Law and the Works of the Law

When Paul says in Romans 3:20 that no human being will be justified by the works of the law, Calvin understands that Paul is not referring only to the ceremonial laws, but to the whole law. For the notion that we can achieve righteousness by keeping the law is opposed to that honoring of God's mercy that is the all-encompassing orientation of all Christian thought and action. Calvin explains that this is why Paul claims that through the law comes the knowledge of sin. The notion that we become righteous by doing the works of the law is already a corruption of the truth.

> Paul does not confuse works with the mercy of God, but removes and eradicates all confidence in works and establishes mercy alone. . . . [Paul] excludes from human righteousness not only works which are morally good, but also all those which believers can possess . . . the merit of works is abolished as the cause of righteousness.[18]

In short, the law is the opponent of faith as the way to human righteousness. "We are in Christ, because we are out of ourselves. We are in

16. *C.C.*, 63; *C.O.*, 50.
17. Ibid.
18. *C.C.*, 71; *C.O.*, 58.

faith, because we rest on God's mercy alone. And we are *freely* in faith, because Christ buries our sins."[19]

Nor is this simply the commencement of our righteousness. Until our death we are righteous only as we rely on our adoption by God in Christ. Our righteousness does not depend on either the law or ourselves, but is to be ascribed to God's mercy alone. That faith alone knows.

How shall we regard the law? As the opponent of faith wherever it is conceived as the way to human righteousness. That view of the law belongs to human corruption. The purpose for which the law was given was to confirm the righteousness of faith, not to teach humans how to obtain righteousness. How does the law confirm the righteousness of faith? By attesting our corruption, our need for the sacrifice of Christ, and also, positively, by the promises of free mercy attached to it—although clearer promises are found in the Prophets.

Calvin finds it important to repeat often that when Paul speaks of the righteousness of faith he does not mean that our faith is our righteousness. Rather, Christ freely transfers to us his own righteousness. The efficient cause of our righteousness is the mercy of God, and Christ is the substance of our righteousness—the Christ who obliterates our sins by his blood.[20] Our faith receives this righteousness and pardon by living by this mercy. But, again, faith is not meritorious. This is shown by the fact that faith never glorifies itself, but always glorifies God's mercy in Christ.

I have highlighted Calvin's emphasis in his Romans commentary on the oppositional relation of law and faith, because that oppositional emphasis demonstrates that Calvin finds Paul giving special force to the point that Christian action is grounded in and directed by God's mercy and is not grounded in and directed by the law. Since that perspective might be taken as a mere slogan, we do well to skip to Calvin's comments on Romans 6 where the issue of holiness emerges.

At the beginning of his commentary on Romans 6, Calvin remarks that the argument that the mercy of God encourages us to sin is a piece of absurdity. The apostle maintains throughout this chapter, Calvin tells us, that those who imagine that Christ bestows free righteousness without bestowing newness of life shamefully rend Christ asunder.[21] Yet, here again, the emphasis is on the mercy of God. Paul does not simply exhort his readers to imitate Christ, Calvin remarks. He has something profounder in mind and does not for a moment relinquish the emphasis on the mercy of God in Christ. Just as Paul

19. *C.C.*, 72; *C.O.*, 58.
20. *C.C.*, 73; *C.O.*, 60.
21. *C.C.*, 121; *C.O.*, 103.

first proclaims that the death of Christ is efficacious to destroy the iniquity of our flesh, he next proclaims that the resurrection of Christ has the power to renew our flesh. It is on this basis that Paul exhorts believers. While in faith believers look to the final resurrection, they already rely now on the present power of Christ's resurrection as they put on Christ. Paul (in 6:5) is not requiring from his hearers any duty that their diligence can achieve, but rather speaks of their ingrafting into Christ, which is accomplished by the hand of God. Paul, indeed, exhorts—exhorts his hearers to conform their thought and actions to him in whom they are ingrafted and in whom they are already who they truly are. Calvin's comments on 12:1, the verse with which Paul commences his exhortations, give us a good sense of Calvin's reading of Paul on the sanctified life.

> Paul has dealt with the necessary matters which concern the building of the kingdom of God: namely we are to seek for righteousness only from . . . God's mercy alone and [recognize] that all our blessings are laid up and daily bestowed upon us in none but Christ. He now proceeds . . . to show how our life is to be formed. Since the person is renewed into heavenly life by the saving knowledge of God and Christ, and that life is formed and regulated by holy instructions, we desire in vain to form our life in a genuine way if we have not first recognized that the origin of all righteousness for humans is to be found in God and Christ. This is what it means for humans to be raised from the dead.
>
> This is the main difference between the Gospel and philosophy. Although the philosophers speak on the subject of morals excellently and with great ability, yet whatever excellency shines forth in their instructions is nothing more than a beautiful superstructure without a foundation. For by omitting the grounds [the mercy of God in Christ] they propound a mutilated instruction. The same manner of teaching obtains among the Roman Catholics. Although they speak of faith in Jesus Christ and the grace of the Holy Spirit, it is clear that their instruction is nearer to philosophers than to Christ and his apostles.
>
> Just as the philosophers, before they lay down laws concerning morals, discuss the end of goodness and enquire into the sources of the virtues from which they, then, derive all duties, so Paul lays down the grounds from which all the parts of holiness flow.[22]

The grounds are "the mercies of God." "I appeal to you therefore, brothers and sisters, by the mercies of God, to present your bodies as a living sacrifice, holy and acceptable to God, which is your reasonable

22. *C.C.*, 262; *C.O.*, 232–33.

worship. Do not be conformed to this world, but be transformed by the renewing of your minds that you may discern what is the will of God—what is good and acceptable and perfect" (Rom. 12:1–2).

Original Sin

Calvin in explaining Romans 5:15 speaks of Christ as the cause of our righteousness, and in explaining Romans 5:12 speaks of Adam as the cause of our sin. Acknowledging that the word "cause" is a crude instrument here, the first assertion seems clearly to accord with what Calvin discerns as the theme of the epistle. God in his mercy transfers Christ's righteousness to humans, who receive and honor that righteousness by faith.

The second assertion is a corollary of the first. The sinful creature is the one who rejects the mercy of God. And Paul relates the sinful creature Adam to the many who sin when he says that "by one man's disobedience the many were made sinners" (Rom. 5:19). Calvin paraphrases this by saying, "Adam is the cause of our sin." Now clearly, the relationship between Adam and us is not one that can be explained in terms of a direct transmission of sin from Adam to us, for then Adam, a creature, rather than God in Christ, would determine our situation, and that assertion violates what Calvin discerns as the primary theme of the epistle.

Does Calvin avoid speaking of a direct transmission of sin from Adam to us? The answer to this question can be found by examining what Calvin says about two differences between Christ and Adam in his comments on Romans 5:17.

(1) "We are condemned by Adam's sin not by imputation alone, as though we were being punished for another's sin, but we suffer condemnation because we too are guilty, since *God holds our nature, corrupted in Adam, guilty of iniquity.*"[23]
(2) "Adam involved the whole race in condemnation."[24] *The condemnation of God is conveyed to us by nature.* Simply by being human, sin dwells in us and we are under condemnation, whereas it is by faith that we receive the righteousness of Christ.

The crucial phrases are "God holds our nature, corrupted in Adam, guilty" and "The condemnation of God is conveyed to us by nature."

23. *C.C.*, 116–17; *C.O.*, 100.
24. *C.C.*, 117; *C.O.*, 100.

These two statements are explained in a later comment (on Rom. 11:32), in which Calvin says that it is God's judgment that has found all humans disobedient; i.e., it is God's judgment (in Christ) that has determined that all are sinners. The relationship between Adam and all others [the substratum of their common nature] is the determination of God's judgment. Calvin explains that what Paul is saying is "that God has so disposed matters by His providence that all humans are guilty of unbelief. His purpose in doing this is to have them subject to His judgment, so that all merit may be buried and salvation depend on His goodness alone. . . . The word mercy is emphatic . . . [no one] obtains salvation from any other source than the mercy of God."[25] Judgment falls on those who refuse mercy.

The relation of Adam and all other humans lies in their common nature, so Calvin may say, "Adam's sin is the cause of our sin." Yet that human nature is not an autonomous entity, but rather is ever held together by God's providential determination, the secret of which is election, election to condemnation and salvation.

So, we turn to the final topic.

Election

Calvin paraphrases God's declaration attested in Romans 9:13 this way: "I chose Jacob and rejected Esau, led by my mercy alone and by no worthiness of his works." Calvin continues, commenting on Romans 9:14, that humans particularly stumble over this teaching about election. Humans think that for God to be righteous he must reward right actions and punish wicked actions. Calvin does not suggest that Paul overturns this axiom formally, but he does indicate that Paul overturns it materially. That is, he overturns the notion that humans can perform righteous actions. Rather, humans are righteous where God bestows the righteousness of Christ upon them and upon their actions by his free mercy. Only faith perceives that the only righteousness of humans depends upon God's free election.

Yet the issue is not yet resolved, Calvin admits—passing on to Romans 9:15, since the complaint is raised over the declaration that God determines some to receive his righteousness while passing by others.

Calvin now enters a thicket. Yet as he begins to explain Paul's account of election, he adheres to his discernment of the primary theme of the epistle. Human righteousness and salvation are the fruit of God's mercy and not of human running and doing. And Calvin further perceives that

25. *C.C.*, 258; *C.O.*, 229.

Paul caps and grounds this declaration with his exposition of God's free election of his creatures. And further still, that the declaration of free election requires that account be taken of the rejected.

It is at this last point that Calvin departs from his discernment of the axis of the epistle. For Paul demonstrates how the rejection of some rests upon the mercy of God in Christ. Calvin misses Paul's argument ("Who are you, a human, to answer back to God?" i.e., to answer back to the mercy of God). Instead of following Paul's argument, Calvin says, "The lot of human beings, before they are born, is assigned to each by the secret will of God."[26] Calvin substitutes here "the secret will of God" for the hidden ways of the gospel, the hidden ways of God's mercy—a mercy that includes a deliberate hardening. (Calvin would say "mercy" instead of "secret will" here if he remembered the axiom that all Christian thought and action honors the mercy of God in Christ.) That the ways of God's mercy are mysterious, Paul admits. But Paul does not refer to a secret will behind God's mercy. God's mercy is not only enacted in Christ, but is grounded in his eternal will to be merciful. Paul does not speak of a secret will of God that eternally wills an eternal mercy and an eternal wrath. That is not to say, evidently, that Paul does not speak of rejection, but he struggles to show, especially in chapter 11, how the enactment of rejection, like the enactment of mercy, is based on God's merciful will and way. Again, God's mercy, enacted in Christ, is the enactment of his eternal intention, his eternal will. Paul understands that the enactment of that will entails judgment—which issues in rejection as well as election. (Human beings, after all, do reject the mercy of God.) Yet, throughout chapters 9–11, but especially in chapter 11, Paul's emphasis is that as Jesus Christ is the enactment of God's eternal will to be merciful, God's will, then, is a living willing, and its enactment is a living enactment. Thus, its fruit among humans is not fixed in a secret will.

Of course, Calvin explains many things that Paul says about election in terms of what he discerns as the primary theme of the epistle. For example, he says repeatedly that the sole cause of election is God's merciful will. It is when he speaks of rejection that he loses hold of the primary theme. But even when speaking of rejection, Calvin does not entirely lose hold of it. An instance of this is his careful account of how the obstinacy of the rejected (e.g., Pharaoh) will not prevent God from carrying out his purpose of delivering his people; and going deeper, how God's work of rejection in no way decisively interferes with his work of election, but mysteriously subserves it.[27] So, even at the point where Calvin loses hold of what he discerns as the primary theme of the epistle

26. *C.R*, 9:14, *C.C.*, 203; *C.O.*, 181.
27. *C.C.*, 206–7; *C.O.*, 183–84.

and scripture, he says things that direct us back to it. Yet it should be acknowledged that where the primary theme of the epistle is taken to be that every truly Christian thought or action is an honoring of the mercy of God in Christ upon human beings, there "some secret will of God" cannot be substituted for "the merciful will of God in Christ."

9

JOHN WESLEY

Victor Shepherd

In his *Notes on the New Testament* John Wesley mentions, in his introduction to Romans, that when Paul is writing to churches that he has planted or visited, he exemplifies a "familiarity" with them that is either "loving or sharp," depending on their deportment.[1] When he writes to congregations that he has never seen, on the other hand, he "proposes the pure, unmixed gospel in a more general manner."[2] Plainly, Wesley's sustained exposition of the law of God, a major motif in Romans and a crucial ingredient in the gospel, pertains to the "pure, unmixed gospel." For Wesley, then, the gospel includes the law, and Romans singularly identifies and amplifies this inclusion.

In order to grasp Wesley's understanding of gospel and law and the manner of their relationship, however, we must look chiefly not to the *Notes*, but to his *Sermons on Several Occasions*. Admittedly, Wesley's single, sustained exposition of Romans is found in his *Notes on the New Testament*.[3] However, the entire exposition there fills only forty-four pages, half of which merely reproduce the English text, leaving but

---

1. John Wesley, *Notes on the New Testament* (Wakefield, U.K.: William Nicholson and Sons, 1872), 355. Hereafter cited as *Notes*.
2. Ibid.
3. Ibid.

twenty-two pages to probe the sixteen chapters of Paul's major work. Wesley's texts for his three major tracts on the law of God are Romans 7:12 and 3:31 (KJV): "Wherefore the law is holy, and the command-ment holy, and just, and good," and "Do we then make void the law through faith? God forbid: yea, we establish the law."[4] Wesley's exposi-tion of Romans 3:31 in the *Sermons* requires twenty-four pages of text, while his comment in the *Notes* is concluded in two lines. Similarly, he uses nineteen pages in the *Sermons* to expound Romans 7:12, but only twenty-six words in the *Notes*. Obviously, his New Testament *Notes* is not a major source of his thought concerning the epistle.

Then will ransacking the Romans references throughout the *Sermons* yield, albeit compositely, Wesley's convictions concerning this epistle? I submit that it will not do so, for at least two reasons. While there are scores of references to Romans in the *Sermons*, there are only twice as many as there are references to 1 John, one of the briefest New Testament Epistles. (This fact alone informs us that Romans does not occupy the place in Wesley that it occupied, for instance, in the sixteenth-century Protestant Reformers.) Second, despite the profusion of references to Romans, many of these references are deployed not exegetically, but rather illustratively; i.e., they are adduced to illustrate or support a theological point that Wesley is making apart from the Romans text. In short, ransacking the references to Romans in the *Sermons* will yield not the singularity of Wesley's approach to this epistle, but rather the singularity of his theology as a whole.

Still, his insistence that the gospel is the substance of the law, together with his insistence that the law is indispensable for the Christian life, goes a long way in comprehending the totality of the gospel. His tenacity on this issue is generated by his understanding of two texts in particular, Romans 7:12 and 3:31.

The work of Martin Luther was instrumental in the spiritual awaken-ing of both John and Charles Wesley. Faith in the saving person and work of Jesus Christ was born in Charles as he read Luther's *Commentary on Galatians* (May 21, 1738), and in his brother three days later as John heard read the preface to Luther's *Commentary on Romans*. Thereupon both men repudiated and forsook the blend of moralism and mysticism they had theretofore regarded as faith. They never looked back from their new understanding and conviction, namely, that Christians are distinguished from unbelievers not by humility, for instance (John had insisted in his pre-Aldersgate sermon, "The Circumcision of the Heart," that humility gives us "a title" to the praise of God),[5] but by that faith

4. John Wesley, *The Works of John Wesley*, vol. 2, bicentennial edition (Nashville: Abingdon, 1984), 4, 20, 23. Hereafter cited as *WJW*.
    5. *WJW*, 1:409.

which grace alone quickens and which embraces Jesus Christ, its author and object. Believers cannot take any credit for faith's commencement or its continuation. Reflecting Calvin's "What can a dead man do to attain life?"[6] Wesley adds, "Of yourselves cometh neither your faith nor your salvation. 'It is the gift of God,' the free, undeserved gift—the faith through which ye are saved, as well as the salvation which he of his own good pleasure, his mere favour, annexes thereto. That ye believe is one instance of his grace; that believing, ye are saved, another."[7]

Initially claiming Luther as an ally, Wesley subsequently thought that the German Reformer's understanding of the relation of law and gospel fostered a cavalier attitude to the specific, concrete obedience that gospel-quickened people are to render God. Thereafter, Wesley insisted on the most delicate balance between faith alone and holy living, without thereby turning the former into a pretext for antinomianism (in this having "faith alone" cut the nerve of faith) or turning the latter into moralism (in this depriving "holy living" of the holy).

Never caviling that "the imputed righteousness of Christ" was synonymous with justification, Wesley was dubious when he heard eighteenth-century Calvinists speak of sanctification as "the imputed obedience of Christ,"[8] regarding "imputed obedience" as dangerous to Christian integrity if not simply self-contradictory. At the same time, he denied any claim to "inherent righteousness," the notion that whatever righteousness believers possess in themselves, however slight, is the *ground* of their justification. He knew that confused Christians could correctly recognize and repudiate an outer "works righteousness" (we are deemed righteous on account of what we do) and in the same instant endorse an inner "works righteousness" wherein we are deemed righteous on account of a so-called godly disposition. In the "stillness controversy" that threatened the nascent Methodist movement, Moravian dissidents maintained that those who lacked assurance of faith were to gain it by remaining "still" in a deliberate inertia wherein they did nothing, attending upon neither scripture nor sermon nor sacrament nor service. In other words, they disdained both the ordinances of God and the concrete obedience that distinguishes genuine faith in Jesus Christ from mere "beliefism." Concerning these people Charles Wesley wrote, "They speak largely and well against expecting to be accepted of God for our virtuous actions; and then teach that we are to be accepted for our virtuous habits or tempers. Still the ground of acceptance is placed

6. John Calvin, *Commentary on John*, 11:26.

7. *WJW*, 1:126.

8. See Randy Maddox, *Responsible Grace: John Wesley's Practical Theology* (Nashville: Abingdon, 1994), chap. 7.

in ourselves. . . . Neither our own inward nor outward righteousness is the ground of our justification."[9]

Wesley saw that his people had to be led to see that the law is to be affirmed not as a moral code (such notions he labeled "heathen"), but rather as an implicate of Jesus Christ and therefore of faith in Christ. Neglect of the law would entail antinomianism, and antinomianism would collapse faith. (Wesley, unlike the Calvinists around him in the Church of England, always maintained that believers could "make shipwreck of faith.") As early as November 17, 1739, his journal reads:

> I left Bristol, and on Saturday came to London. The first person I met with there was one whom I had left strong in faith and zealous of good works. But now she told me Mr. Molther had fully convinced her that she *never had any faith at all*," and had advised her, till she received faith, "to be *still, ceasing from outward works*," which she had accordingly done and did not doubt but in a short time she should find the advantage of it.
>
> In the evening Mr. Bray also was highly commending "the being *still* before the Lord." He likewise spoke largely of "the great danger that attended the doing of outward works."[10]

The "stillness" controversy, of course, was one aspect of a twofold problem with respect to the relation of law to faith, the two aspects of the problem belonging to "enthusiasts" and "formalists" in turn. Wesley customarily described those with a defective attitude to the gospel as "enthusiasts" who elevated their experience or opinion above scripture, while "formalists" were those who claimed to be possessed of saving faith but possessed only a theological ideation. Antinomians clearly belonged among the enthusiasts, and moralists among the formalists. Wesley knew from the outset of the Awakening that he would have to address both parties.

While Wesley continued to preach and teach with respect to the dangers of the misuse of the law, he did not write a tract on the topic until 1750. From 1748 to 1750, however, he had published thirteen sermons, *Upon Our Lord's Sermon on the Mount*. He subsequently insisted that the aim of these thirteen was "to assert and prove every branch of *gospel obedience* as indispensably necessary to gospel salvation."[11] Now he reckoned it necessary to develop an argument on the relation of law and gospel as a sequel lest the latter suggest either antinomianism to those who thought gospel and faith to eclipse the law, or moralism to

9. Charles Wesley, preface to *Hymns and Sacred Poems, 1739*, quoted in J. Tyson, *Charles Wesley: A Reader* (Oxford: Oxford University Press, 1989).

10. *WJW*, 19:119.

11. Letter, Nov. 17, 1759; emphasis his. *WJW*, 1:466.

those who thought the law to be a code against which people measured themselves and preened themselves, aided and abetted in this by an influential Arian Christology and the semi-Pelagian soteriology that was so common in eighteenth-century Anglicanism.

Wesley wrote the three tracts *The Original, Nature, Properties and Use of the Law*, *The Law Established through Faith (I)*, and *The Law Established through Faith (II)* in the way Luther had written his "occasional" theology; namely, as tracts produced to provide immediate assistance for people whom the gospel had brought to faith and whose discipleship was threatened by theological distortions that claimed to reflect "the faith once for all delivered to the saints" (Jude 3) but in fact contradicted it, and contradicted it so as to imperil those whom the Wesleyan movement's evangelism had "brought to the birth" and thereby nullify a grace-wrought testimony through ensuing disgrace. Wesley knew precisely what was at stake here: nothing less than the spiritual well-being of the Methodist converts, the public reputation of the Societies, and the future of the movement. Antinomianism would derail the movement through outer degradation; moralism would derail it as surely through inner enervation.

While Wesley would certainly have preached and taught on these matters between 1738 and 1750, there is no record that the three homilies were ever preached. He wrote the three to be printed, distributed, and read.

Without thinking himself at all overstated, Luther had maintained that theologians are defined by their ability to distinguish between law and gospel.[12] Wesley begins his exposition with a statement similarly global: "Perhaps there are few subjects within the whole compass of religion so little understood as this."[13] Immediately he highlights the nature of the misunderstanding: readers of the Romans epistle assume that the apostle's reference to the law pertains either to the Jewish law or to the old Roman law. As Gentiles they dismiss the law inasmuch as they are not Jewish; as moderns they dismiss it inasmuch as they are not ancients.

The Mosaic law "inflamed" sin, "showed" sin, but could not remedy sin, and therefore bore fruit unto death as it incited believers to an obedience they could not attain.[14] Believers (i.e., Christians) are wedded to the "body of Christ" (i.e., to Christ himself), and this law is expected to be fruitful

---

12. See Gerhard Ebeling, *Luther: An Introduction to His Thought* (London: Collins, 1994), 111.

13. *WJW*, 2:4.

14. Wesley's understanding of the logic of Torah is now recognized as highly questionable.

unto life. Believers, wedded to Christ, are delivered from "that whole moral as well as ceremonial economy,"[15] since Christ's death has slain this economy, and it subsequently has as little claim upon believers as a dead marriage partner has upon the survivor. The result is that believers are to serve "him who died for us and rose again";[16] i.e., believers are to serve Jesus Christ as a present, living person. Implicitly Wesley is asserting the Mosaic economy to be the Torah abstracted from the gospel, from Christ himself; explicitly he evinces his misunderstanding when he states that the service believers render the living person of Jesus Christ "in a new spiritual dispensation" is contrasted with the "bare outward service" rendered the Mosaic economy.[17] While the Mosaic dispensation has been set aside, the law as such has not been and cannot be, just because (as will be made plain later) Jesus Christ is the substance of the law. In this regard Wesley's understanding and Calvin's are identical.

"Moral" Law

Like the magisterial reformers before him, Wesley first identifies the moral law as that law which antedates Moses[18]—antedates, in fact, the creation of the terrestrial world, but not the creation as such, since the "morning stars" of the creation were angelic intelligences with a capacity to know God.[19] These angelic intelligences were created with understanding to discern truth from falsehood and goodness from evil, and "as necessary result of this, with liberty, a capacity of choosing the one and refusing the other."[20]

Several matters call for comment here. While Wesley's vocabulary might suggest he is adopting the moralism he eschews, it must be understood that liberty is not that freedom wherewith only Jesus Christ can set us free. Liberty is the pre-fallen creature's uncoerced response to the truth and reality and goodness of God. In mentioning "liberty" Wesley wishes to emphasize that these intelligences are agents, not automatons, and neither an aspect of God nor an emanation from God. Their uncoerced affirmation of God is essential to them as creatures. Freedom, to be distinguished from liberty, will be the Christ-wrought capacity to obey Jesus Christ, as believers, now redeemed and reconciled,

---

15. *WJW,* 2:5.

16. Ibid.

17. Ibid. Wesley failed to see that the Torah never enjoins "bare outward service."

18. J. T. McNeill, "Natural Law in the Teaching of the Reformers," *Journal of Religion* 26 (1946): 168–82.

19. *WJW,* 2:6.

20. Ibid.

find restored in them that *imago Dei* that the fall has defaced. In the second place Wesley maintains that the end of "moral" law, for these unfallen intelligences, is knowing God. Then plainly "moral" is not the word he wants in his discussion of "moral law." In the third place, moral law is that by which these creatures could serve God and therein find their service "rewardable in itself."[21] The service of *God* (by means of the "moral" law) is such a delight, a fulfillment, that it is inconceivable because inherently inappropriate that "something" be granted as the law's reward. In other words, the moral law (plainly misnamed) is that by which the living God invites creatures to know him and enjoy him. Their knowledge of God, indistinguishable from their service of God (here the force of *law* is retained), is inherently the reward of God. In saying that the law that gave these intelligences is "a complete model of all truth so far as was intelligible to a finite being,"[22] Wesley is plainly borrowing from his coming pronouncements concerning Jesus Christ as the substance of the law.

When God created humankind he gave it the same law, inscribed on humankind's heart as on angels', "to the intent that it might never be far off, never hard to be understood; but always at hand, and always shining with clear light."[23] While the law was "well-nigh" (i.e., almost) effaced in the fall, it was never obliterated. Undeniably, then, the law of God inscribed on the heart is identical with the *imago Dei* in Wesley's understanding. In the wake of the fall the *imago* is defaced but never effaced, or else the sinner would not be human. For exactly the same reason, Wesley maintains that the inscribed law cannot be obliterated. Law as the *imago Dei* is the irreducible, indefeasible humanness in which we are created, regardless of the extent to which we contradict it as fallen creatures.

Then Wesley adds that through the reconciliation that God fashioned "through the Son of his love," God "in some measure re-inscribed the law on the heart of his dark, sinful creature."[24] "In some measure" indicates that Wesley does not want to predicate of the atonement as such what the church catholic reserves for incorporation in Christ, namely, that the *imago Dei* is restored only as we "put on" Christ through faith, as he is "formed" in us. On the other hand, Wesley insists on a christological determination of that work of God whereby God gives up on no one, abandons no one, but rather reasserts his blessing and claim. The "reinscription" of the law, effected through the atonement, is of course

21. Ibid.
22. *WJW*, 2:6.
23. *WJW*, 2:7.
24. Ibid.

a work of Christ. Wesley is not speaking here of the person united to Christ in faith; he's insisting, nevertheless, that in the act of God *extra nos, pro nobis,* but not yet *in nobis,* there has been reengraved that which the fall had well-nigh effaced. The question can always be asked, "If 'well-nigh' means 'not entirely,' then is reinscription necessary?" Wesley would argue, in sound theological fashion, that we ought always to argue from actuality to necessity (i.e., God's act forestalls all speculation as to its necessity). Reinscription, then, is the claim of Jesus Christ specifically, the reassertion of *his ownership* in the reclamation of the sinner. The reinscription effected through the atonement means that what is reinscribed (the law) is nothing less than the claim of the Son, who has come to fallen creatures as Salvager. This action of the Salvager upon *all* humankind entails the following:

[1] His claim, while admittedly authoritative (or else his claim is hollow), is never authoritarian, authoritarianism meaning here the assertion of a demand that is arbitrary, since the demander is not entitled to it, and compliance with which demand is therefore coerced. Instead, because the claim is one with God's mercy ("the *Son* of God's love"), rather than extraneous to that mercy and unrelated to it, the claim is an implicate of this mercy and therefore not alien to the fallen creature.

[2] This claim pertains to the essence of humankind's humanness. To be human is to be made by the Son for the Son, and, in the wake of the fall, to be cherished by the Son, sought by him, and reconfirmed as the one upon whom the Son's mercy-wrought ownership is restated.

[3] The grace that is God's action and provision in his Son is also that grace now at work preveniently in all people everywhere, preparing them for the day when their hearing the gospel of grace resonates within them on account of the grace with which they are graced now unknowingly. In other words, while I am not aware that Wesley ever speaks formally of Jesus Christ as the substance of prevenient grace, plainly "the Son of his love" *is* this as he forges himself within all men and women everywhere, apart from which the explicit declaration of the gospel would be pointless. While Wesley agrees entirely with the magisterial reformers in their understanding of "total depravity,"[25] and therefore agrees that in the wake of the fall humankind is dead of itself *coram Deo,* he insists that all fallen people are beneficiaries of that reinscription, which is nothing less and nothing other than the action of the Crucified upon them.

[4] A corollary of the foregoing is the truth that no human is God-forsaken. God's act of reconciliation, the heart of which is the Son's utter and *actual* forsakenness at the hands of the Father, means that *for the Son's sake* no one is God-forsaken now nor can be.

25. *WJW,* 1:118.

[5] Since only by grace can grace be discerned, and since only by grace can anyone respond to grace, then the action of the Son in the cross is an instance of a visitation of God's grace vouchsafed to all humankind apart from which fallen people would be neither response-able nor response-ible. In a word, apart from the reinscription of the law (the substance of which is the atonement wrought in the Son), fallen humankind would find the gospel of grace inherently incomprehensible.

[6] Since the reinscription of the law arises from the cross, the crown and climax of God's work, and presupposes incarnation and atonement, the so-called natural law is never merely natural, but is always graced, such grace always being constitutive of humankind. This grace, it must be noted, is not an outer structure whose inner content is human achievement. Wesley bears no resemblance to Gabriel Biel and other medieval scholastics akin to Biel. This grace, rather, means that those who hear the gospel do not add to or bring to the proclamation of the gospel a "faith" that is their self-fashioned "contribution" (as it were). Faith ever remains God's gift.[26] At the same time, the gift has to be exercised; faith is always a human affirmation and activity or else it is not a human who responds. Here Wesley is strong where the magisterial reformers were weak in their insufficient recognition that faith, even as God's gift, must ever be a human activity. Wesley's understanding of reinscription (i.e., tantamount to prevenient grace) means that what God wills for people (faith in Jesus Christ) God must also will in them, or else faith is a human invention; at the same time, what God wills in them God must will in them not so as to coerce them, but rather so as to have them now *will for themselves* in a genuinely *human* act what he has already willed for them and in them—or else they simply haven't responded.

The so-called natural law is thoroughly christological.

Notwithstanding the discussion just concluded, Wesley maintains that humankind's flight from God finds God choosing a "peculiar people" (Gen. 6:12) "to whom he gave a more perfect knowledge of his law."[27] What is the force of "more perfect"? Does Wesley mean here a psycho-religious intensity—i.e., Israel's awareness of the law of God is extraordinarily vivid? Or does he mean not increased vividness, but rather greater subtlety and specificity concerning the details of the law? He indicates that he has neither in mind in view of the fact that the Ten Commandments are but the "heads" of the law, the law being much more extensive than the heads. Moreover, these "heads" were given to Israel because the people were "slow of understanding"; i.e., they lacked familiarity with subtle details.

26. *WJW*, 1:126.
27. *WJW*, 2:7.

I contend he means a deeper understanding of God's self-sacrificing love for his people. Since it is the Son's sacrifice that reinscribes the law, a "more perfect" knowledge of the law must pertain to that sacrifice willed and enacted by the Godhead in concert on behalf of sinners. In virtue of God's election, Israel is made aware of God's self-sacrificing love (albeit by anticipation of the death of the Nazarene).Gentiles, on the other hand, who are taught the Ten Commandments, have only the "heads" of the law.

Wesley's conclusion to his discussion in this part of his tract—"And thus it is that the law of God made known to them that know not God"—may appear to contradict the argument I have advanced. After all, if they know the law of God without knowing God, what do they know? A moral code? They know something other than a moral code, however, for "moral code" operates in the orbit of an ethic rooted in metaphysics; Wesley's insistence that they are aware of a *claim* upon them operates in the orbit of the presence and power of the living God. In short, they are aware of a claim upon them without knowing precisely *who* has claimed them. For this reason, says Wesley, their knowing the law of God "does not suffice."[28] Why not? He adds, "They cannot by this means comprehend the height and length and breadth thereof."[29] Thereof? Of what? Obviously, of the law. Yet the indisputable reference to Ephesians 3:18 speaks of Christ's love for us. Wesley's next sentence, "Plainly God alone can reveal this by his Spirit,"[30] grants readers a greater glimpse of what he has in mind as he renders "this" explicit by quoting Jeremiah 31:31–33, where God promises to write the law on the hearts of his people. It can only be concluded that for Wesley *the law of God written on the heart* and *the love of Christ* are identical.

Earlier, Wesley had said that knowing the law of God does not suffice. It is evident now that what does not suffice is that love of Christ which is *pro nobis* but not yet *in nobis* in the absence of faith. As Jesus Christ is embraced in faith, the love of Christ takes root in us; as this occurs the law of God comes to be written on the heart. Plainly Jesus Christ, the gospel, and the substance of the law are the same.

The Nature of the Law

Having discussed the "original" of the law at length, and having hinted many times over at the nature of the law in its christological substance,

28. *WJW,* 2:8.
29. Ibid.
30. Ibid.

Wesley now discusses the nature of the law in terms that permit no other interpretation than that Christ is Torah incarnate.

The law is "an incorruptible picture of the high and holy One that inhabiteth eternity."[31] Here, it must be noted, "picture" does not mean "illustration only" in the sense that a picture of an object is not the object itself. The language Wesley uses throughout his discussion of the nature of the law indicates that by *picture* he means exactly what Calvin means by *mirror. Mirror,* for Calvin, is never mirror only or mirror-image only in the sense that the reflection lacks the ontic status of what is reflected. When Calvin says that Jesus Christ mirrors the Father or that the Son mirrors our election, he means that Jesus Christ is our effectual election, *is* the electing God electing us, and this truth and reality is both operative and known to be operative in Christ alone. *Mirror* for Calvin never implies that "image" lacks substance. For Calvin the purpose of the mirror is to render substance accessible and knowable.

In the same vein *picture* for Wesley is the effectual presence of substance. This is evident when he speaks in the same paragraph of the *law* as "the face of God unveiled."[32] Admittedly, in his homily on the law Wesley does not link explicitly the law as the face of God unveiled with 2 Corinthians 4:3–6 (where Jesus Christ is spoken of in this manner). Still, in his New Testament *Notes* on 2 Corinthians 4 he does, and his exegetical comments are as profound as they are subtle. In commenting on "But if our gospel also is veiled," Wesley adds parenthetically, "As well as the law of Moses," and then goes on to say, "The gospel is clear, open and simple, except to the wilfully blind and unbelievers . . . [the gospel itself] has no veil upon it,"[33] and by implication, neither has the law of Moses. Wesley avers that there was a veil on the face of Moses, while the law of Moses is as transparent as the gospel of Christ. Lest anyone think the foregoing comment strained, Wesley underlines it in his discussion of 2 Corinthians 4:6. Here he states that the glory of God (which shines in the face of Christ) is God's glorious love and God's glorious image, and the face of Christ reflects this glory "more resplendently than the face of Moses."[34] Once again, however, "more" is predicated of the face of Christ compared to the face of Moses, but not compared to the law of Moses. In his *Notes* Wesley points out by way of illustration that God is not merely the author of light but *is* light itself,[35] and this light shines in the face of Christ; i.e., God manifests *himself* in the face of Christ.

31. *WJW*, 2:9.
32. Ibid.
33. *Notes*, 2 Cor. 4:3–6.
34. Ibid.
35. Ibid.

To recapitulate: Wesley says that the law is the face of God unveiled. Paul says Jesus Christ is this. For Wesley, Jesus Christ is plainly the substance of the law.

My interpretation of Wesley here is supported by his remark (still in the same paragraph of his homily) that the law is "God manifested to his creatures as they are able to bear it."[36] Wesley's unqualified assertion here must be allowed its full weight: the law is not a message from God or truth of God but is rather God himself disclosing himself; i.e., God is both the author and object of revelation, and all of this in such a manner as to preserve us, as Wesley once again echoes John Calvin's ubiquitous notion that God "accommodates" himself to us finite, frail creatures lest his glorious self-disclosure annihilate us.[37] Wesley then adds with limpid simplicity, "[The law] is the heart of God disclosed to man,"[38] when the heart of God, in light of the incarnation, can only be the gospel.

Temporarily puzzling, then, is Wesley's comment, "Yea, in some sense we may apply to the law what the Apostle says of his [i.e., God's] Son—it is the 'streaming forth' or the outbeaming 'of his glory,' the express image of his person."[39] Does "in some sense" mean that Wesley is now retracting what he has stated concerning the relationship of the law to Christ? Bewilderment vanishes, however, with Wesley's commentary on Hebrews 1:3. Here he declares without qualification that glory is "the nature of God revealed in its brightness";[40] i.e., the law can only be God's nature shining compellingly. Concerning Hebrews' "the express image of his [God's] person," Wesley adds, "Whatever the Father is, is exhibited in the Son."[41] Insisting in his commentary that *person* and *substance* are synonyms, Wesley states that the Son as express image of God's person means that the Son is possessed of "the unchangeable perpetuity of divine life and power."[42]

Clearly, Wesley is predicating of the law what has been predicated of the Son. This is possible only if the Son is the substance of the law. Then what does he mean by his caution, "in some sense"? He gives no indication. In light of his understanding of the relation of law to God and to the gospel, it appears he hesitated with the same hesitation that dogged Calvin before him; viz., if gospel and law are identical in es-

36. *WJW*, 2:9.
37. See F. L. Battles, "God Was Accommodating Himself to Human Capacity," in *Interpreting John Calvin* (Grand Rapids: Baker, 1996).
38. *WJW*, 2:9.
39. Ibid.
40. *Notes*, Heb. 1:3.
41. Ibid.
42. Ibid.

sence, wherein do they differ? Calvin resorted to such expressions as "less clear," "more brightly," etc.[43] Wesley reflects Calvin's vocabulary in the speaking of the law as "these faint pictures to shadow out the deep things of God."[44]

Still expounding the first of his three homilies on the law (Rom. 7:12), Wesley circles back to 2 Corinthians 4:3–6, referring once again to the "unveiled face" of God, albeit this time through a seemingly circuitous reference to Cicero. Cicero had said, "If virtue could assume such a shape as that we could behold her with our eyes, what wonderful love she would excite in us."[45] Wesley immediately adds, "It is done already. The law of God is all virtues in one, in such a shape as to be beheld with open face by all those whose eyes God hath enlightened."[46] His summary comment here is, "What is the law except divine virtue and wisdom assuming a visible form?"[47] Does "virtue" take Wesley back to the moralism he seeks to avoid? It might if *virtue* were to be understood in a classical sense. The context of Wesley's reference to Cicero, however, makes it plain that *virtue* here *with respect to the law* is the claim of God. And the claim of God, whose unveiled face is seen in the Son, reinterprets all such expressions as *virtue*. Additionally, lying behind the Ciceronian reference to virtue is Wesley's insistence on the substantial identity of Christ and the law. His point in the reference to Cicero (virtue, once beheld, quickens love in the beholder) is amplified in his 1745 tract, *A Farther Appeal to Men of Reason and Religion, Part II*. Here he speaks of God's opening the eyes of our understanding, only to add that the immediate consequence of such "seeing" is loving God.[48] And we cannot love God, he continues, without "a tender love to the whole of human kind."[49] The law of God, then, is virtue only in the sense that the law grants us understanding of the nature of God in such wise that our understanding unfailingly gives rise to love for God and neighbor. The perhaps dubious reference to Cicero, then, merely highlights Wesley's insistence that to "see" the law (i.e., understand it) is invariably to love it; better, love him whose face and heart the law is. Wesley's christological understanding of the law contradicts any putative moralism, however dangerous it may have been for him to adduce a reference to Cicero when so much of

43. See Victor A. Shepherd, *The Nature and Function of Faith in the Theology of John Calvin* (Macon, GA: Mercer University Press, 1983), 129–78.

44. *WJW*, 2:10.

45. *WJW*, 2:9.

46. Ibid.

47. Ibid.

48. *WJW*, 11:269.

49. Ibid.

eighteenth-century Anglicanism was only too ready to think of law in terms of moralism.

Wesley knows that no language is adequate to the wonder, glory, and magnificence of the law, aware as he is of the "shortness, even impropriety, there is in these and all other human expressions."[50] Still, he resorts to them just because they are the only expressions humans have. Therefore, he circles around the law again, approaching it now from a different angle of vision, declaring it to be "supreme, unchangeable reason; it is unalterable rectitude; it is the everlasting fitness of all things are or ever were created." It must be noted once more that by "unchangeable reason" and "everlasting fitness" Wesley is not departing from Christology and migrating toward moralism. As early as 1733, in *The Circumcision of the Heart,* he deplored all attempts at "grounding religion in 'the eternal *fitness* of things,' or 'the intrinsic *excellence* of virtue,' and the *beauty* of actions flowing from it—on the *reasons,* as they term them, of good and evil, and the relations of beings to each other."[51] Wesley denounces all efforts at grounding "religion" in moralism of any sort, even moralism supplemented by rationalism and aesthetics, all such moralism aiming at a righteousness other than that which believers receive through faith in Christ. It must be noted that Wesley penned even this criticism before the Aldersgate episode of 1738, after which he never failed to declare justification by faith.

If, then, the foregoing is what Wesley can't mean by "unchanging reason" and "everlasting fitness," what *does* he mean? It appears that *reason* has to be understood as *logos,* where *logos* means "word, reason, rationality, intelligibility." The logos of God is unchangeable in that God is unchangeable. The logos of God is the outer expression of God's "innerness," now imprinted indelibly on creaturely actuality in its entirety. In other words, since the Son of God is the logos of God, and since the Son of God and the law of God are substantially identical, then the law of God is the logos of God now rendered incarnate in Jesus of Nazareth.

And the "fitness of all things"? Wesley appears to have in mind here the "fitting-ness" of all things in the sense of Colossians 1:17: "In him [i.e., Christ] all things hold together." In his commentary on this text Wesley writes, "*And by him all things consist*—the original expression not only implies that he sustains all things in being, but more directly, *All things were and are compacted in him, into one system.* He is the cement and support of the universe. And is he less than the supreme God?"[52]

50. *WJW,* 2:10.
51. *WJW,* 1:410; emphasis his.
52. *Notes,* Col. 1:17.

In fact, Wesley's *Notes* on Colossians 1:15–18 predicate of Christ what his homilies on the law predicate of the law; e.g., "the glorious pre-eminence of Christ over the highest angels" means that Christ is "begotten before every creature; subsisting before all worlds, before all time, from all eternity."[53] This is precisely how he spoke of the law in the early part of his homily. Now in the same homily Wesley brings forward a concatenation of English expressions even as, regrettably, he does not supply the Greek he has in mind. He describes the law as "a copy of the eternal mind," "a transcript of the divine nature," "the fairest offspring of the everlasting Father," the brightest efflux of his eternal wisdom," and "the visible beauty of the most high."[54]

Once again, then, while some expressions Wesley uses concerning the law might be read, at first sight, as turning obedience to Christ into moralism, "first sight" can never be "last word": Wesley's antimoralistic rigor remains undiluted.

In his final comment on the nature of the law, Wesley says that the angels delight in the law and marvel at it, as will "every wise believer, every well-instructed child of God upon earth."[55] Surely angels and humans, recognizing the Christoform nature of the law, marvel at it because it is the God-authored vehicle of God himself; they delight in it because God himself is their consummate blessing. It is little wonder Wesley pronounces the law *"ever* blessed,"[56] *ever* denying any suggestion that the law of God might be provisional only, to be honored in one era but not in another. *Ever* suggests instead *eternal,* pertaining to the Godhead itself.

The Properties of the Law

Holy

Having discussed the nature of God's law, Wesley attends to its properties, first among which, following Romans 7:12, the text of his homily, the law is holy; even ". . . internally and essentially holy."[57] By "internally" Wesley intends "inherently."[58] Since God alone is inherently holy, Wesley

---

53. Ibid., Col. 1:15.
54. *WJW,* 2:10. Note here the similarity with respect to the reference in Cicero, where Wesley discussed the force of "beauty" and "visible."
55. *WJW,* 2:10.
56. Ibid.; emphasis mine.
57. *WJW,* 2:11.
58. See footnote 30, *WJW,* 2:11, where the editor comments on this meaning throughout all the editions of this homily in Wesley's lifetime.

understands the law of God to be God himself in his inherent holiness, fostering in his people the holiness he purposes for them. When the law is "transcribed"[59] into "life" and into "the soul," the result is the "pure, clean, unpolluted worship of God," when by "worship" Wesley characteristically has in mind a godliness that is the sanctification of all of life.[60]

Wesley maintains that the law must be holy, otherwise "it could not be the immediate offspring, and much less the express resemblance of God, who is essential holiness."[61] This statement is rich. Plainly the law can be holy only because it is substantially identical with the God who is essentially holy. To forfend any suggestion of subordinationism or even Arianism, Wesley maintains that the law is not merely the immediate offspring of God (allowing the interpretation "made not begotten"), but is rather the "express resemblance." Again, without citing either the scripture passage or the Greek word he has in mind, he evidently means *eikon*—identity, not similarity. The law as holy is the *"eikon"* or image of God who is essentially holy; i.e., the law is not merely functionally holy, an instrument or tool that God deploys to effect holiness (of some sort) in his people. ("Of some sort" must be added, since only if the law is one with the God who is essentially holy is God-in-his-holiness forging holiness in his people by means of the law.) Since the law is essentially holy, Wesley reminds us, it is blasphemous to speak of it as sin or the cause of sin, even though the law, upon meeting sin, exposes sin.[62]

Just

The law is also just:

> It renders all their due. It prescribes exactly what is right, precisely what ought to be done, said or thought, both with regard to the author of our being, with regard to ourselves, and with regard to every creature which he has made. It is adapted in all respects to the nature of things, of the whole universe and every individual. It is suited to all the circumstances of each, and to all their mutual relations, whether such as have existed from the beginning, or such as commenced in any following period. It is exactly agreeable to the fitness of things, whether essential or accidental. It clashes with none of these in any degree, nor is ever unconnected with them. If the word be taken in that sense, there is nothing *arbitrary* in the law of God: although still the whole and every part thereof is totally

59. See above, where Wesley speaks of the law as "transcript."
60. *WJW,* 2:11.
61. Ibid.
62. Ibid.

dependent on his will, so that "Thy will be done" is the supreme universal law in earth and heaven.[63]

Many aspects of this extended passage deserve comment.

[1] God's law is equated with God's will, and God's will is God himself in the act of willing.[64]

[2] God's law is his intention for every aspect of the creation.

[3] The law pertains to the creature as created or the creature as found, to the creature as intended or the creature as instantiated, in the wake of the distortions of the fall and the complexities of world-occurrence.

[4] The law befits "exactly" all things, whether essential or accidental; i.e., the law of God comprehends the totality of the creaturely order: original, fallen, essential, accidental. There is nothing, no one, no situation, development or circumstance that is law-exempt. The ground of this, of course, is that there is nothing that has not been made through the Son for the Son.

[5] The law cannot clash with "any of these" for the same reason that it cannot be unconnected with them: the "connection" and the "fit" are rooted in the fact that the law, characterized by God's essence, cannot be the contradiction of anything that has been made but can only be its "whence," its "whither," its fulfillment, its blessing.

[6] There is nothing arbitrary in the law of God. (i) There could not be, since the law is the "transcript" or "efflux" of God. (ii) No one can repudiate the law on the ground that the law is arbitrary and therein a surd element whose imposition on humankind renders human existence ultimately absurd. If the law were arbitrary it would never subserve the human good but would at best be "unconnected" with that good, and at worst contradict it.

Wesley underlines once more that all things, together with their "essential relations to each other," are the work of God's hands; and for this reason there arises the "fitness" of all things. The law as "the immutable rule of right and wrong" depends on this "fitness."[65] All of this—the nature of all that exists, its interconnectedness or "fitted-ness"—occurs through the will of God, by which they "are and were created."[66] With this last statement Wesley has adduced Revelation 4:11. While he does not amplify the scriptural text, he plainly has it in mind. Revelation 4:11 states that by God's will there has been created all that exists. The immediate context of the passage informs us that the seer looks into

---

63. *WJW*, 2:12; emphasis his.
64. "The will of God is God himself" (*WJW*, 2:13).
65. *WJW*, 2:13.
66. Ibid.

heaven and sees the throne and the exalted Lord Jesus seated upon the throne. Lightning, voices, and peals of thunder issue from the throne—a reminder of Sinai, and an especially pointed reminder that the throne of God is essentially related to the promulgation of the law at Sinai, even as the Trisagion of the worshiper recognizes in God the holiness that characterizes God, throne, *and law*.[67] And of course Revelation 11:15 insists that the one seated on the throne is none other than Christ, for to him there has passed sovereignty over the world. The antinomians, then, are without excuse: the law can no more cease to be good than can God. In the same way, antinomians who claim to have embraced Christ yet disdain the law have embraced only a chimera.

If the antinomians are self-contradicted, what about the moralists? Wesley immediately adds, ". . . it may be granted . . . that in every particular case God wills this or this (suppose that men should honour their parents) because it is right, agreeable to the fitness of things, to the relation wherein they stand."[68] In other words, the law of God comprehends all of creaturely existence in its multidimensionality and its interconnectedness. Obviously, the law cannot be a moral code, notwithstanding the reference to the fifth commandment, since no code comprehends what Wesley says the law comprehends. The law comprehends what it does in that the substance of the law is Christ, through whom and for whom all things have been made and in whom all things hold together or "fit."

Good

Not only is the law holy and just, it is also good, and good in that it flows from the goodness of God, which goodness inclined God "to impart that divine copy of himself to the holy angels."[69] Here Wesley reinforces his point against the antinomians, that the law is good because it is a "copy" of God, only to strengthen the case for the law by adding that God's motive in supplying the law was his "tender love" in manifesting his will "afresh to fallen man."[70] In fact, Wesley insists, love alone moved God to publish the law in the wake of the fall, to send prophets to declare the self-same law to the sin-hardened, and finally to send the only begotten Son to "confirm every jot and tittle" of the law with a view to writing it in the hearts of all his children; and all of this with

67. See G. B. Caird, *The Revelation of St John the Divine* (London: A & C Black, 1966).
68. *WJW*, 2:13.
69. Ibid.
70. Ibid.

the eschatological result that the Son can deliver his "mediatorial function" to the Father.[71] Plainly, Wesley sees the promulgation of the law comprehended in the one and only Mediator himself; i.e., the law is the Mediator claiming those whom he has visited and acted for in light of his "tender love." Not surprisingly, then, Wesley climaxes the accolades he heaps upon the law (e.g., "sweeter than honey in the honeycomb") with "mild and kind" and "wherein are hid all the treasures of divine knowledge and love."[72] "Mild and kind" points unambiguously to Matthew 11:29–30, where Jesus insists that his yoke (a common metaphor for the Torah in the Old Testament) is "easy" and "light" just because he himself is gentle. The second reference is Colossians 2:3, a passage in which Paul refers to Christ alone. For Wesley, then, "law" and "Jesus Christ" imply each other.

The enthusiast-antinomians think they can be the beneficiaries of Christ while disdaining the law. The formalist-moralists, on the other hand, think they can benefit from the law while disdaining Christ. Both are wrong, and wrong not because the antinomians lack morals while the moralists lack religion. Morals added to antinominans and religion added to moralists would still leave both sunk alike in unbelief and condemnation. Both groups fail to understand that the law is good in itself because it is God authored and Son (substance) informed, and that it effects good (i.e., godliness) in those who honor it. Failing here, they fail to understand that a fruit of the law in believers is that righteousness of which Isaiah 32:17 ("And the effect of righteousness will be peace, and the result of righteousness, quietness and trust for ever" [RSV]) speaks. Their ignorance is only highlighted when Wesley, eschewing both antinomianism and moralism, maintains that righteousness is not merely an effect of the law (this might lend itself to a moralistic misinterpretation); rather, "the law itself is righteousness," even as he glories in the truth that Christ alone is ever our righteousness.[73]

Conclusion

Many New Testament exegetes have maintained that "Christ our righteousness" is the central theme of Romans, while others have insisted chapters 9–11 are the pivot of the epistle, and with it the relation of Torah to Jesus Christ. Wesley would spend little time adjudicating this issue. For in the introduction to Romans found in his New Testament

71. *WJW,* 2:14.
72. Ibid.
73. Ibid.

Notes Wesley maintains that in the Romans epistle in particular Paul "labours . . . to produce in those to whom he writes a deep sense of the excellency of the gospel, and [labours] to engage them to act suitably to it."[74] Wesley's exposition of the constellation of gospel, law, Christ, righteousness, and faith, his exposition in the *Sermons,* supports what he insists in the *Notes* is Paul's intention in Romans, viz., a magnification of the beauty, attractiveness, and winsomeness of the gospel, and therein of believers' self-abandonment to its claim upon them, which is nothing other than their self-abandonment to the One who is their life, their comfort, and their eternal blessing.

74. *Notes,* 355.

10

CHARLES HODGE

Mark Noll

In January of 1870 Charles Hodge published a retrospective history of the *Biblical Repertory and Princeton Review*, the theological quarterly that he had been editing for nearly half a century. Only shortly before, Hodge had described labors on this journal as being encumbered with "a ball-and-chain" that he would have gladly relinquished many times over. Yet despite its burden, there had been "compensation" in editing the journal; in particular, "the high privilege and honour of making it an organ for upholding sound Presbyterianism, the cause of the country, and the honour of our common Redeemer."[1] Hodge, his colleagues at Princeton, and a host of friends, associates, and former students around the United States, and even farther afield, had made the *Princeton Review* in its long career a notable landmark for a type of conservative Calvinist theology that, even by the end of Hodge's life, was becoming increasingly rare. While much of the Protestant world was hastening toward progressive neologism, revivalistic reaction, anti-intellectual pietism, or Spirit-led individualism, Hodge and company were trying

1. Charles Hodge, "The *Princeton Review* on the State of the Country and of the Church," *Biblical Repertory and Princeton Review* 37 (1865): 657. Hereafter cited as *BRPR*.

to hold fast to what they considered the time-tested verities of historical confessional Protestantism.[2]

In his 1870 retrospective of the *Princeton Review,* Hodge took pains to spell out exactly what he considered the critical teachings of "sound Presbyterianism": "men are born into the world, since the fall, in a state of sin and condemnation; . . . this fact was due to the sin of Adam; . . . men are dependent on the Holy Spirit for their regeneration; and . . . it is due to the sovereign and supernatural interposition of the Spirit that one man is converted and not another."[3] As clearly as Hodge could state the doctrines for which the *Princeton Review* had stood, he was even more definite about the teachings of his day that it had withstood as dangerous perversions of classical Reformed theology:

> . . . that all sin consists in the voluntary violation of known law; that men, since the fall, are not born in a state of sin; that they are not chargeable with guilt or moral pollution until, having arrived at the years of discretion, they deliberately violate the divine law; that all men have plenary ability to avoid all sin; and, having sinned, to return unto God and do all that he requires at their hands; that God cannot prevent sin, or the present amount of sin, in a moral system; that he cannot effectually control the acts of free agents without destroying their liberty; that in conversion it is man, and not God, who determines who do, and who do not, turn unto God; that election is founded on the foresight of this self-determined repentance on the part of the sinner.[4]

Charles Hodge's forcefulness in stating what he did, and did not, consider proper Christian teaching concerning human nature, the character of sin, and the nature of salvation made him renowned among friends and foes in his own day and has sustained his reputation among critics, admirers, and the historically curious to the present.

At the foundation of Hodge's conservative Presbyterian theology—at the root of his lifelong effort to preserve "the honour of our common Redeemer" against a swelling tide of human-centered religion—was his engagement with the book of Romans.

2. For earlier efforts to take the measure of Hodge and his theology, see Mark A. Noll, "Introduction," in *Charles Hodge: The Way of Life,* ed. Mark A. Noll (New York: Paulist Press, 1987); and the introduction and notes to *The Princeton Theology, 1812–1921: Scripture, Science, and Theological Method from Archibald Alexander to Benjamin Breckinridge Warfield,* 2nd ed., ed. Mark A. Noll (Grand Rapids: Baker Academic, 2001). The sections in this paper on Moses Stuart and Albert Barnes are adapted from Noll, *America's God: From Jonathan Edwards to Abraham Lincoln* (New York: Oxford University Press, 2002).

3. Charles Hodge, "Retrospect of the History of the *Princeton Review,*" *BRPR: Index Volume* (Philadelphia, 1870–71), 12.

4. Ibid., 12–13.

As at so many other moments in the history of Christianity, so also for Hodge, commentary on the book of Romans operated at many levels and therefore could be examined from many angles. A fully developed study of Hodge on Romans would include at least four major considerations.

First, it would treat his personal understanding of the text as a literary document and his personal response to Paul's message as a theological challenge. Pursuing this inquiry would lead to deeper insight into the tension that marked Hodge's entire career between, on the one hand, his Baconian tendency to define Christianity as a set of propositions and, on the other, his pietistic tendency to define the faith as an affective relationship with Jesus Christ.[5]

Second, a full study would consider Hodge's work on Romans as a testimony to the state of biblical scholarship during the dawning of academic self-consciousness in the United States.[6] Hodge's commentary on Romans appeared during the first decade of serious American interest in modern biblical scholarship from the continent. Hodge himself had been one of the first American theologians to study in Europe, and so his commentary offers an important test case for how Americans were absorbing European understandings of philology, history, philosophy, and scientific method as applied to the scriptures. Hodge's own situation is particularly interesting, since during his time in Europe he established a close bond with Friedrich August Gottreu Tholuck (1799–1877) of Halle, who was not only a leading proponent of the pietistic *Vermittlungstheologie*, but also the author himself of an influential commentary on Romans in 1824, which both Hodge and Hodge's American opponents put to use for their own expositions of the epistle.[7]

Third, Hodge's work on Romans could also be studied for its place in the ancient stream of commentary on this central New Testament

5. This tension is a major theme in Noll, "Charles Hodge as an Expositor of the Spiritual Life," in *Charles Hodge Revisited: A Critical Appraisal of His Life and Work*, eds. John W. Stewart and James H. Moorehead (Grand Rapids: Eerdmans, 2002).

6. For guidance, see Thomas H. Olbricht, "Charles Hodge as an American New Testament Interpreter," *Journal of Presbyterian History* 57 (Summer 1979): 117–33; and Noll, "Charles Hodge," in *Historical Handbook of Major Biblical Interpreters*, ed. Donald K. McKim (Downers Grove, IL: InterVarsity Press, 1998), 325–30.

7. For an introduction, see Claude Welch, *Protestant Thought in the Nineteenth Century*, vol. 1 (New Haven: Yale University Press, 1972), 218–19. It is interesting to note that Hodge became acquainted with Tholuck at about the same time that Tholuck met E. B. Pusey. Tholuck remained good friends with both throughout their long lives, even though Hodge became one of the strongest American critics of the Oxford Movement, which Pusey led. See Albert Geck, "Friendship in Faith: Edward Bouverie Pusey und Friedrich August Gottreu Tholuck im Kampf gegen Rationalismus und Pantheismus. Schlaglichter auf eine englisch-deutsche Korrespondenz," *Pietismus und Neuzeit* 27 (2001): 91–117 (the same issue of this periodical contains a number of other studies on Tholuck).

epistle. In particular, Hodge's use of prior authorities merits close attention, because he based much of his own defense of imputation and
penal substitutionary atonement on earlier commentators who had also
highlighted these teachings in the apostle Paul. Hodge thus represented
an important way station for an exegetical tradition with roots in Augustine and Anselm and a later flowering that continues to the present
in expositors such as Martyn Lloyd-Jones, Leon Morris, John Murray,
J. I. Packer, and John R. W. Stott.[8]

As fruitful as examination of these other perspectives might be, I
will examine Hodge on Romans from yet a fourth angle. Since Hodge's
commentary turns out to have played a key role in a grand American
controversy over cardinal principles of Christian theology, it is also
important to understand its appearance and its arguments against
the backdrop of local circumstances. However much Hodge's writing
might contribute to the broad and general history of the study of Romans, it also illuminates in unusual fashion a particularly important
moment in the history of American theological development. What
was at issue when Hodge published his commentary was nothing less
than the character of the Christian gospel itself. But in order to see how
Hodge's work contributed to far-reaching discussion of fundamental
theological assertions, it is necessary to say something first about Hodge
himself, the circumstances in which his commentary was written, and
about those whose work on Romans set the challenge to which Hodge's
commentary was a response.

Hodge and His Context

Charles Hodge was born in Philadelphia in 1797.[9] By the time of
his death in 1878, he had personally instructed more theological students at Princeton Seminary than had attended any other postgraduate

8. For a sampling of modern reference to Hodge's commentary, see John R. W. Stott,
Romans: God's Good News for the World (Downers Grove, IL: InterVarsity Press, 1994),
110, 114, 127, 145, 152, 156; Leon Morris, *The Epistle to the Romans* (Grand Rapids: Eerdmans, 1988), 65, 69, 147, 223, 232, 240, 241, and many other pages; John Murray, *The
Epistle to the Romans* (Grand Rapids: Eerdmans, 1968), 31, 168, 200; James Montgomery
Boice, *Romans*, vol. 2, *The Reign of Grace, Romans 5–8* (Grand Rapids: Baker, 1992), 513,
566, 579; Douglas Moo, *The Epistle to the Romans* (Grand Rapids: Eerdmans, 1996), 75,
307, 318, 321, 326, 345.

9. The basic biographical source remains A. A. Hodge, *The Life of Charles Hodge* (New
York: Charles Scribner's Sons, 1880). For a recent updating, see Noll, "Charles Hodge,"
in *American National Biography*, vol. 10, ed. John A. Garraty and Mark C. Carnes (New
York: Oxford University Press, 1999), 906–9.

educational institution of any kind in the United States. Hodge was a graduate of the College of New Jersey, but his main educational and spiritual formation was undertaken by Archibald Alexander, with whom he studied at the new Princeton Seminary from 1816 to 1818. From Alexander, Hodge learned the singular combination of commitments that defined his own exposition of "the Princeton theology"—heartfelt piety, commitment to the inspiration of scripture, devotion to the Westminster Confession and Catechisms, confidence in the European Calvinism of savants such as François Turretin (1623–1787), and intuitive reliance upon Scottish commonsense moral philosophy. Alexander's interest in Hodge took on wider significance when he recruited Hodge to teach the biblical languages at Princeton and then in 1820 persuaded the Presbyterian General Assembly to ratify this appointment. Hodge spent most of the rest of his life, with but two significant breaks, at Princeton. The first of those breaks occurred in 1820, when he traveled through New England and met several leading Congregationalists, including Moses Stuart of Andover Seminary and Nathaniel W. Taylor of the Yale Divinity School, with whom he later engaged in vigorous theological polemic. The second extended from October 1826 to September 1828, when he traveled to Europe, with most of his time spent at Halle and Berlin, where he became friends not only with Tholuck, but also with several other young leaders of confessional and pietistic movements, like Ernst Wilhelm Hengstenberg and J. A. W. Neander. He also came away from Europe with a deep respect for the thoroughness of German scholarship, the power of preachers such as F. D. E. Schleiermacher, and the moving character of German church music. At the same time, he found German speculative theology most uncongenial. To him, post-Kantian philosophy overestimated the creative power of the human spirit, and the vogue for Hegel was entirely unfathomable. He also thought that the theology of Schleiermacher, which grounded religion on a feeling of utter dependence, debased sound thinking as well as sound theology. In Europe he sharpened an earlier sense that proper Christian theology could be undermined in two ways—by overemphasizing either philosophical rationalism or inner subjectivity.

Hodge's theological reputation arose from the skill (or, as his opponents would have it, the obduracy) with which he defended confessional Calvinism. In the pages of the *Princeton Review*, which he founded in 1825, he chastised Nathaniel William Taylor and the "New Haven theology" for departing from the high Calvinism of Jonathan Edwards.[10] He attacked the revivalism of Charles Finney for promoting

10. On the career of that journal, see Noll, "The Princeton Theological Review: 1825–1929," *Westminster Theological Journal* 50 (Fall 1988): 283–304.

a presumptuous confidence in human potency. He called to account the Mercersburg theologians, John W. Nevin and Philip Schaff, for wandering into mysticism. He directed telling shafts at England's Oxford Movement and German romantic theologians. He defended a high view of the Bible's inspiration against both Roman Catholic arguments for apostolic hierarchy and the first waves of continental biblical criticism. And he offered encouragement to Calvinist theological movements in other places (especially, after 1843, the Free Church of Scotland) and, more generally, to expressions of Protestant confessionalism (as in many warm, if not entirely comprehending, commendations of Luther, Lutherans, and Lutheranism).

When Hodge published his commentary on the book of Romans in 1835, it represented the culmination of an unusual set of personal, ecclesiastical, and theological developments. In light of his own biography, that a commentary on Romans appeared at all was something of a marvel. For most of the five years between 1833 and 1838, Hodge suffered a debilitating pain in his thigh (he called it "rheumatism"). For much of this period he was confined to a couch with his leg in a splint. During the months when he wrote his Romans commentary, "he was most heroically treated with violent counter-irritants. His hip, and thigh, and knee were over and over again blistered, cupped, rubbed with tartar emetic, and iodine; treated with issues, and setons, and the moxa, i.e., burnt with actual fire from the hip to the knee."[11] Most of the writing he did during this period—which included many long articles in the *Princeton Review* and a compendious history of Presbyterianism in America as well as the commentary on Romans—he penned "upon a board covered with leather held upon his breast by his left arm."[12] Princeton students regularly met him for lectures and recitations around his bed of infirmity.

Hodge's ecclesiastical anguish through these same years was, if anything, sharper than his physical pain. This was an era of theological crisis for American Presbyterians.[13] Among Hodge's party of traditionalists, nervousness centered on the apparent seepage of New England views into their denomination. The particular cause of complaint was the teaching of Nathaniel W. Taylor at the Yale Divinity School that traditional doctrines of original sin, human solidarity with Adam, and the vicarious atonement in Christ were exegetically superfluous and morally suspect. In the tumultuous Presbyterian debate that led in 1837 to the

11. A. A. Hodge, *Life of Charles Hodge*, 237.
12. Ibid., 239.
13. The outstanding study remains George M. Marsden, *The Evangelical Mind and the New School Presbyterian Experience* (New Haven: Yale University Press, 1970).

schism of the denomination into Old School and New School factions, Hodge played the part of a moderate conservative. When, however, that division occurred, he cast his lot unreservedly with the Old School and soon became one of its theological champions.

The theology that Hodge championed was being refined through an extensive series of first-order controversies. These controversies were the antecedents of his work on Romans. The great provocation for his own work was provided by a true landmark in American biblical scholarship, Moses Stuart's *Commentary on the Epistle to the Romans*, which appeared in 1832. Very little in the early United States had survived the assault on tradition associated with the American Revolution. Reverence for the Bible was an exception, and the revival of evangelical fortunes that was under way by the early decades of the century was being driven by lay appropriation of the scriptures. When American seminaries began to achieve a certain degree of professionalization, as they were doing by the 1820s, it was no surprise that the publications of biblical exegetes received a great deal of attention. Nor is it surprising, given the theological climate of the late 1820s and following years, that some of this biblical commentary would become matter for great controversy. No American biblical scholar enjoyed a higher reputation in this era than Moses Stuart of Andover, and no work of early American biblical scholarship generated sharper controversy than Stuart's *Romans*.

Moses Stuart (1780–1852) remains a respected figure as the pioneer of academic biblical scholarship in America.[14] To peers, his dedication as a professor at Andover to mastering, teaching, and then promoting biblical Hebrew was legendary. He was honored almost as much for his willingness to study the latest German scholarship while maintaining conservative opinions on the inspiration of the scriptures, the integrity of the Old Testament, and the reality of biblical miracles. Most Protestants were also grateful for his decades-long opposition toward the Unitarians. At the same time, however, Stuart was suspect to some New England conservatives and to almost all Old School Presbyterians for his theological pedigree and for what they considered the tendentious theological agenda at work in his commentaries.

From 1806 until his call to Andover in 1810, Stuart served as minister of New Haven's First Church, where his pastorate was notable for its successful revivals, and for his friendship with the young N. W. Taylor, who succeeded him at the First Church when Stuart removed to Ando-

14. See Jerry Wayne Brown, *The Rise of Biblical Criticism in America, 1800–1870: The New England Scholars* (Middletown, CT: Wesleyan University Press, 1969), 45–59; a useful monograph is John H. Giltner, *Moses Stuart: The Father of Biblical Science in America*, Society of Biblical Literature Centennial Publications (Atlanta: Scholars Press, 1988).

ver. As Taylor's opinions became better known, the friends of orthodoxy were not reassured by Stuart's low-key but unmistakable support for the New Haven theology.

Although Stuart's commentary on Romans of 1832 was hailed universally as a monument to scholarship, orthodox reviewers were troubled by what seemed to be Stuart's aggressive promotion of New Haven conclusions, especially in commenting on the critical passage in chapter 5 that had usually been read by traditional Protestants, as well as many Roman Catholics, to teach human solidarity with Adam, the doctrine of imputation (both Adam's sin to humanity and Christ's righteousness to the redeemed), and the determinative work of the Holy Spirit in converting the lost.

Stuart's learning was on full display as he took up this passage, but so also was what his biographer calls a weakness for "the push of theological prejudice." In summary, Stuart held that the apostle Paul taught that all humans did sin as a result of Adam's own transgression, but that the connection between Adam and later humanity was circumstantial rather than federal (as the Westminster Confession and Hodge affirmed), organic (as held by Jonathan Edwards), or imputed (as maintained by traditional theologians generally). In addition, Stuart maintained that sinfulness and the guilt of sin came to humans only when they themselves sinned, never as a result of the disposition of an underlying character. The result, in John Giltner's conclusion, was to "provide the New Haven 'liberals,' Taylor chief among them, a solid exegetical ground for their speculative conclusions," and to make Stuart "the first American Calvinist biblical scholar to offer extended exegetical support for what was perceived to be a significant divergence from the received theological tradition."[15]

What makes Stuart's commentary especially important in the history of American theology was the prominence in his work of what might be called local warrants, that is, deference to a distinctly American ideology of freedom and a distinctly American trust in commonsense moral reasoning. These principles had become everywhere ascendant by the 1820s in the new United States, and they were on display as well in Stuart's work on Romans.[16]

When, for example, Stuart expanded upon the interpretative cruxes of Romans 5:12–19, he used standard warrants of early-nineteenth-century intellectual method to bolster his conclusions. Against Jonathan Edwards's account of original sin as the participation of all humanity

15. Giltner, *Moses Stuart*, 110, 112–13, 116.
16. For an explanation of how these principles became important for theology, see Noll, *America's God*.

in Adam, as also against the traditional idea that the guilt and penalty of Adam's sin were imputed to later humanity, Stuart claimed that a proper understanding of "moral government" could not support the older theories. By contrast, he felt that "the whole doctrine of moral retribution, as built on the principles of moral justice . . . at the very first view of it which is taken by our conscience and our sense of right and wrong" supported the notion that sinfulness lay ultimately in sinning itself, with no "original sin" as that notion had been developed in traditional Christian theology.[17] According to Stuart, theologians had been misled by their own "philosophizing," and "the speculations of eighteen centuries" had distorted "the simple facts as stated by the Apostle Paul." As Stuart read those "facts," he wanted still to affirm that "Adam involved all his race in a state of sin and death," but he refused to use a stronger word than "involved."[18] As he drew such conclusions, Stuart sounded most like N. W. Taylor. For example, "It is in opposition to the immutable principles of our moral nature, to predicate sin in its proper sense of any being that acts without free choice and knowledge of rule." Furthermore, if humans would only realize that they alone were ultimately responsible for their own offensiveness before God, they would align their doctrines with "an immutable law of moral sense" and let their reasoning rest on "self evident principles."[19] Stuart admitted that it was difficult in the extreme to affirm both that Adam's sin influenced later humanity to scorn God and that later humanity scorned God on its own, but he was also confident that a theological system much more like N. W. Taylor's (whom he did not name) than Jonathan Edwards's (whom he named repeatedly) was in accord "with the Scriptures and with our moral sense and judgment."[20]

Presbyterians like Hodge who were disconcerted by Stuart as a representative of New England Congregationalism were even more alarmed when Stuart's interpretations of sin, imputation, and atonement began to be publicized from within their own ranks.[21] Here the focus of attention was Albert Barnes (1798–1870), a rising light of the New School.

17. Moses Stuart, *A Commentary on the Epistle to the Romans with a Translation and Various Excursus*, 2nd ed. (Andover, MA: Flagg and Gould, 1835), 585, 593. (The commentary appeared in four editions, with at least fourteen printings, between 1832 and 1865.)

18. Ibid., 599.

19. Ibid., 610, 614, 615.

20. Ibid., 616.

21. For a solid discussion, see Stephen J. Stein, "Stuart and Hodge on Romans 5:12–21: An Exegetical Controversy about Original Sin," *Journal of Presbyterian History* 47 (December 1969): 340–58. Somewhat less helpful is Elwyn A. Smith, "The Doctrine of Imputation and the Presbyterian Schism of 1837–1838," *Journal of the Presbyterian Historical Society* 38 (September 1960): 129–51.

Barnes had studied with Archibald Alexander and the young Charles Hodge at Princeton Seminary, where he graduated in 1824. From his first pastorate at Morristown, New Jersey, Barnes was widely regarded as a minister to watch—as a leader of pious good sense and exactly the right kind of energetic activism by those who would eventually form the New School, but also as a dangerously uncritical adherent of New England principles and a precariously earnest moral reformer by some who would later constitute the Old School. Barnes gained national prominence in 1829 with the publication of a sermon entitled "The Way of Salvation," which to Presbyterian moderates and conservatives sounded suspiciously similar to what New Haven theologians were propounding. According to Barnes, there was no federal or organic solidarity with Adam; Christ's atonement created the conditions for all to be saved yet was applied to no one in particular; and humans possessed a power within themselves from their own natural resources to choose God. Barnes did stress the work of the Holy Spirit in the process of conversion, yet not so clearly as to distinguish his views from those of N. W. Taylor, who also spoke regularly of the Holy Spirit as a necessary influence in, but not the fundamental cause of, conversion.

Like Stuart, Barnes also at key points drew on the era's prominent ideologies to carry his message. As he denied the imputation of Adam's sin, for example, Barnes held up the standard of "moral government" and "the facts" it taught by showing that God was always "equitable" in treating humanity.[22] When he affirmed, for example, that the atonement "had not respect so much to *individuals*, as to the *law* and *perfection of God*," he argued that it was "a matter of common sense" that God does not require more of people "than *in any sense* they are able to perform."[23] Barnes's own stress on how the sovereignty of God was the key matter in human salvation reassured Presbyterian readers that he was not simply repeating principles from the New Haven theologians, but to many of those same readers the similarities with New England were too striking to ignore.

Problems with Barnes's theology were compounded many times over when in 1834 he published a lay-oriented, popular set of notes on the Epistle to the Romans.[24] In this work, Barnes went even further than Stuart in revising older Reformed doctrines of imputation, solidarity with Adam, and union with Christ.

---

22. Albert Barnes, *The Way of Salvation . . . Together with Mr. Barnes' Defence of the Sermon*, 7th ed. (New York, 1836), 15–16n, 16.

23. Ibid., 21, 24n.

24. Albert Barnes, *Notes on the New Testament* (1835; reprint, Grand Rapids: Baker, 1949).

The timing of Barnes's publication on Romans was critical for general Presbyterian history. From 1832 to 1835, ferment boiled over in several local controversies where traditionalists accused ministers of false teaching derived from New England. Ecclesiastical trials arising from these charges took place among Presbyterians in Pennsylvania, Indiana, Illinois, and most spectacularly for Lyman Beecher in Cincinnati. With respect to Barnes, the Old School's specific offense was not just that he seemed to have swallowed Moses Stuart's conclusions whole.[25] It was also that he did so with engaging prose and in an accessible format that any literate layperson could read.

Hodge's Commentary on Romans

Turmoil within the Presbyterian church, the challenge of Moses Stuart's detailed and academic treatment of Romans, as well as Albert Barnes's provocative popularization were working together to pose the question that Hodge set out to answer with his own commentary from 1835.

Although Hodge was still relatively young as he bent to the task of publishing on this epistle, he was able to draw on more than a decade of concentrated study. From 1822 he had been lecturing each year on the Pauline Epistles.[26] During his time in Germany he had recorded Tholuck's opinions that "the doctrine of depravity was the most important doctrine of the gospel" and that "justification . . . [was] founded on the imputed righteousness of Christ."[27] His foreign sojourn had been filled to the full with up-to-date philological, linguistic, and exegetical study. When he returned from Germany in 1828, he had taken the first opportunity to tell the Princeton students, "Wherever you find vital piety . . . , there you find the doctrines of the fall, of depravity, of regeneration, of atonement, and of the deity of Jesus Christ."[28] In 1830 he published long essays in the *Princeton Review* articulating traditional Reformed theology on regeneration and imputation.[29] The next year he followed with another

25. Ibid., 141. For example, Barnes on Romans 5:19 ("many were made sinners"): "There is not the slightest intimation that it was by imputation. The whole scope of the argument is, moreover, against this; for the object of the apostle is not to show that they were charged with the sin of another, but that they were in fact *sinners* themselves."

26. A. A. Hodge, *Life of Charles Hodge*, 98.

27. Ibid., 118 (from journal dated March 4, 1827).

28. Hodge, "Introductory Lecture. Delivered in the Theological Seminary . . . Nov. 7, 1828," *BRPR*, new series, 1 (1829): 94–95.

29. Hodge, "Regeneration and the Manner of Its Occurrence," *BRPR* 2 (1830): 250–96; "Review of an Article in the *Christian Spectator* . . . on Imputation," *BRPR* 2 (1830): 425–72.

lengthy essay on imputation itself.[30] In 1832 he took to task the whole drift of theology in New England with another formidable paper.[31] In 1833 and 1835 he published long reviews of the commentaries by Stuart and Barnes. In both cases he expressed appreciation—to Stuart for his scholarship, to Barnes for his rhetorical skills.[32] But in both cases as well, he was unrelenting in his criticism. After focusing on Stuart's treatment of 5:12–19, for example, Hodge concluded "that the doctrine of imputation is not touched either by Professor Stuart's exegesis or metaphysics."[33] Then just as his own nearly 600-page commentary was coming from the press, Hodge also brought out a 175-page series of "Questions" on Romans that he had prepared for Bible and Sunday school classes. When, therefore, Hodge published his own commentary in 1835, it came as the climax of a long period of intense concentration on the exegesis of this one book, but also of the theological issues that epistle so centrally addressed.[34]

The introduction to Hodge's commentary, which was heavily dependent on contemporary German scholars whom Hodge trusted, addressed the apostle Paul, the situation of the church at Rome, circumstances of the writing of the epistle, its "authenticity," and its outline. But by keeping the introduction short, Hodge could get down to business right away. Throughout, his main focus was on understanding the apostle's depiction of justification by faith. In that effort, the perils through which Hodge wanted to steer the reader were, on one side, Roman Catholic notions about justification arising from infused righteousness and, on the other, New England views about personal agency being foundational to personal salvation.

Hodge's sense of the epistle was clear from his first extended comments on the theme of justification. His words on 1:17 are indicative: "From this contrast between a righteousness which is our own, which is of works, and that which is not our own, which is of God, from God, the gift of God, it is plain that the [righteousness of God] of which the apostle here speaks, is that [righteousness] by which we are made [righ-

30. Hodge, "The *Christian Spectator* on the Doctrine of Imputation," *BRPR* 3 (1831): 407–43.

31. Hodge, "The New Divinity Tried," *BRPR* 4 (1832): 278–304.

32. Hodge, "Stuart on Romans," *BRPR* 5 (1833): 381–416; "Barnes on the Epistle to the Romans," *BRPR* 7 (1835): 285–340.

33. Hodge, "Stuart on Romans," quoting Hodge, *Essays and Reviews* (New York: R. Carter, 1856; reprint, New York: Garland, 1987), 85.

34. Charles Hodge, *Commentary on the Epistle to the Romans.* For citations, I have used a 1993 reprint from Eerdmans in Grand Rapids of an 1886 reprint of Hodge's second edition from 1864. The main difference between the original commentary from 1835, which I have also consulted, and Hodge's second edition from 1864 is that there are more quotations from Barnes and Stuart in 1835 and more quotations from authorities supporting Hodge's conclusions in 1864.

teous before God]; it is a righteousness which he gives and which he approves." Hodge then cited six modern commentators, with Tholuck first in line, who also affirmed this concept of righteousness, and then he quoted another modern German who underscored his judgment: "All interpretations which overlook the idea of imputation, as is done in the explanations given by the Romanists, and also in that of Grotius, are false." Already in his remarks on the epistle's first chapter, Hodge's main direction was clear: "The nature of this righteousness, it is one great design of this epistle, and of the whole gospel to unfold. . . . it will present itself at every step of our progress."[35]

Similar arguments and conclusions came again to the fore when Hodge got to the second half of chapter 3. His comment on 3:23 affirmed human solidarity with Adam in the fact of sin, and his reading of 3:25 provided an occasion to underscore the objective basis of the atonement. That affirmation also offers a sense of how Hodge marshaled his arguments:

> The obvious meaning . . . of this important passage is, that God has publicly set forth the Lord Jesus Christ, in the sight of the intelligent universe, as a propitiatory sacrifice for the sins of men. It is the essential idea of such a sacrifice, that it is a satisfaction to justice. It terminates on God. Its primary design is not to produce any subjective change in the offerer, but to appease God. Such is the meaning of the word, from which we have no right to depart. Such also is the idea which it of necessity would convey to every Gentile and every Jewish reader, and therefore such was the idea which the apostle intended to express. For if we are not to understand the language of the Bible in its historical sense, that is, in the sense in which the sacred writers knew it would be understood by those to whom they wrote, it ceases to have any determinate meaning whatever, and may be explained according to the private opinion of every interpreter.[36]

In dealing with the themes of chapter 3, Hodge also paused to draw a contrast between the Germans, who in his view treated Paul fairly, even when they disagreed with him, and Americans, who were prone to force Paul into their own procrustean assumptions. The specific issue was a contention from some New England theologians that 3:27 supported a governmental view of the atonement. The suggestion was to Hodge indicative of a major problem: "In Germany, the subjection of the Bible to philosophy has come to an end. In this country, it is still struggling for liberty."[37]

---

35. Hodge, *Commentary on Romans* (1864), 31.
36. Ibid., 93.
37. Ibid., 99.

Hodge's lengthy discussion of 5:12–21 manifested the full range of his exegetical equipment and bore the full weight of his main argument. His discussion of this section of the epistle occupied over 11 percent of the total commentary in both the 1835 and 1864 editions. The commentary was particularly full at 5:12—in the King James Version, which was Hodge's default text: "Wherefore, as by one man sin entered into the world, and death by sin; and so death passed upon all men, for that all have sinned." In discussing this critical verse, Hodge addressed what it meant for sin to enter the world through one man, what it meant for death to come to all because of sin, and what it meant for death to be connected to the fact that all sinned.

Hodge's treatment of the conjunction in 5:12 was characteristic of his work in the commentary as a whole. At the outset he labored to identify his interpretation with the linguistically correct reading: "The ordinary and natural force of the word expresses a perfectly good sense: 'All men die, *because* all sinned.'"[38] Then he canvassed alternative views on the question of how human sinfulness was connected to Adam with erroneous or inadequate ones examined before he presented his own interpretation. First, against the view held by Moses Stuart, N. W. Taylor, and some of the New School Presbyterians, who regarded human sinfulness as arising only from the sinful deeds that individuals committed themselves, Hodge fired salvo after salvo. Such a reading was rejected by "the almost unanimous judgment of the Church"; it was inconsistent with the aorist tense; it was inconsistent with "the literal, simple force of the word"; it was inconsistent with the whole passage's focus on Adam; and it destroyed the analogy between Adam and Christ. In sum, Stuart's picture of sinfulness was "contrary not only to this whole passage, but all Paul's teaching, and to the whole gospel." Moreover, that teaching was simply false: "It is not true that all die because all personally sin; death is more extensive than personal transgression. This is a fact of experience, and is asserted by the apostle in what follows."[39]

Second, Hodge examined the interpretation of the passage that treated it as if human sinfulness arose from a corruption inherited from Adam. Showing that this second interpretation was substandard did take a little finesse, for Hodge conceded that Calvin could be enlisted in its defense. But Hodge was able to his own satisfaction to show that Calvin also relativized this reading by other exegetical conclusions. And so he put that interpretation to rest.

Third, he made quick work also of Jonathan Edwards's interpretation that since all individuals actually existed by a kind of seminal Platonism

38. Ibid., 148.
39. Ibid., 149.

in Adam, death was a consequence that came to all humans because all humans were really "in Adam."

Finally, Hodge came to what he considered the correct interpretation, that "all sinned in Adam as their head and representative."[40] At this point he then developed the notion of Adam as federal or covenantal head of the whole human race, which Hodge held to be both demanded exegetically and confirmed by the historic usage of the church.

At the end of his consideration of 5:12–21, Hodge was at pains to make sure that his conclusions would not be obscured:

> The doctrine of imputation is clearly taught in this passage. This doctrine does not include the idea of a mysterious identity of Adam and his race; nor that of a transfer of the moral turpitude of his sin to his descendants. It does not teach that his offence was personally or properly the sin of all men, or that his act was, in any mysterious sense, the act of his posterity. Neither does it imply, in reference to the righteousness of Christ, that his righteousness becomes personally and inherently ours, or that his moral excellence is in any way transferred from him to believers. The sin of Adam, therefore, is no ground to us of remorse; and the righteousness of Christ is no ground of self-complacency in those to whom it is imputed. This doctrine merely teaches, that in virtue of the union, representative and natural, between Adam and his posterity, his sin is the ground of their condemnation, that is, of their subjection to penal evils; and that in virtue of the union between Christ and his people, his righteousness is the ground of their justification. This doctrine is taught almost in so many words in verses 12, 15–19. It is so clearly stated, so often repeated or assumed, and so formally proved, that very few commentators of any class fail to acknowledge, in one form or another, that it is the doctrine of the apostle.[41]

This conclusion then made way for Hodge's broader interpretation of the whole epistle:

> The design of the apostle being to illustrate the nature and to confirm the certainty of our justification, it is the leading doctrine of this passage, that our acceptance with God is founded neither on our faith nor our good works, but on the obedience or righteousness of Christ, which to us is a free gift. This is the fundamental doctrine of the gospel, verses 18, 19.[42]

As then supplemented by similar exegesis for the rest of the book, Hodge's work represented a strong restatement of a traditionally Augustinian understanding of the apostle Paul's main arguments.

40. Ibid., 151.
41. Ibid., 178.
42. Ibid., 190.

His exegesis was not, however, without its suspect maneuvers. When convenient, he also could draw freely upon his era's standard epistemological warrants. The same assumptions of a distinctly American ideology that he saw distorting the work of others sometimes, in other words, became quite useful for his own purposes. In particular, Hodge on several occasions used commonsense intuitions about the way things simply had to be as a standard by which to measure the text. Thus, in his commentary on Romans 5:12, Hodge's argument against Jonathan Edwards's sense of sinful human unity in Adam was not in the least exegetical: "It is a monstrous evil to make the Bible contradict the common sense and common consciousness of men. This is to make God contradict himself."[43]

Hodge could also reveal himself at times as an ordinary Victorian sentimentalist. A case in point is revealed by how hard nineteenth-century intuitions about the innocence of children bore down upon Hodge. As a classical Calvinist Hodge had to preserve human unity in Adam, but as a sensitive Victorian, he had somehow to get dying infants into heaven. His answer to the dilemma was a theory of imputation that made an ingenious distinction between imputed sin (which only grace could overcome) and actual sinning (which condemned people to hell). That Hodge found in scripture a theology of covenant to support his Victorian position suggests how complicated the exchange of social conventions and objective research actually can be for all biblical exegesis.[44] And so on this subject he concluded, "If, without personal participation in the sin of Adam, all men are subject to death, may we not hope that, without personal acceptance of the righteousness of Christ, all who die in infancy are saved?"[45]

Conclusion

Hodge was by no means finished with the great issues of human nature, human sin, justification, imputation, and atonement after he brought out his commentary in 1835. The very next year he published a major essay in the *Princeton Review* on another recently published German commentary on Romans.[46] In 1839 he published, also in the

---

43. Ibid., 151.

44. For an excellent discussion, see George P. Hutchinson, *The Problem of Original Sin in American Presbyterian Theology* (Nutley, NJ: Presbyterian and Reformed Pub. Co., 1972), 31–35.

45. Hodge, *Commentary on Romans*, 190.

46. Hodge, "Rückert on Romans," *BRPR* 8 (1836): 39–51.

Review, a major collection, "Testimonies on the Doctrine of Imputation," from throughout the church's history, which supported his own conclusions.[47] In many of his weighty essays on the New England theology, Charles Finney's revivalism, and modern European theologies, themes of justification, the vicarious atonement, and federal headship figured prominently. And toward the end of his life, Hodge reprised many of the subjects he had first developed with Stuart and Barnes in view as a very substantial chapter in his *Systematic Theology*.[48]

As for the commentary itself, it was very well received by the public in general, and it was soon recognized as a major statement of traditional Reformed theology even by those who disagreed with its conclusions. In its first three years, either the full commentary or a 350-page abridgment was brought out by four different Philadelphia publishers, as well as by publishers in New York and London, often with multiple printings. At least seventy different editions have been published since 1835, many with multiple printings; the commentary has never been out of print; it has been translated into many languages (the first, French, in 1840); and it is available in at least two editions today.[49]

A final assessment of Hodge's work as commentator is complicated because of the early stage of modern biblical scholarship in which he worked out his conclusions and because all of the voices with whom he was in dialogue were also so clearly arguing to particular theological conclusions. One of the most helpful general comments on Hodge the exegete came from B. B. Warfield, a successor to Hodge's chair of theology at Princeton, who had observed Hodge while a student at the seminary in the early 1870s and who recorded his observations shortly after Hodge's death. The balance of his conclusions nicely summarize the strengths and weaknesses found in Hodge's commentary on Romans:

> I thought then, and I think now, that Dr. Hodge's sense of the general meaning of a passage was unsurpassed. . . . Nothing could surpass the clearness with which he set forth the general argument and the main connections of thought. Neither could anything surpass the analytical subtlety with which he extracted the doctrinal contents of passages. . . . He seemed to look through a passage, catch its main drift and all its theological bearings, and state the result in crisp sentences, which would have been worthy of Bacon; all at a single movement of mind. He had, however, no taste

47. Hodge, "Testimonies on the Doctrine of the Imputation," *BRPR* 11 (1839): 553–79.

48. Hodge, *Systematic Theology*, 3 vols. (New York: C. Scribner, 1872–73), especially 3:180–92 ("Protestant Doctrine of Sin"), 3:192–205 ("Immediate Imputation"), and 3:205–14 ("Mediate Imputation").

49. Information on editions and printings is from World Cat.

for the technicalities of Exegesis. . . . [O]n such points he was seldom wholly satisfactory. . . . He made no claim, again, to critical acumen; and in questions of textual criticism he constantly went astray. . . . Even here he was the clear, analytical thinker, rather than a patient collector and weigher of detailed evidence. He was great here [as an exegete], but not at his greatest. Theology was his first love.[50]

For a historical judgment with American history primarily in view, it is obvious that Charles Hodge understood, internalized, and revivified an important Augustinian strand of Pauline interpretation. Without the kind of work on display in the Romans commentary, it is hard to imagine that Hodge's kind of Reformed theology could have flourished as it did in the nineteenth century, and survived as it has into the twenty-first century. In Hodge's view sin was the curse of the race, as sin was the curse of every human being. But in his view as well, precisely because all humans died in Adam, so could the whole body of the faithful be made alive in Jesus Christ. Hodge did not impose his theology on the book of Romans. Rather, he found it there. When American thought in general was pushing resolutely toward self-assertion, self-definition, and self-choosing, and when strands of Reformed theology elsewhere in the Western world were growing weary of their own traditions, Hodge stood fast for a theology of inherited human sinfulness in Adam, of federal headship in both Adam and Christ, but most of all for objective justification in Jesus Christ. He thought he was supported in these views by the book of Romans. Given the circumstances of his time and place, he made a good case.

50. Warfield, quoted in A. A. Hodge, *Life of Charles Hodge*, 589–90.

11

JOHN WILLIAM COLENSO

Timothy Larsen

On Sunday, January 5, 1866, Bishop Colenso of Natal was publicly and solemnly declared to be excommunicated. His Metropolitan, Robert Gray, bishop of Cape Town, pronounced in the sentence that he, "by the authority of Christ committed unto us, pass upon John William Colenso, D.D., the sentence of greater excommunication, thereby separating him from the Communion of the Church of Christ . . . he is, according to our Lord's command . . . to be taken by the whole multitude of the faithful as a heathen man and a publican."[1] Colenso thus appears to have the peculiar distinction of being the only Anglican bishop to receive a sentence of excommunication in at least the last three hundred years. This sentence was based upon his having been found guilty of heresy at an ecclesiastical trial—a trial he did not recognize as legitimate and therefore did not attend. The evidence offered at his trial to support the charge that he was teaching error was derived entirely from three books he had published, the first of which was his commentary on Romans,

1. Charles Gray, *Life of Robert Gray, Bishop of Cape Town and Metropolitan of Africa* (London: Rivingtons, 1883), 2:248. I am grateful to Jeffrey Greenman, Paul Friesen, Sandy Finlayson, and Robert Derrenbacker, all of whom read an earlier draft of this chapter and commented upon it.

St. Paul's Epistle to the Romans: Newly Translated, and Explained from a Missionary Point of View (1861).

Colenso's trial was a dubious affair—even in ecclesiastical terms—and a legal challenge revealed that the letters of patent for both the bishops of Natal and Cape Town were invalid, as they had been drawn up after the South African legislature had already been established, an administrative muddle that resulted in Colenso retaining the legal right to be the bishop of Natal. Nevertheless, the vast majority of bishops in the Anglican Communion considered him spiritually deposed. When he returned to his own cathedral in 1865, the dean informed him dramatically that he was not impressed by mere legalities: "It is written, 'That which ye shall bind on earth is bound in heaven.' That sentence stands ratified before the Throne of the Almighty. Fear God, and depart from evil."[2] Even the archbishop of Canterbury himself, C. T. Longley, who needed to walk particularly carefully in such matters, told Colenso bluntly in 1866, "I have no hesitation in avowing that, according to my belief, you have been duly and canonically deposed from your spiritual office."[3] When the first Lambeth Conference of the bishops of the Anglican Communion was held, Colenso did not receive an invitation. With the approval of Convocation, W. K. Macrorie was consecrated bishop of Maritzburg in 1869, a diocese geographically identical to the bishop of Natal's. If Colenso, in the eyes of British law, retained his bishopric, and if it is not the place of a historian to pronounce whether his status was altered in the eyes of the Almighty, it can nevertheless certainly be said that Colenso became isolated and cut off from the rest of his fellow bishops to an extent without parallel.

The bishop of Natal is often discussed in current works of scholarship— just to focus on the subjects at hand—both for his controversial religious views and his work in the field of biblical studies. Nevertheless, attention has naturally focused on his studies of the Pentateuch and the book of Joshua, which represented his true life's work in terms of scholarship and which provoked the general furor that made his public reputation.[4] A by-product of this focus has been that, especially outside of South Africa, his intriguing commentary on Romans has not received the attention it deserves, either in recent scholarship or during his own lifetime.[5] In En-

---

2. Gray, *Gray*, 2:239.

3. Ibid., 2:245–46.

4. For this controversy, see Timothy Larsen, *Contested Christianity: The Political and Social Contexts of Victorian Theology* (Waco: Baylor University Press, 2004), chap. 5.

5. Professor Jonathan A. Draper of the University of Natal is the only person I know of who has written works focused upon Colenso's *Romans*, and he has done so repeatedly. See, for example, his "Hermeneutical Drama on the Colonial Stage: Liminal Space and Creativity in Colenso's *Commentary on Romans*," *Journal of Theology for Southern Africa* 103 (March 1999); "Bishop John William Colenso's Interpretation to the Zulu People of

gland, his Old Testament work was formally investigated and condemned by Convocation in 1863, but the Anglican hierarchy chose to ignore his New Testament study. On the other hand, people were hardly likely to cite his Pauline commentary as an authoritative or insightful source once he had been so widely labeled a heretic, and thus Colenso's *Romans* largely fell out of sight. Nevertheless, it is a volume well worth exploring, due to the telling way that it illuminates the contours and limits of mid-nineteenth-century liberal Anglican thought.

Colenso's *Romans* was a reflection of and a contribution to Broad Church Anglicanism. The notion of the "Broad Church party" was developed and popularized by W. J. Conybeare in an essay published in the *Edinburgh Review* in 1853 in which he devised a striking taxonomy of Anglican churchmanship. The three basic parties in his scheme were High, Low, and Broad. Conybeare subdivided the High and Low parties in a tripartite manner, arguing that they had "exaggerated" and "stagnant" factions. The exaggerated were identified as Tractarians for the High, and Recordite Evangelicals (after their newspaper, the *Record*) for the Low. Stagnant High churchmen were given the inevitable appellation "High and Dry," while the corresponding group in the other camp were creatively dubbed "Low and Slow." No label was offered for stagnant Broad churchmen, but the High Church newspaper, the *Guardian*, helpfully suggested "Smart and Shallow," arguably implying that Conybeare himself belonged in this category.[6] There is now a general scholarly consensus that there was no Broad Church "party," that is, no such organized group with its own machinery for united action, such as newspapers and societies.[7] Nevertheless, "Broad Church" is a useful label for a certain type of Victorian churchman. These churchmen can be distinguished by two traits, either of which would usually warrant the label, but they were often both held together. The first was an instinct toward comprehensiveness or inclusiveness in the national church. This meant that they were not apt to want to throw anyone out who wished to stay in, and they were open to finding ways for others to come in, perhaps

---

the *Sola Fide* in Paul's Letter to the Romans," *SBL 2000 Seminar Papers;* and "The Bishop and the Bricoleur: Bishop John William Colenso's *Commentary on Romans*," and "Magema Kamagwaza Fuze's *The Black People and Whence They Came*," in *The Bible in Africa: Transactions, Trajectories, and Trends*, ed. G. O. West and M. W. Dube (Leiden: Brill, 2000).

6. W. J. Conybeare, "Church Parties," ed. Arthur Burns, in *From Cranmer to Davidson: A Church of England Miscellany*, ed. Stephen Taylor (Woodbridge, U.K.: Boydell Press, 1999), 241. This reprint of Conybeare's article benefits from Burns's meticulous research and generous, informative introduction and notes.

7. See, for example, John Wolffe, "Anglicanism," in *Nineteenth-Century English Religious Traditions: Retrospect and Prospect*, ed. D. G. Paz (Westport, CT: Greenwood Press, 1995), 12–16. Conybeare, "Church Parties," 251.

even going so far as envisioning a place for Unitarians. The second trait was a more liberal theological outlook; a suspicion that some precise doctrinal positions from the past had become a liability in the light of modern thought and sensibilities and a hope that these themes might now be articulated in a less rigid and more acceptable manner.

Colenso is often painted as a loner, a maverick, a crank, a rogue bishop. While such a portrait does capture some realities, his *Romans* is better understood as a reflection of a particular, wider school of theology: mid-Victorian liberal Anglicanism. Although he would soon develop a reputation as a leading English champion of the modern discipline of biblical criticism, Colenso's *Romans* was in no sense a contribution to that field. Not even making it to the first hurdle, he assumed without even bothering to argue it that all thirteen letters traditionally attributed to Paul were actually written by him.[8] Jeff Guy claims that the bishop of Natal's "historical sense," that is, his discussion of the original recipients of the Epistle to the Romans, is "immediately impressive."[9] In truth, however, this portion of Colenso's work is transparently subservient to and skewed by his theological agenda: he needed the original audience to be narrow, proud, exclusivistic, misguided Jews who did not really understand the gospel in order to apply his version of its message to his contemporary target—a Christian world that he viewed as narrow, proud, exclusivistic, misguided, and failing to understand the gospel. Galatians would have been a more apt choice for his theme. Indeed, sometimes Colenso's historical reconstruction is downright risible: "May it not be that the twenty-eight persons mentioned by name, and the others referred to in Rom. xvi., comprise really the whole register, as it were, the *church-roll*, of believers at that time in Rome?"[10] The bishop of Natal may deserve to be included in the story that encompasses De Wette and Ewald, but a case cannot be made for mentioning him alongside F. C. Baur and J. B. Lightfoot.

Although inconsequential if judged as a work of biblical criticism, Colenso's *Romans* may be deemed something of a tour de force when it is seen for what it is, a daring and ambitious contribution to Broad Church theology. The bishop of Natal managed to tackle an impressive range of topics and targets under the structure of a Pauline commentary. He attacks High Church thought repeatedly, and when the restrictions of his project did not afford sufficient possibilities for countering their "sacramental system," he even included as an appendix his "Sermon on

---

8. J. W. Colenso, *St. Paul's Epistle to the Romans: Newly Translated, and Explained from a Missionary Point of View* (New York: Appleton, 1863 [1861]), 244–45.

9. Jeff Guy, *The Heretic: A Study of the Life of John William Colenso, 1814–1883* (Pietermaritzburg, South Africa: University of Natal Press, 1983), 73.

10. Colenso, *Romans*, 29.

the Eucharist" in order to finish the work. Low churchmen receive their fair share of attacks as well, especially Calvinists, and High and Low are perhaps simultaneous targets in his polemics against substitutionary atonement and endless punishment. Positively, he argued for a recognition of the fatherhood of God over all humanity, for justification and righteousness as the possession of all human beings through the work of Christ, for a form of universalism, and for human sensibilities as a locus of authority in matters of doctrine.

One might well wonder why he chose a study of Romans as a way of presenting such a theological vision. Romans, after all, has always been the favorite of Calvinists, whose doctrinal distinctives he abhorred. Peter Hinchliff convincingly suggested that Colenso chose Romans for the very reason that it was often used to support views to which he objected, as a way of capturing "the enemy's citadel."[11] Nevertheless, it is also possible to argue his choice more positively, as a reflection of Broad Church values and preoccupations. St. Paul was a hero for mid-Victorian liberal Anglicans. A focus on Paul was an expression of their resolute identity as Protestants. Their self-conscious Protestantism, in turn, was a way, negatively, of being anti-Tractarian and, positively, of asserting the principle of religious freedom. The most influential liberal Anglican theological mind of the period, F. D. Maurice, whose thought was the dominant influence on Colenso's own theological development, described himself in his *Theological Essays* as "a very vehement Protestant."[12] Colenso himself commented in 1864 that he was fighting "for a great principle—no less than the essential principle of Protestantism—free enquiry."[13] Indeed, the bishop of Natal was in no way inventing a new approach for liberal Anglicans by writing a Pauline commentary. Thomas Arnold himself, who is usually identified as a father of Broad churchmanship, had set an agenda of Pauline studies: "Arnold had even planned a sort of Rugby 'Paul'; and as early as 1836 was at work on the first epistle to the Thessalonians."[14] His student and biographer, and a leading Broad Church clergyman, A. P. Stanley, adopted the project, dividing the work between himself and his friend, the great liberal Anglican scholar Benjamin Jowett, a fellow of Balliol College, Oxford. They published their Pauline commentaries in 1855. Romans was handled by Jowett, and his work was sufficiently stamped with liberal Anglicanism to draw accusations that it was unortho-

11. Peter Hinchliff, *John William Colenso: Bishop of Natal* (London: Thomas Nelson and Sons, 1964), 79.

12. F. D. Maurice, *Theological Essays* (London: James Clarke, 1957 [1853]), 106.

13. Guy, *Heretic*, 144.

14. J. Estlin Carpenter, *The Bible in the Nineteenth Century* (London: Longmans, Green, 1903), 25. See A. P. Stanley, *The Life and Correspondence of Thomas Arnold, D.D.*, vol. 1 (New York: Charles Scribner's Sons, n.d.[1844]), 193.

dox, especially on the atonement. Jowett had to endure the humiliation of being required to resubscribe to the Thirty-nine Articles in order to keep his post.[15] Another bright student of Arnold's, and a contemporary of Stanley's at Rugby, was C. J. Vaughan, who was also a clergyman, and who published a work on Romans in 1859. Likewise, W. J. Conybeare, who "himself must of course be consigned to the broad church," published in the early 1850s, with J. S. Howson, an oft-reprinted work, *The Life and Epistles of St Paul*.[16] In short, far from being enemy territory, studies of Romans were a well-established tradition within liberal Anglicanism.

Colenso's *Romans* was entirely steeped in this world of mid-Victorian Broad churchmanship. One would never know from his commentary that Luther or Calvin or any other figure in the first eighteen centuries of Christian history or in any country besides England or in any tradition beside Anglicanism had ever written a commentary on Romans. Indeed, almost the only people whose works he cites, and he cites theirs repeatedly, are Jowett, Vaughan, and Conybeare and Howson. The bishop of Natal was joining a conversation that his contemporaries in England were already having. Colenso's particular brand of Broad churchmanship, however, is best situated by recalling his friendship with and unabashed admiration of F. D. Maurice. Maurice had been forced out of his post at King's College London due to charges that his *Theological Essays* (1853) contained unorthodox elements. In particular, his effort in that volume to turn the notion of endless punishment into an open question aroused opposition. While Maurice was enduring these attacks, Colenso courageously dedicated a volume of sermons to his friend and mentor, drawing fire on himself in the process. In 1856 the bishop of Natal described his own churchmanship by referring to himself simply as a "Maurician."[17] Colenso's *Romans* repeatedly evokes the feel of Maurice's *Theological Essays*.[18] Nevertheless, Colenso was far more bold in his theological assertions, and one gains the impression

---

15. See Peter Hinchliff, *Benjamin Jowett and the Christian Religion* (Oxford: Clarendon Press, 1987), 45–68.

16. Conybeare, "Church Parties," 233, 239.

17. Wyn Rees, *Colenso Letters from Natal* (Pietermaritzburg, South Africa: Shuter and Shooter, 1958), 20.

18. For example, anyone who has read Maurice's essay "On the Sense of Righteousness in Men, and Their Discovery of a Redeemer" can hear its echo in Colenso's comments: "But all men, everywhere, have had all along, and still have, a belief in such Divine Forgiveness . . . coupled with the very sense of sin, there is a dim sense of a righteousness which they already possess" (Colenso, *Romans*, 50). The Wesleyan George Osborn was scandalized by one passage that, arguably, was actually a penetrating insight in the Maurician mode: "He speaks of it with a levity which is perfectly shocking. 'Will it be said,' he asks, 'that after death still comes the judgment? *Why, yes, and before death too.*' We doubt if the theological literature of the English Church, vast and varied as it is, can supply a

that Maurice essentially wanted to find a more congenial route to the same old doctrines, while Colenso was beginning to wonder whether some of them might no longer be worth revisiting.

The key to Colenso's *Romans* is its objectification of the work of Christ in relationship to human beings, and the universalization of the scope of its application, under the umbrella of the fatherhood of God toward all humanity. The benefits of the gospel have already been freely applied to all: "under the new covenant of the Grace of God in the Gospel, all human beings were declared to be accepted before God."[19] This stance, of course, has implications for numerous doctrines. On justification: "the justification here spoken of extends to *all*, to those who have never heard the name of Christ, and who cannot have exercised a living faith in Christ, as well as to Christians."[20] Indeed, Colenso treats Romans 5:18 as the theological center of the epistle, a verse that he translates thus: "So then, just as through one fault, *it passed* unto all men, unto condemnation, so also, through one righteous act, *it passed* unto all men, unto justification of life."[21] "All" receiving justification being the salient point.

Other doctrines implicated include original sin: "the whole human race are looked upon and dealt with as righteous creatures, in Jesus Christ their Head. The curse of their sinful nature has been taken away altogether. . . . The whole human race is made righteous, and released from any fear of judgment on this account."[22] Naturally, such a theological vision was more easily found in some portions of scripture than in others. Colenso handled the text "there is none righteous, not even one" (3:10) as follows:

> The Psalmist in this passage is describing the *general* depravity of the age in which he lived, in terms very similar to those of the prophet Elijah: "I *only* am left, and they seek my life." And yet came the answer of God to him: "There are seven thousand left in Israel, who have not bowed the knee to Baal;" . . . So, though the words before us give such a gloomy account of the state of things in Israel, we must not suppose it to have been really so very bad as the Psalmist imagined, and his language implies.[23]

On Romans 8:14 the bishop was reduced to asserting, "St. Paul does not say, 'All, who are being *led* by God's Spirit, *they*, and none other, are

---

parallel to this passage" (*London Review* [April 1862]: 37). For the passage quoted, see Colenso, *Romans*, 128.

19. Colenso, *Romans*, 70.
20. Ibid., 82.
21. Ibid., 109.
22. Ibid., 115, 116–17.
23. Ibid., 78.

the sons of God."[24] Moreover, Colenso was sometimes ready to charge headlong at the standard assumptions made regarding some particularly cherished texts, including ones in parts of scripture other than Romans. On the account of Nicodemus asking Jesus how an adult might be born from above, he defiantly claimed:

> Nicodemus, in point of fact, was already thus born again, thus born from above; he had already received that second spiritual birth, though he did not know it. . . . we have already died unto sin, and risen again unto righteousness, in our very birth-hour, through the gracious gift of God, by that mysterious union with Christ our Head, which we all enjoy through the grace of our Heavenly Father, as members of the great human family.[25]

Colenso was so thorough in sweeping away traditional notions regarding salvation history, the work of Christ, and soteriology, and so unsystematic in what he offered in their place, that the *London Review* could offer a delicious caricature of one of his discussions: "We are redeemed, he tells us, from a personification!"[26]

One of the more counterintuitive of his universalizing maneuvers—and one particularly annoying to High churchmen—was his treatment of the Eucharist, of which he averred that

> all men are everywhere partaking, through God's mercy, and so receiving all the life they have, as redeemed creatures, whether they feed upon it by living faith or not, whether they know the precious gift of God's grace or not, whether they heed or disregard it.[27]

Thus, on the strength of these words, Colenso's view of the benefit that comes to believers when they receive the sacrament was somewhat mischievously summarized at his trial: "they do not cease at that moment to be partakers of the food which every other moment of their lives they are receiving from God."[28]

This inclusive approach did not mean that human beings were exempt from divine judgment. Penalties did not await individuals on account of original sin, but people would receive punishment, according to the bishop of Natal, for willful transgressions of what they knew to be right. However,

---

24. Ibid., 162.
25. Ibid., 16, 121.
26. *London Review* (April 1862), 26.
27. Colenso, *Romans*, 122.
28. *Trial of the Bishop of Natal for Erroneous Teaching: Before the Metropolitan Bishop of Cape Town, and the Bishops of Graham's Town and the Orange Free State as Assessors* (Cape Town: Cape Argus Office, 1863), 326.

he suspected that punishments beyond the grave were not retributive, but only remedial. Such a view led on to his innovative approach to the subject of future states. Colenso began by renouncing the traditional view:

> I now declare that I can no longer maintain, or give utterance to, the doctrine of the endlessness of "future punishments,"—that I dare not dogmatise at all on this matter,—that I can only lay my hand upon my mouth and leave it in the hands of the righteous and merciful Judge. But I see that the word "eternal" does not mean "endless." And, for such reasons as the following, I entertain the "hidden hope" that there are remedial processes, when this life is ended, of which at present we know nothing, but which the Lord, the Righteous Judge, will administer, as He in His Wisdom shall see to be good.[29]

The wording of this passage turned out to be something of a gift for Colenso's critics. The archdeacon of George observed at his trial that the bishop of Natal "no sooner put his hand upon his mouth than he takes it down again, and inculates naked Universalism."[30] A leading Methodist, George Osborn, observed dryly in the *London Review*, "he calls it the 'hidden hope,' but in what sense it is 'hidden' we have no idea."[31] Lewis Grout, who was serving in Natal under the auspices of the American Board of Commissioners for Foreign Missions when Colenso published his *Romans*, had a point when he argued, "And yet the condition and prospects of man beyond the grave are points on which he seems to have felt the deepest, to have labored the hardest, in[deed] that for which he would seem to have written the book."[32] It is certainly fair to say that, far from shying away from this subject, Colenso actually explores it enthusiastically and at length. The conclusion of all this labor is the suggestion that hell is actually only purgatory; in other words, that all people might ultimately be admitted into the presence of God after having undergone a period of remedial punishment. One of his more enterprising scriptural expositions along this line was Colenso's treatment of the gospel story of Dives and Lazarus:

> We have in this chapter the story of Lazarus, in which our Lord assumes that, even in the place of torment, there will be loving, tender thoughts, in

29. Colenso, *Romans*, 168.

30. *Trial*, 186.

31. *London Review* (April 1862): 38. It is beyond the scope of this study to evaluate the ideas of Colenso's critics, but it seems right to note that Osborn also maintained the decidedly obscurantist position that no fresh attempts should be made to translate the Bible into English, but rather the Authorized Version should be all in all.

32. Lewis Grout, "Colenso on the Doctrines: A Review of . . . [Colenso's *Romans*]," (September 1869): 469–70. I have not identified the journal that carried this article. The copy I consulted is a separately bound one in the Yale Divinity School Library.

a brother's heart. If there can be such, as they cannot come from the Spirit of Evil, they must be believed to come from the Spirit of all Goodness. While there is life, there is hope. In fact, the rich man is represented as *less* selfish in the flames of hell than he was in this life. The Eternal Fire has already wrought some good result in him.[33]

Osborn quipped that, according to the bishop of Natal's view, John 3:16 "ought to read,—He gave His only begotten Son, that all men might have everlasting life in the end, and that those who believe might have it a little sooner than the rest."[34]

Colenso also made a point of rejecting substitutionary atonement:

Once for all let it be stated distinctly, there is not a single passage in the whole of the New Testament, which supports the dogma of modern theology, that our Lord died for our sins, in the sense of dying *instead of* us, dying *in our place*, or dying so as to *bear the punishment or penalty* of our sins. . . . And the truth is that our Blessed Lord certainly, whatever he did, did *not "die in our stead."*[35]

Likewise he repeatedly attacked Calvinism:

The error of the Calvinist is in supposing that this asserts for the Almighty the power to act, by the exercise of an arbitrary prerogative, in choosing whom He will save and whom He will cast away. In point of fact, the whole tenor and object of the Apostle's words is expressly to do away with the notion of an arbitrary election. It was just that which the Jew of his day relied on. He was one of the elect. The Jews were the Calvinists of those days, and believed themselves, as God's chosen people, sure of the kingdom.[36]

Colenso's sympathetic Victorian biographer sanguinely declared that his *Romans* destroyed for all time "the tyranny of the Westminster Confession."[37]

The bishop of Natal's attack on Calvinism was central to his alternative reading of Romans, a reading that was based on applying teaching regarding the inclusion of Gentiles into salvation history to un-Christianized people as well. For example, his exposition of Romans 2:26, which he translated as, "If, then, the Uncircumcision keep the requirements of the Law, shall not his uncircumcision be reckoned as

33. Colenso, *Romans*, 180.
34. *London Review* (April 1862): 45.
35. Colenso, *Romans*, 105.
36. Ibid., 197.
37. G. W. Cox, *The Life of John William Colenso, D.D. Bishop of Natal*, vol. 1 (London: W. Ridgway, 1888), 148.

circumcision?" was, "If, then, an unbaptized heathen does that which is good and right and true, shall not his unbaptized state be reckoned for baptism?"[38] One of the most interesting passages in his *Romans* where Colenso sticks particularly close to the text and patiently expounds it is his handling of the analogy of the potter and the clay in Romans 9. Here is but a portion of it:

> [T]hat St. Paul is not arguing . . . that the Potter has power to make out of the same lump, *at the same time,* two vessels, at his own arbitrary will, one for honour, and the other for dishonour (so as to support the Calvinistic view), will be plain, if we turn to the passage in Jeremiah, to which he is evidently referring (Jer. xviii. 3–6). . . . So, then, the Great Potter, when a vessel is marred in His Hand in the making, when He sees that a people, or a Church, or an individual, will not answer to the end for which He fashioned it, will make it into another vessel for His use, as it seemeth good to Him, to make it. He will not cast it away, but refashion it, to serve for a lower and less honourable use in His Kingdom.[39]

All these stances, of course, reflected a romanticist perspective, a sensibility that was typical of liberal churchmen, especially those, like Colenso, who stood intellectually in the Colridgean tradition. The bishop of Natal felt in his bones that doctrines such as endless punishment, substitutionary atonement, and double predestination could not be true, ought not to be true: they were wrong and therefore it was revolting to teach them; they were revolting and therefore wrong. This was so clear to him that he did not hesitate to assert that such instincts were, in themselves, an authority in matters of doctrine—in fact, the highest authority:

> For we must never forget that this witness within our hearts is the Voice of God. . . . God, then, has given this Light of the inner man to be the very guide and polestar of our lives. . . . By that Light, the sayings and doings of good men, the acts of the Church, the proceedings and decisions of her Fathers and Councils, the writings of Prophets and Apostles, the words recorded to have been uttered by our Blessed Lord Himself, must all be tried. . . . no seeming authority of the Church or Scripture *ought* to persuade a man to believe anything, which contradicts that moral law, that sense of righteousness, and purity, and truth, and love, which God's own finger has written upon his heart. The voice of that inner witness is closer to him than any that can reach him from without, and ought to reign supreme in his whole being.[40]

38. Colenso, *Romans*, 73.
39. Ibid., 201–2.
40. Ibid., 175–77.

Thus we have the principle teachings of Colenso's *Romans:* the fatherhood of God toward the whole human family, an objectified and universalized work of Christ, future punishment as temporary and remedial, substitutionary atonement and Calvinism as misguided and offensive, and the inner light as the final authority in matters of faith and practice.

Colenso's *Romans* inevitably was denounced by both High churchmen and evangelicals. The High Church newspaper, the *Guardian,* judged that the bishop of Natal had joined forces intellectually with Arians, Socinians, and, worst of all, Anabaptists, "those pestilent heretics—of all sectaries the most obnoxious to our Reformers."[41] Likewise the High Church journal, the *Christian Remembrancer,* referred to it as "Bishop Colenso's unhappy 'Commentary on the Romans' (Macmillan), which, we fear, will incur further and more painful notoriety."[42] The Wesleyan, and therefore evangelical, *London Review,* also pronounced that the bishop was borrowing arguments from Socinians and Arians, but it also could not resist endorsing his anti-Calvinism: "In so far as he testifies to the universal benignity of Almighty God,—to the possibility of salvation for all men, notwithstanding the ruin brought upon them by the first father, Adam,—and to the supply of means, which, if duly improved, might issue in universal salvation, we, as evangelical Arminians, go heartily with him."[43] Affinities notwithstanding, however, its final verdict was that he was preaching "another gospel," biblical parlance for deadly heresy.

The really intriguing question, though, is: what did his fellow Broad churchmen think of Colenso's *Romans*? This question is surprisingly difficult to answer. Almost all the leading Broad churchmen are on record criticizing Colenso's first volume on the Pentateuch, but it is remarkably hard to find opinions regarding his Pauline commentary. The bishop of Natal did not consult his Broad Church friends and contacts in England before publishing his *Romans* but rather approached them shortly thereafter with his controversial work on the Old Testament, and this new sensation naturally drew away all their attention. The few clues that exist indicate that Broad churchmen were initially sympathetic or at least tolerant of the book, but reluctant to endorse a volume that might end up at the center of a very hot controversy. Of course, once Colenso had been widely branded a heretic for his Pentateuch studies, then there was a strong incentive to suppress any favorable views that might have been held of his *Romans.* Two instances have been found of liberal Anglican reactions to Colenso's Pauline commentary before his Old Testament studies had come on the scene.

41. *Guardian*, April 9, 1862, 353–54.
42. *Christian Remembrancer* (April 1862): 506.
43. *London Review* (April 1862): 32.

The *Spectator,* the only organ of liberal Anglican opinion, offered a brief notice. Observing that the bishop claimed it to be a commentary from a missionary point of view, it went on to say (to quote almost the entire review):

> It must be confessed, however, that the right reverend divine has terribly overlaid the text of the apostle with notes and explanations, extremely wearisome to ordinary readers, and not always easily understood. The introduction, on the other hand, is very interesting, and clears up much of the obscurity relating to the class of persons to whom this epistle was originally written. At the same time we are at a loss to perceive the especial connexion between either notes or introduction and the "great work in Zululand."[44]

This is, at best, decidedly cool. On the other hand, Colenso's stunningly bold handling of theological issues—which no reviewer could fail to perceive—is not censured at all. The paper seems to have covered its own position against attack with the phrase "not always easily understood," leaving itself open to arguing later that if certain passages are to be understood in the unorthodox sense now being attributed to them, then it could not go along with them. In short, nothing was said to hint to the reader that even a whiff of suspected heresy might arise from this volume, but, on the other hand, neither could it justly be said that the paper had reviewed it favorably.

A. C. Tait, then bishop of London, took an almost identical tack, albeit paradoxically and ingeniously both defending and failing to endorse it more comprehensively. Bishop Gray had asked the English bishops to take notice of the dangerous tendency of Colenso's *Romans.* The bishops duly met twice to consider the volume, and this happened before the bishop of Natal's Old Testament studies complicated the picture. Most of the bishops disapproved of Colenso's *Romans,* but Bishop Tait's resolute opposition to any action being taken, despite his stand being a solitary or near solitary one, prevented any united action and thereby successfully thwarted any public response from the bishops at all. Bishop Gray's report of a later episcopal discussion of these meetings is revealing:

> The Archbishop of York then asked why the Bishops who met to discuss the book [Colenso's *Romans*] at the time referred to had come to no conclusion; to which the Bishop of London replied that he believed he was the reason. Many of the Bishops wanted them to inhibit. "I would not inhibit," he said; "I have never read the book, and I hope never to do so." . . . "It is not my business to do so," the Bishop of London replied with much warmth, "I have little time for reading, and when I do read, I wish to read good books." . . .

44. *Spectator,* December 7, 1861.

> [Gray] ought to have dealt with it himself, and not brought unfair extracts from it, which did not represent its teaching, before them. He went on to accuse the Bishop of Oxford of having also dealt unfairly about the book.[45]

Gray, of course, was a hostile source, but, for what it is worth, his account accords with that of his cocombatant and ally, Bishop Wilberforce of Oxford.[46] Neither Gray nor Wilberforce commented on the irony that Tait could simultaneously claim that he had not read the book and that its contents had been misrepresented. There is, however, a ring of truth to this. It was in Tait's interest to have not read the book just as it was in the *Spectator*'s interest not to have fully understood it; both stances saved them from the precarious position of publicly approving of the contents of a volume that might shortly come under official censure. On the other hand, Tait clearly viewed the controversy through the lens of competing churchmanships. Tait and A. P. Stanley, who also defended Colenso as opportunities arose, both viewed Gray as a rabid High churchman who needed to be disabused of the notion that he had been deputized to decide what was and was not permissible for Anglicans.[47]

Apparently, no comment by F. D. Maurice on Colenso's *Romans* has survived. This is a pity. Colenso, a friend and disciple of Maurice before his Pauline commentary, was disowned by him for life once Maurice had read his first volume on the Pentateuch. One cannot help but wonder if the bishop of Natal's *Romans* counted as the last crop of the old dispensation or the firstfruits of the new in Maurice's reckoning. Maurice's son and biographer wrote intriguingly, "Whatever may be the merits of that question [whether or not Colenso's *Romans* deserved censure], it is necessary as a matter of historical accuracy that it should be kept clear from that of the Book on the Pentateuch, which was not published till late in the year 1862."[48] This arguably reads as an apologetic for favorable things that Maurice might have said at the time about the bishop's Pauline commentary. Nevertheless, it is highly unlikely that Maurice gave the volume his unqualified approval: both Bishop Gray and Colenso himself suspected in advance that he would disapprove of some portions of it.

The timing of Colenso's *Romans* did him no favors. When a provincial clergyman was accused of heterodox views, Jowett replied to his letter

---

45. Gray, *Gray*, 2:42.

46. R. G. Wilberforce, *Life of the Right Reverend Samuel Wilberforce, D.D.*, vol. 3 (London: John Murray, 1882), 114–16.

47. See Gray, *Gray*, 2:275, where it is recorded that Stanley defended Colenso by offering a "highly declamatory speech" attacking Gray as an advanced ritualist "likely to deprive his Comprovincials for not using incense, or wafer bread, or the like."

48. Frederick Maurice, *The Life of Frederick Denison Maurice*, vol. 1 (New York: Charles Scribner's, 1884), 421.

in July 1861—around the very time that the bishop of Natal's Pauline study was coming out in England—commenting wearily that it was "a dreary time for clergymen of liberal opinions."[49] English Broad churchmen were already embroiled in a life-or-death struggle within the church in the wake of the publication of *Essays and Reviews* the year before, an edited volume of liberal Anglican thought that drew fierce fire on several prominent Broad churchmen, not least Jowett himself. In such a climate, there were no troops to spare in order to open a second front to defend Colenso's *Romans,* and his study of the Pentateuch sealed the matter. There was an unwritten rule among liberal Anglicans that they were to be careful not to push matters too far. A. P. Stanley's comment to Jowett about Colenso's study of the Pentateuch was telling: "No man ought ever to write himself down as a heretic."[50] In 1855 Conybeare had added an "exaggerated" category to the Broad Church party as well, conceding that such people were really "concealed infidels."[51] In one sense, Colenso seems to have wished to lead Broad churchmen from the front. He wrote to a friend just after the publication of his *Romans:* "My own feeling is that the 'Essayists & Reviewers' must go on with me—& I must confess I anticipate (not of course from my works but from the whole movement now begun) a complete Revolution in the religious time of England."[52] The *London Review* declared that he had won this leadership bid, saying of Colenso's *Romans* that the "tone of the book, in fact, is that of a school [later explicitly named as Broad churchmen] of which we must now, we fear, pronounce Bishop Colenso the most distinguished member."[53]

Colenso became the bishop who didn't give a damn, not only in the sense that he rejected the doctrine of endless punishment, replaced hell with purgatory, and defended universalism, but also in the sense that he abandoned Broad Church caution and was ready to proclaim what he perceived to be the truth irrespective of the repercussions. He was willing to publish and be damned. Colenso wrote to Gray himself in response to the bishop of Cape Town's initial alarm at his *Romans:*

> But the die is cast—the book will be reprinted & published in England I imagine before any letter from me could prevent it—and were it otherwise, I could not recal [*sic*] what I have written, or withhold it, though all my friends advised me to do so. This is not a time for halting between

49. Evelyn Abbott and Lewis Campbell, *The Life and Letters of Benjamin Jowett, M.A.,* vol. 1 (London: John Murray, 1897), 304.
50. R. E. Prothero and G. G. Bradley, *The Life and Correspondence of Arthur Penrhyn Stanley, D.D.,* vol. 2 (London: John Murray, 1894), 100.
51. Conybeare, "Church Parties," 242.
52. Colenso to Bleek, September 4, 1861: Guy, *Heretic,* 108.
53. *London Review* (April 1862), 3.

two opinions, or concealing what appears to be the truth from the fear of consequences. A conflict is coming, as I believe, & near at hand, from which we cannot escape.[54]

Colenso wrote to a friend to whom he was sending a copy of his *Romans:* "I fully expect that it will be violently attacked by High Church and Low. I am not sure that Mr. Maurice will agree with all of it. But this is not the time to care for things of this kind."[55]

The evangelical newspaper, the *Record,* carried a letter that claimed that "Bishop Colenso has imprudently outstripped the reserve of his friends."[56] At his trial, his accusers took pains to show that Colenso was not a representative Broad churchman, but rather a rogue heretic. Cleverly, they quoted both Coleridge and Arnold approvingly, tacitly contrasting their place within the pale with his alleged one without.[57] Again and again, it was argued that Colenso was isolated and alone:

> But it appears that the Bishop contradicts truths in which all schools of theology within our Church agree, and that his opinions are wholly outside the limits of the questions discussed between them. . . . We do not recognize opinions held by any of the religious "schools" of thought in the Church of England. The Bishop is charged with teaching, as well as holding, opinions strange to all English Church people, and beyond the wide latitude which seems to be allowed in our Church.[58]

It was claimed that Colenso had been drawn further and further from all known Anglican views by "the giddy vortex of his error."[59]

One could argue that Colenso ran too far ahead of his fellow liberal Anglicans, and rather than thereby becoming their acknowledged leader, as he might have hoped, he simply drew the enemy's fire upon himself as the rest headed for cover. He wrote in a letter in 1864 that he did not

> think the "Broad Church," First (Maurice, Kingsley, &c) or Second (Stanley) will ever open the Ch. of England. Yet it *may* be done, I am convinced, or, at least, I am very hopeful that it may be done, eventually, by the simple statement of the *truth*. That must be the rallying principle—"the Truth, the whole Truth, as far as we know it, & nothing but the Truth." How, you will say, can this be published *within* the Natl.

54. Colenso to Gray, July 29, 1861: Guy, *Heretic,* 106.
55. Cox, *Colenso,* 1:126.
56. *Record,* November 17, 1862, 4.
57. See, for example, *Trial,* 75, 111.
58. *Trial,* 294, 322.
59. Ibid., 191.

Church? Well! if it cannot be published *within* the Church, it must be published at all hazards.[60]

The bishop privately fumed that the leading English Broad churchmen were cowards.[61] They, in turn, complained that he was reckless and seemingly untethered. Maurice wrote to a friend about Colenso in 1862, "I agree with you that it is very difficult to say to what point of disbelief he may go."[62] After a meeting with the bishop of Natal in 1863, Tait wrote despairingly of him in his diary: "He seems to me very wild, and to be likely to go very far in discarding the old faith."[63]

It is not clear how far he did end up going. A case can be made that Colenso eventually adopted Unitarian views.[64] Nevertheless, for this very reason, Colenso's case serves to illuminate the distinctive situation of Broad churchmen particularly clearly. The nature of the distinctive views of Anglican evangelicals and High churchmen meant that their exaggerated forms were self-limiting. Those who followed High Church arguments too far from the heart of Anglicanism were eventually inclined to accept the logic of their own position and convert to Rome. Likewise, those whose burgeoning evangelical distinctives began to chafe against the *via media* might finally discover that dissent was their true home, perhaps even becoming Baptists or joining the Brethren.[65] There was no parallel logical development for Broad churchmen, however. A certain kind of liberal thought might draw some Broad churchmen toward Unitarianism, but this was a move toward an intellectual or theological stance, not an alternative denomination. Broad churchmen, after all, stood for comprehension. The logic of their exaggerated form led not to their leaving the church for the Unitarian camp, but rather their allowing the Unitarian camp to find a home within the church. In that sense, Colenso was being true to his Broad Church principles by refusing to resign his bishopric. He confided to a friend in 1862:

My *present* intention is to abide in my post, so long as the Law allows me to retain it, & to fight from the vantage ground which the Providence of

60. Colenso to Bleek, April 5, 1864: Guy, *Heretic*, 147–48.

61. Colenso to Shepstone, June 2, 1863: Cox, *Colenso*, 1:239.

62. Maurice, *Maurice*, 2:423.

63. March 5, 1863: R. T. Davidson and William Benham, *Life of Archibald Campbell Tait, Archbishop of Canterbury*, vol. 1 (London: Macmillan, 1891), 347.

64. Hinchliff, *Colenso*, 176. See also Gerald Parsons, "Friendship and Theology: Unitarians and Bishop Colenso, 1862–1865," *Transactions of the Unitarian Historical Society* 22, no. 2 (April 2000).

65. For a study of such cases, see Grayson Carter, *Anglican Evangelicals: Protestant Secessions from the Via Media, c. 1800–1850* (Oxford: Oxford University Press, 2001).

God has thus given me the battle of freedom for the Ch. of England. It *may* be—& I am not alone in this thought, though I can scarcely say that we have at this time any hope or prospect of immediate success—that our National Church will really have her borders enlarged, to take in *all* devout minds of all Creeds, at least, of every possible modification of Christian belief, upon the basis of the Lord's prayer. We shall make an effort for this, I think, if my book has any effect, & the battle may be won at last, if the victors have to tread over our graves.[66]

The Lord's Prayer was a telling choice for setting the minimum boundaries, as it contains no trinitarian ideas, no Christology at all, no affirmation of the miraculous, no doctrine of scripture, no views on future states, the incarnation, the atonement, or the resurrection. Frances Power Cobbe, herself a Unitarian, suggested that Colenso ought to abandon Anglican for Unitarian worship, but the bishop of Natal—again, in true Broad Church fashion—replied, "I do not wish to leave the National Church and become a sectarian."[67] A comparison can be made with the Congregationalist Old Testament scholar Samuel Davidson, who was also accused of unorthodoxy for his biblical studies in the mid-Victorian era, but who, unlike Colenso, did eventually decide to worship with Unitarians.[68] Such a change was much more natural for someone like Davidson, who was already a part of chapel culture, than for lovers of the national church, as liberal Anglicans generally were.

This study of the bishop of Natal's *Romans* serves to remind us that the image of Colenso the maverick heretic needs to be balanced with an emphasis on Colenso the true Broad churchman. He did not want to push on the pillars of Anglicanism until the whole temple collapsed on their heads; rather, he longed to enlarge the place of their tent, to lengthen their cords. In his *Romans*, Colenso took these Broad Church ecclesiastical instincts unto a theological plane, developing a view of the work of Christ that expanded the camp of the justified and the righteous to include even the "heathen." It is therefore particularly ironic that the sentence of excommunication pronounced against him because of this very theological work declared that he should henceforth be treated as a heathen man. In his *Romans*, Colenso had articulated a theological vision that assured him that he need not fear how the Almighty might respond to such an injunction.

66. Colenso to Bleek, October 4, 1862: Guy, *Heretic*, 118–19.
67. Guy, *Heretic*, 149.
68. A. J. Davidson, *The Autobiography and Diary of Samuel Davidson* (Edinburgh: T & T Clark, 1899).

12

KARL BARTH

John Webster

In this chapter I want to argue what appears to be a completely self-evident thesis, namely, that Karl Barth's commentary *The Epistle to the Romans* is just that: a commentary on the Epistle to the Romans. This strikingly obvious point has, however, been less than plain to most of the commentators on Barth's commentary, who have generally considered that the real significance of Barth's *Romans* lies elsewhere: in what it indicates about his hermeneutics, or about his attitude to such diverse cultural phenomena as expressionism or the Russian Revolution; or again, in what it can tell us about such matters as Barth's commitment to a consistently eschatological or dialectical interpretation of Christianity at this point in his theological development. Barth's commentary is, no doubt, instructive in reconstructing what he thought about such matters; but when they dominate the reception of Barth's *Römerbrief*, the first casualty is the fact that what Barth is doing is writing a commentary on a New Testament letter. By way of contrast, my suggestion is that *Romans* is not primarily a hermeneutical manifesto, or a piece of irregular dogmatics (that is, a set of theological reflections only loosely attached to the Pauline text); still less is it an encoded set of sociopolitical experiences or directives. It is a commentary, intended by Barth as such; and whatever abiding interest and worth it may have stands or falls by its success in fulfilling that intention. Barth meant what he said in his preface to Hoskyns's idiosyncratic translation of the second edition: "My sole aim was to interpret Scripture."[1]

In what follows, I begin by locating my suggestions about the interpretation of Barth's *Romans* in relation to some of the trends of interpretation of his biblical writings, especially of the Romans commentary; from there, I move to ask about the significance of the fact that Barth chose the literary form of the biblical commentary for his first major publication; I go on to offer an analysis of some of the distinguishing features of Barth's approach to the task of commentary; and I close by drawing some lessons both about Barth and about the art of commentary writing.

I

There are at least three related clusters of issues that press themselves upon our attention in the matter of the relation between Barth's work and Holy Scripture. A first set of questions concerns what might rather loosely be termed Barth's doctrine of scripture. Properly speaking, of course, Barth does not have a doctrine of scripture, but more a "scripture principle." That is to say, what Barth has to say about the nature of scripture is a function of other, more primary, dogmatic convictions, most of all convictions about the character, instruments and ends of God's self-revealing activity; these convictions are not freestanding, but rather corollaries or extensions of the doctrine of the Trinity. Barth has a great deal to say about the nature of scripture and about the significance for theology and church of the scripture principle—in, for example, public addresses in the latter years of his ministry in Safenwil; in the Göttingen lectures on Calvin and the theology of the Reformed confessional writings; in the treatment of topics such as biblical inspiration and authority or canon in all three of his dogmatics cycles (the Göttingen dogmatics, the *Christliche Dogmatik*, and the *Church Dogmatics*); and, at the end of his career, in the delightful treatment of the Word of God in *Evangelical Theology*.[2] Yet for all its importance in interpreting Barth's work, there has been almost no serious scholarly attention to this theme; Klaas Runia's study of forty years ago, *Karl Barth's Doctrine of Holy Scripture*,[3] is the only substantial exception. The reasons for the

1. Karl Barth, *The Epistle to the Romans* (London: Oxford University Press, 1933), 11.

2. Karl Barth, *Evangelical Theology* (London: Weidenfeld and Nicolson, 1963), 15–36.

3. Klaas Runia, *Karl Barth's Doctrine of Holy Scripture* (Grand Rapids: Eerdmans, 1962).

neglect are, in part, a general lack of interest in bibliology (as distinct from hermeneutics) on the part of mainstream academic theology, and the fact that of late students of Barth's writings have shown a marked tendency to concentrate upon his use of scripture rather than upon his theological understanding of its nature. This question, however much in need of revisiting, will not be at the center of our concern here.

A second cluster of questions concerns Barth's hermeneutics. Much more attention has been devoted to this matter—whether to mapping Barth's attitude to the remarkably high profile accorded to the human activity of interpreting in the tradition that stretches from Schleiermacher through Dilthey and Bultmann to Ebeling and beyond (a tradition with which Barth had little sympathy and, especially in its more tortured "new hermeneutic" presentations, even less patience); or, more narrowly, to Barth's understanding of the nature and tasks of biblical interpretation; or, more narrowly again, to his various attempts to position himself vis-à-vis dominant interpretative conventions, above all, of course, the historical-critical method. Some of the questions raised in this field are certainly germane to our understanding of what is happening in Barth's *Romans*, though, as I shall try to show, they should not be allowed to overwhelm Barth's commentary with hermeneutical theory. Gadamer's much-quoted judgment that *Romans* is "a kind of hermeneutical manifesto," or Jüngel's suggestion that *Romans* is a "hermeneutical metacritique,"[4] are at best only half-truths.

A third set of issues concerns Barth's exegetical practice. A good deal of work in this area was stimulated by Hans Frei's account of the place of Barth in the modern history of theological hermeneutics, and has, accordingly, concentrated on those issues that Frei identified as of central significance: the importance of the narrative genre for the Christology of the New Testament, and the fate of the so-called plain sense of scripture. Though the studies that Frei's work stimulated have proved illuminating for some parts of Barth's work, notably the doctrine of reconciliation in the later volumes of the *Church Dogmatics*, they suffer from a number of limitations. They are often reductionist in their presentation of Barth's exegesis and inattentive to the variety of his exegetical strategies; they are often heavily overtheorized, with the result that Barth's exegesis is explicated in terms of—for example—its consonance with literary or cultural theory, or with philosophical ideas of personal identity; they tend to undervalue Barth's specifically theological realism by assimilating his exegesis to postcritical conceptions of textual

4. Hans-Georg Gadamer, *Truth and Method* (London: Sheed and Ward, 1979), 463; Eberhard Jüngel, "Barth's Theological Beginnings," in *Karl Barth: A Theological Legacy* (Philadelphia: Westminster, 1986), 74.

reference; and they have a restrictive focus on the *Church Dogmatics*, and therefore only on the kinds of exegesis that Barth undertook in the course of his doctrinal writing. What is almost never taken into account in presentations of Barth's exegesis is the considerable bulk of what he wrote by way of biblical commentary. This includes not only the two commentaries on Romans from 1919 and 1922, but also other published commentaries—on 1 Corinthians,[5] Philippians,[6] and Romans once again (this time the extramural lectures from the beginning of World War II published as *A Shorter Commentary on Romans*).[7] In addition to these published materials, there is an even more substantial body of material in the texts of Barth's exegetical lectures in which he taught his way through New Testament texts in *Lectio Continua* fashion, covering Ephesians, James, Colossians, the Sermon on the Mount, and 1 Peter, along with the lectures on the first six chapters of the fourth Gospel, which are now available in German and, in part, in English translation.[8] In view of the very significant proportion of his energies that Barth gave to the production of these materials, the lack of any thorough study of his work as commentator is both surprising and regrettable.[9] The importance of such a study would be twofold. It would, first, allow us to see Barth at work more directly, fully, and exclusively on the biblical texts than is usual in either his dogmatic or his homiletic writings, free from the pressure of other concerns, and so more able to concentrate on the text in its entirety and sequence. And, second, it would enable students of Barth's work to address a largely unasked question, namely, what may be learned about the overall character of Barth's theological commitments from the fact that he expended much labor on biblical commentary.

This paper offers an introductory sketch of one section of such a thorough study of Barth's work as biblical commentator by looking at the second edition of Barth's *Romans*. I focus on the second edition simply because it is by far the better known of the two editions of the

5. Karl Barth, *The Resurrection of the Dead* (London: Hodder and Stoughton, 1933).

6. Karl Barth, *The Epistle to the Philippians* (London: SCM Press, 1962).

7. Karl Barth, *A Shorter Commentary on Romans* (London: SCM Press, 1959).

8. Karl Barth, *Erklärung des Johannes Evangeliums 1–8* (Zurich: Theologischer Verlag Zurich, 1976); Karl Barth, *Witness to the Word: A Commentary on John 1* (Grand Rapids: Eerdmans, 1986).

9. A beginning is made in David P. Henry's comparison of Barth's practices as commentator in the two editions of *Der Römerbrief* against the background of some standard German commentaries from the early twentieth century; but, quite apart from its restricted focus on only a portion of Romans 5, Henry's work suffers from some mischaracterizations of both Barth's exegetical practice and his theological commitments. See David P. Henry, *The Early Development of the Hermeneutic of Karl Barth as Evidenced by His Appropriation of Romans 5.12–21* (Macon, GA: Mercer University Press, 1985).

Römerbrief (and, it should be noted, the differences between the two editions, though real, are easy to overemphasize: there is substantial continuity of content between the two editions, and there are only minor differences in exegetical practice). We begin by asking why it is that this extraordinary text, produced in a period of almost manic activity between October 1920 and September 1921 and finished just before Barth took up his chair in Göttingen, has very rarely been considered to be *commentary*.

II

As we shall see, conventional critical-historical scholarship (whether of Barth's contemporaries or our own) has not found it easy to consider Barth's *Romans* as a commentary. James Barr, in the course of an intemperate attack on Barth's exegesis in *The Concept of Biblical Theology*, suggests that so strong are Barth's theological concerns that *Romans* "almost ceases to be a commentary: the earlier stage, the asking what Paul actually thought, often dropped out of sight, and what remains is a theological essay planted upon the Pauline text."[10] And even those friendly to Barth have often stumbled into the same trap, namely, that of ignoring or minimizing the commentary genre and interpreting the *Römerbrief* in other ways. Three particular interpretative trends are worth noting.

First, the most common manner of dealing with Barth's *Romans*, even on the part of some of the most sophisticated and perspicacious readers, has been to offer a *thematic* analysis of his text. This is particularly evident amongst those concerned with the question of the relation between *Romans* and Barth's later work, who often quarry the commentary for evidence of Barth's handling of theological themes in order to establish contrast (or, on occasions, continuity) with the treatment of similar topics in the *Church Dogmatics*. To cite one of many examples, Werner Ruschke (in a work notable for its careful attention to the character of Barth's early work, to its constructive elements, and to its essential continuity with the later developments of Barth's thinking) argues that although the *form* of Barth's *Romans* is that of exegetical *Erklärung*, it is best read as what Barth would later call "irregular dogmatics," that is, "free discussion of the problems that arise from Church proclamation from the standpoint of the question of dogma."[11] From this point of view, Ruschke comments,

10. James Barr, *The Concept of Biblical Theology: An Old Testament Perspective* (London: SCM Press, 1999), 57.
11. Karl Barth, *Church Dogmatics*, vol. I/1 (Edinburgh: T & T Clark, 1975), 277f.

"it is . . . completely legitimate to read and interpret Barth's expositions of Romans as an early example of his dogmatic work."[12] Ruschke is simply one instance of the trend to isolate certain theological themes in *Romans;* the effect is that of loosening the all-important anchorage of Barth's comments in the texts on which they are intended to comment, so that Barth's text comes to have a life of its own. *Romans* is, of course, instructive for what Barth has to say about such topics as eschatology, dialectic, revelation, resurrection, "the origin," and many others, and for tracing the development of Barth's thinking on such matters. But what Barth has to say is quite seriously misconstrued if it is not understood as directed both in substance and in order by and toward the Pauline text. In *Romans* Barth is not trying to tell us what he thinks but what Paul thinks. Looking back in 1932, Barth noted that

> in writing this book, I set out neither to compose a free fantasia upon the theme of religion, nor to evolve a philosophy of it. My sole aim was to interpret Scripture. . . . I shall not be impressed in the least . . . by general propositions concerning the value or lack of value of my "spiritual outlook," or of my "religious position," or my "general view of life." My book deals with one issue, and with one issue only. Did Paul think and speak in general and in detail in the manner in which I have interpreted him as thinking and speaking? Or did he think and speak altogether differently?[13]

Second, and closely related, much interpretation of Barth's *Romans* has been preoccupied with historico-genetic issues, treating *Romans* as a key text for understanding the relation of Barth's earlier theology to his context and for plotting the development of his work. A number of different lines of inquiry into *Romans* have been pursued. Some have sought to explain *Romans* in terms of its sociopolitical context, proposing that the commentary in both editions is to be read as "an attempt to hear the word of Paul as the Word of God in the midst of absolutely concrete political realities."[14] Thus, for example, part of what led Barth to abandon the organic eschatology of the first edition in favor of a more consistently dialectical approach was "the pressure of the revolutionary crowd."[15] Others cast the net more widely, setting *Romans* in the con-

12. Werner M. Ruschke, *Entstehung und Ausführung der Diastasentheologie in Karl Barths zweitem "Römerbrief"* (Neukirchen: Neukirchener Verlag, 1987), 8.

13. *Romans,* ixf.

14. Timothy Gorringe, *Karl Barth: Against Hegemony* (Oxford: Oxford University Press, 1999), 48.

15. Ibid., 55. See also Friedrich-Wilhelm Marquardt, *Theologie und Sozialismus: Das Beispiel Karl Barths* (Munich: Kaiser, 1972); and Peter Winzeler, *Widerstehende Theologie: Karl Barth, 1920–35* (Stuttgart: Alektor Verlag, 1982).

text of the wider European culture at the end of the second decade of the 1900s—expressionism, a usually ill-defined sense of cultural crisis associated with the dissolution of stable social, literary, and linguistic forms, often judged to be deconstruction *avant la lettre*,[16] or a putative "anti-historical revolution" that caught up the leading figures of the dialectical theology circle and fostered a highly negative attitude toward the historicized renderings of the context and procedures of Christian theology offered by a figure such as Troeltsch.[17] Again one example will suffice. In his recent book, *Karl Barth and the Strange New World within the Bible,* Neil MacDonald proposes that *Romans* must be understood as an attempt to respond to what are termed the "meta-dilemmas of the Enlightenment," namely, the impossibility after Hume of continuing to deploy the historically realist procedures of classical dogmatics. For MacDonald, Overbeck is the key figure in Barth's response to these dilemmas. "Overbeck believed that one did non-theology or nothing. It is in this sense that he made explicit what was implicit in Hume. . . . Overbeck's dilemma is of immense importance to understanding Barth's theology . . . it is the key to *what it is* Barth is doing as a theologian."[18] Barth's response is that "*contra* Overbeck and Hume . . . *theology* must be reestablished with audacity"; the possibility for its reestablishment was given to Barth when he discovered the new world of the Bible as "theological truth which, in the fulness of time, he characterised as a *sui generis historicality constitutive of a theological* historicality."[19] Whether or not Barth's discovery in *Romans* is analogous to the work of Wittengenstein, Kraus, and Schoenberg, is, I think, a largely unanswerable question. But what has to be noted here are the losses entailed by interpreting *Romans* as an answer to the question "Into which cultural peer group can *Romans II* be best assimilated?"[20] The loss is this: the content of *Romans* is drastically foreshortened, and its form as a running commentary on Paul is simply factored out. "*Romans II* is a relentless

16. Neil B. MacDonald, *Karl Barth and the Strange New World within the Bible* (Carlisle, U.K.: Paternoster, 2000); Stephen H. Webb, *Refiguring Theology: The Rhetoric of Karl Barth* (Albany: SUNY Press, 1991); Richard H. Roberts, "Barth and the Eschatology of Weimar," in *A Theology on Its Way? Essays on Karl Barth* (Edinburgh: T & T Clark, 1991); and, William S. Johnson, *The Mystery of God: Karl Barth and the Postmodern Foundations of Theology* (Louisville: Westminster/John Knox Press, 1997).

17. Friedrich-Wilhelm Graf, "Die 'antihistorische Revolution,' in der Protestantischen Theologie der zwanziger Jahre," in *Vernunft des Glaubens*, eds. Jan Rohls and Gunther Wenz (Göttingen: Vandenhoeck und Ruprecht, 1988), 377–405; Kurt Nowak, "Die 'antihistorische Revolution,'" in *Troeltsch-Studien* 4, ed. Horst Renz and Friedrich-Wilhelm Graf (Gütersloh: Mohn, 1987), 133–71.

18. MacDonald, *Karl Barth,* 16f.

19. Ibid., 18.

20. Ibid., 23.

first-order exposition"—not, note, of the Epistle to the Romans, but "of the theme 'God is God.'"[21] In other words, what Barth is doing in *Romans* is precisely what in the preface to the English translation he denied that he was doing: "free theologizing."[22]

The shortcoming of many of the genetic-historical studies of *Romans* is not simply that of historical impressionism, but more that, in order to plot Barth on a proposed cultural or social trajectory, they have to transform his text into something other than it is, against both its plain sense and Barth's declared intentions. This by no means suggests the unimportance of genetic issues; quite the opposite: it suggests that the question of Barth's context and development needs more careful study, study that will give due weight to his chosen literary form of the biblical commentary and not reduce its integrity by thematic presentation or reductive causal analysis. Probably the most important direction in Barth studies over the last fifteen years or so has been the replacement of a dominant paradigm of Barth's development "from dialectic to analogy" by a much more textually scrupulous presentation of the continuity of Barth's thinking from 1915 to the end of his life. Yet even here, much remains to be done, above all in giving proper attention to the importance of Barth's discovery of the Reformed *Schriftprinzip* and to his work as biblical exegete and commentator.

A third trend in interpretation of Barth's *Romans* that has tended to sidestep the significance of his work as commentator is the disproportionate amount of scholarly attention devoted to the prefaces that Barth wrote for the various editions of the *Römerbrief*. Using the prefaces as the interpretative key to the commentary can have the effect of suggesting that the primary importance of Barth's exegesis is that it illustrates some hermeneutical theory. That there are hermeneutical and exegetical implications to be drawn from Barth's commentary, and that some of them are indicated in the prefaces, is beyond doubt. Moreover, when given careful historical placement, the published (and draft) prefaces shed a good deal of light on Barth's intentions as commentator, as Richard Burnett's study shows to great effect.[23] But, in the end, the heart of the matter is not method, but practice and content: exegetical work on the *Sache* of the text. Whatever interest Barth may have had in formal, procedural matters was entirely subservient to the real business of the commentary: exegesis as that activity by which the church lays itself open to the divine Word to which scripture bears witness. "The purpose

21. Ibid., 62.
22. *Romans*, ix.
23. Richard E. Burnett, *Karl Barth's Theological Exegesis* (Tübingen: Mohr Siebeck, 2001).

of this book," Barth wrote to his English readers in 1932, "neither was nor is to delight or to annoy its readers by setting out a New Theology. The purpose was and is to direct them to Holy Scripture, to the Epistle of Paul to the Romans, in order that, whether they be delighted or annoyed . . . they may at least be brought face to face with the subject matter of the Scriptures."[24]

Thematic and genetic of *Romans,* and those dominated by the issues raised in Barth's various prefaces, all find it difficult to give persuasive answers to two questions: Why did Barth write a *commentary?* And why did he write *this kind of commentary?* We turn next to develop some initial answers to these questions.

III

Why did Barth write a commentary? The long answer runs: Barth wrote a commentary because since his decisive turn from liberal Protestantism in the summer of 1915 he had acquired a deep and permanent conviction of the unsurpassable majesty, freedom, and originality of God; one of the corollaries of that conviction was the relativization of all human attempts to attain to the knowledge of God through creaturely acts and experiences, forestalled as they are by the gratuitous divine Word-act that is encountered through the witness of Holy Scripture and to which the church and its theology must attend and submit. The short answer runs: Barth wrote a commentary on Romans because of convictions about God, revelation, scripture, and the theology of the church.

What drove Barth to produce the *Römerbrief,* therefore, was the *Sache,* the substance or matter, of the Christian gospel. His exegetical labor was thus not driven by hermeneutical or exegetical principles, or even at this stage by dogmatic principles; still less was it the result of being tied "to the linguistic world of the Bible."[25] Rather, it was precipitated by beliefs about God and the economy of God's acts toward his creatures, beliefs which were themselves generated by and sustained through attention to scripture and which could best be articulated by scrupulous scriptural exegesis. In the famous lecture "The New World in the Bible," delivered at his friend Thurneysen's church in Leutwil in 1916, Barth already made clear that what riveted his attention to scripture was its content: "Within

24. *Romans,* x.
25. Mary K. Cunningham, *What Is Theological Exegesis? Interpretation and Use of Scripture in Barth's Doctrine of Election* (Valley Forge, PA: Trinity Press International, 1995), 83.

the Bible there is a strange new world, the world of God";[26] or again, "it is certain that the Bible, if we read it carefully, makes straight for the one point where we must decide to accept or reject the sovereignty of God."[27] It is just this—the sovereign, utterly alive, and communicative God—which Barth finds to be the substance of the Letter to the Romans.

> God, the pure and absolute boundary and beginning of all that we are and have and do; God, who is distinguished qualitatively from men and from everything human, and must never be identified with anything which we name, or experience, or conceive, or worship, as God; . . . God, the "Yes" in our "No" and the "No" in our "Yes," the First and the Last and, consequently, the Unknown, who is never a known thing in the midst of other known things; God, the Lord, the Creator, the Redeemer:—this is the Living God. In the Gospel, in the Message of Salvation of Jesus Christ, this Hidden, Living God has revealed Himself, as He is. Above and beyond the apparently infinite series of possibilities and visibilities in this world there breaks forth, like a flash of lightning, impossibility and invisibility, not as some separate, second, other thing, but as the Truth of God which is now hidden as the Primal Origin to which all things are related, as the dissolution of all relativity, and therefore as the reality of all relative realities.[28]

"In the Gospel"—and therefore through the service of Holy Scripture—"this Hidden, Living God has revealed Himself, as He is." And so to speak of this God we must first attend to the sovereign, divine self-utterance in the biblical witness.[29] Thus, as Ingrid Spieckermann has suggested, because from 1915 onward the development of Barth's thought is constituted by a "turn towards theological objectivity,"[30] it is no mere accident that the first period of Barth's theological work "is very definitely a period of *scriptural exegesis*," and that "the first documents of this theological . . . rethinking are expositions of *Scripture*."[31]

26. Karl Barth, "The Strange New World within the Bible," in Barth, *The Word of God and the Word of Man*, trans. Douglas Horton (London: Hodder and Stoughton, 1928), 35.

27. Ibid., 41.

28. *Romans*, 330f.

29. The link between Barth's astonished recovery of an understanding of divine sovereignty and the importance of the biblical witness is noted by, for example, Burnett, *Karl Barth's Theological Exegesis*, 35f.; and especially by Helmut Kirschstein, *Der souveräne Gott und die heilige Schrift: Einführung in die Biblische Hermeneutik Karl Barths* (Aachen: Shaker Verlag, 1998), and Cornelis van der Kooi, *Anfängliche Theologie: Der Denkweg des jungen Karl Barths (1909 bis 1927)* (Munich: Kaiser, 1987), who argues that for Barth, in exegesis one is "nothing less than on the way to understanding God in his revelation, understanding his self-explication" (106).

30. Ingrid Spieckermann, *Gotteserkenntnis: Ein Beitrag zur Grundfrage der neuen Theologie Karl Barths* (Munich: Kaiser, 1985), 73.

31. Ibid., 77.

The Romans commentary is thus bound up with a complex of convictions (or, perhaps better, instincts) about divine aseity, about the spontaneity of God in self-communication, and about the function of scripture as witness to revelation. These convictions were not to receive formal dogmatic articulation until the 1923 lectures on the Reformed confessional writings and the *Göttingen Dogmatics,* but what is brought to expression in those academic texts is already present and operative in what Barth wrote about Paul at the end of his pastorate.

But why choose the *commentary* as the literary form for articulating these convictions? After all, the convictions could be and were expressed in other ways: in occasional lectures and addresses, in sermons, and, after Barth's move from Safenwil, in the growing bulk of his academic lectures on historical and dogmatic theology, a little clumsily at first but then with remarkable confidence and incisiveness as Barth made the lecture genre his own. Why then the commentary? Barth does not reflect explicitly on his reasons for choosing the genre, but two points may be in order. One is the example of Calvin, celebrated as a model exegete in the preface to the second edition of *Romans.* When Barth lectured on Calvin's theology in 1922, very soon after the appearance of the commentary, what he praised in Calvin's exegesis was "its extraordinary objectivity. . . . We can learn from Calvin what it means to stay close to the text, to focus with tense attention on what is actually there. Everything else *derives* from this. But it has to *derive* from this. If it does not, then the expounding is not real questioning and readiness to listen."[32] "Staying close to the text," we may reflect, meant expanding "what is actually there" in its integrity. This leads to a second point: the commentary *Gattung* is particularly suitable to respecting the integrity of the biblical text, precisely because both its substance and its sequence are completely determined by the text itself. Of all forms, commentary is least likely to overwhelm the text and so most likely to fit Barth's conviction that—again as he put it with reference to Calvin—"Exegesis has to be a conversation in which one speaks and the other listens. Listening . . . is the task of the exegete."[33]

IV

The form of the commentary thus offered Barth a genre that embodied conviction about Holy Scripture as testimony to the divine Word, a conviction that scripture is (as he put it in the preface to the first volume

32. Karl Barth, *The Theology of Calvin* (Grand Rapids: Eerdmans, 1991), 389.
33. Ibid.

of the *Church Dogmatics*) "the basic text upon which all the rest and everything of our own can only wait and comment."[34] However, writing a commentary under the impress of this conviction about God, revelation, and the nature of Holy Scripture involved Barth in a radical reworking of the genre of the biblical commentary as it had developed at the hands of professional exegetes. What sort of redefinition was involved?

A good deal of light is shed on that question by a statement in the course of Barth's discussion of biblical hermeneutics in *Church Dogmatics* I/2: "The fact that we have to understand and expound the Bible as a human word can . . . be explained . . . in this way: that we have to listen to what it says to us as a human word. We have to understand it as a human word in the light of what it says."[35] Biblical interpretation, and therefore biblical commentary, is to be determined by the fact that the human word of the biblical text is what it is: a human word that describes or intends divine revelation. It is what it says. And hence what it says, it says as a human word; what matters about it as a human word is what it says. Or, as Barth put it in the preface to the second edition of *Romans:* "Criticism applied to historical documents means for me the measuring of words and phrases against the matter [*Sache*] of which the documents speak. . . . The relation of the words to the Word in the words must be disclosed."[36] What is involved in this commentarial task of laying bare the relation of the human word of the biblical text to the divine Word that is its matter?

First, the text must be read and commented upon as the human word that it is. Accordingly, in *Romans* Barth is by no means unconcerned with the text; on the contrary, the language, the argumentative sequence and the subject matter of Paul's text are all thoroughly determinative of his commentary. Whatever else might be meant by the term, Barth's commentary is clearly concerned with the literal sense, that is with the text in its explicit, surface grammatical meaning. As he was to note in commending Calvin's commentaries in 1922, the exegete is responsible "to derive fruitful doctrine *from* the actual wording and historical circumstances, not by ignoring them."[37] But, crucially, where Barth differs from most of his (and many of our) contemporaries is that this focus upon the text as the human historical word that it is *demands,* and does not *exclude,* the attempt on the part of the commentator to hear the "Word in the words," precisely because the human word of the text is a human word that bears to its listeners a divine Word. Not to listen for the divine Word in the text's

34. Barth, *Church Dogmatics*, vol. I/1, xii.
35. Karl Barth, *Church Dogmatics*, vol. I/2 (Edinburgh: T & T Clark, 1957), 466.
36. *Romans*, 8 (translation altered).
37. Barth, *The Theology of Calvin*, 389.

words, systematically to exclude consideration of this witnessing function of the text, is not to hear the human word at all. And it is this failure—the failure to grasp the real nature of the human word of the text by neglecting or banishing the relation of the textual word to the divine Word—that is central to Barth's unease with the dominance of the historical-critical method in the professional commentaries of his day.

The famous opening words of the preface to the first edition of the *Römerbrief* run:

> Paul, as a child of his age, addressed his contemporaries. It is, however, far more important that, as Prophet and Apostle of the Kingdom of God, he veritably speaks to all men of every age. The differences between then and now, there and here, no doubt require careful investigation and consideration. But the purpose of such investigation can only be to demonstrate that these differences are, in fact, purely trivial.[38]

On the basis of such statements, Barth's exegesis is routinely criticized as idealist or dualist, lifting the text out of historical communicative practices: "The meaning the interpreter finds in the text is unperceivable, unhistorical, transcendent truth. All truth is transcendent; nothing whatever of time and space has any meaning except with reference to the unperceivable, unhistorical work."[39] But this is seriously to misread Barth. His objection to the dominance of historical criticism is that it is ensnared in a notion of history and of historical texts that so emphasizes the sheer distance of the scriptural text from the present that it makes impossible any idea that the text performs a function in divine revelation. Insisting on the historical gulf between text and interpreter, historical criticism—at least when it thinks of its work as a sufficient account of the text—reinforces a view of the text as alien, as an object for historical explanation. "My complaint," Barth responded to professional exegetical critics of the first edition,

> is that recent commentators confine themselves to an interpretation of the text which seems to me no commentary at all, but merely the first step towards such a commentary. Recent commentaries contain no more than a reconstruction of the text, a rendering of the Greek words and phrases by their precise equivalents, a number of additional notes in which archaeological and philological material is gathered together, and a more or less plausible arrangement of the subject-matter in such a manner that it may be made historically and psychologically intelligible.[40]

38. *Romans*, 1.
39. Henry, *Early Development*, 186.
40. *Romans*, 6.

For the historical critic, the text is definable without residue as a linguistic, religious-psychological entity from the past. For Barth, such features of the text, though real, are by no means its only properties; for him the text's matter is prophetic and apostolic speech, and so the historical gulf that separates it from its contemporary readers is by no means constitutive of the entirety of the work of exegesis. What is common to both the text and its present-day readers is the *Sache* of the text, which is the communicative Word of God; text and interpreter are bound together before this *Sache*. And so once again Barth praises Calvin's exegetical procedure:

> How energetically Calvin, having first established what stands in the text, sets himself to re-think the whole material and to wrestle with it, till the walls which separate the sixteenth century from the first become transparent! Paul speaks, and the man of the sixteenth century hears. The conversation between the original record and the reader moves round the subject-matter, until a distinction between yesterday and today becomes impossible.[41]

None of this means that Barth rejects what Peter Stuhlmacher calls the "instrumental use" of historical criticism.[42] Responding to critics of the first edition such as Jülicher and Lietzmann, Barth argued that: "There is no difference of opinion with regard to the need of applying historical criticism as a prolegomenon to the understanding to the Epistle. So long as the critic is occupied in this preliminary work I follow him carefully and gratefully. So long as it is simply a question of establishing what stands in the text, I have never dreamed of doing anything else than sit attentively at the feet of such learned men."[43] Historical criticism is necessary to establish *was da steht* in the human word; but its assumption that the historical distance between text and interpreter determines the text's function is for Barth a refusal of a properly theological reading of the historical character of the text—a refusal to see the historical text as having a place in the divine economy. As Barth put it in a lecture from April 1920 (six months before he began the feverish rewriting of the Romans commentary), "intelligent and fruitful discussion of the Bible begins when the judgement as to its human, its historical and psychological character has been made and *put behind* us"[44]—not "put behind"

41. Ibid., 7.
42. Peter Stuhlmacher, *Historical Criticism and the Theological Interpretation of Scripture* (Philadelphia: Fortress Press, 1977), 49.
43. Ibid., 7.
44. Karl Barth, "Biblical Questions, Insights and Vistas," in *The Word of God and the Word of Man*, trans. Douglas Horton (Boston: Pilgrim Press, 1928), 60f.

in the sense of dismissed as irrelevant, but rather grasped as what it is: the necessary human properties of a text that sets before the commentator a certain *Sache,* so that the interpreter's concern is properly with "the special *content* of this human document, the remarkable *something* . . . the Biblical *object*."[45] Even in its humanness, the text, as bearer of this *Sache,* is more than a "psychologically and historically conceivable magnitude."[46] To read it as such is simply to fail to understand the human word in the light of what it says.

Because it is oriented to *was da steht,* Barth's commentary is an attempt to be led by what Paul says towards the *Sache* that Paul indicates. It is this that is meant by theological exegesis or, a little more precisely, by *theologische Sachexegese.*[47] Once again some careful delineation is necessary. Theological exegesis is not to be thought of as the addition of an extra layer of religious, doctrinal, pastoral, or spiritual interpretation to a basic commentarial framework supplied by historical criticism. David Henry, for example, sees Barth's commentary as composed of rather rudimentary historical-critical materials to which are added Barth's "convictions."[48] But this partitioning of the material does not do justice to what Barth is about. Partly that is because it makes Barth into a pious exegete such as his father, Fritz Barth, making cautious use of historical-critical tools and adding pastoral application. But the problem is much more that to locate the distinctiveness of theological exegesis in the convictions of the exegete is simply to put the emphasis in the wrong place, making theological exegesis a matter of the commentator's subjectivity or use of the text. It is not a matter of Barth seeking "a closer relationship between the text and its interpreter despite their undeniable historical distance";[49] rather, theological exegesis is rooted in the exegete's acknowledgment of objective properties that the text acquires in serving to indicate the self-revelation of God. Theological exegesis is not a construal or deployment of the text, or a matter of interpretative attitude or disposition. It is, once more, a reading of the human word in the light of what it says.

Similarly, theological exegesis is not to be misunderstood as *thematic* exegesis. Barth was painfully aware of being misinterpreted at this point: "I know that I have laid myself open to the charge of imposing a meaning upon the text rather than extracting its meaning from it, and

45. Ibid., 61.

46. Ibid., 68.

47. Cf. Walter Lindemann, *Karl Barth und die Kritische Schriftauslegung* (Hamburg: Reich, 1973).

48. Henry, *Early Development,* 94, 119.

49. Eberhard Jüngel, "Barth's Theological Beginnings," in Jüngel, *Karl Barth: A Theological Legacy,* trans. Garrett E. Paul (Philadelphia: Westminster Press, 1986), 76.

that my method implies this."[50] But though there are exceptions, Barth's usual commentarial practice does not bear this out, for he is scrupulous in following the sense and sequence of Paul's text. A passage in one of the draft prefaces to the first edition runs: "Because this book is not my dogmatic but an exegetical work, I was not able to say everything about each of the topics touched upon, but only about that which lies directly in the path of Paul's words. One is not allowed, therefore, to read its statements as a treatise but rather should be interested, first of all, in the understanding of the text itself. My statements have no importance of their own."[51] That catches exactly Barth's procedure in writing a theological commentary. As James Martin notes apropos of Barth's slightly later lectures on the fourth Gospel, "Barth is a theological exegete, not a dogmatic one."[52]

Theological exegesis, then, refers neither to the religious subjectivity of the commentator nor to a thematic reordering of the content of the biblical text. In essence, theological exegesis is an attempt to identify and rearticulate the matter of the text, *was da steht*. In the case of Barth's Romans commentary, this involves allowing the matter to be the organizing principle of the commentator's presentation, though without in any way supplanting or eclipsing the language, form, and sequence of the text itself. It is, therefore, by no means incidental that Barth offers a *lectio continua*, a running restatement of the text in its given order and not a study of Paul's theology (or of his own). In an analysis of the commentary genre, Paul Griffiths identifies a number of essential properties of the commentary, two of which are particularly applicable in the case of Barth's *Romans*. First, not only must a commentary have "a direct relation to some other work," which obviously is the case in *Romans*, but this relation must be demonstrated in the commentary by "overt signs of another work"—such as quotation, paraphrase, or summary.[53] Barth's procedure clearly secures this: each section contains his own translation of the Greek text, and then a sequential exposition in which the text is quoted and then re-presented with lengthy interpolations that are attempts to restate the text, not so as to improve upon it or trace its genesis, but so as to indicate it and draw the attention of the reader to its details and its argumentative scope. Second, the signs of the presence of the primary text upon which

50. *Romans*, 10.

51. Preface draft Romans III, cited by Burnett, *Karl Barth's Theological Exegesis*, 289.

52. James P. Martin, "The Gospel of John," in *Karl Barth in Re-View*, ed. H. Martin Rumscheidt (Pittsburgh: Pickwick Press, 1979), 41.

53. Paul Griffiths, *Religious Reading: The Place of Reading in the Practice of Religion* (Oxford: Oxford University Press, 1999), 81.

comment is offered must "outweigh other elements" in the commentary.[54] We have already noted how Barth intended his commentary to be just that—not a set of reflections, but an attempt to interpret "the text of the Epistle": "I should be altogether misunderstood if my readers refused to credit me with the honesty of, at any rate, *intending* to *explain* the text."[55] Even though we may judge that on occasions Barth did not achieve the right sort of subservience of his text to the biblical text, the intention of his method is beyond doubt. Because of this, it is unsurprising that Barth's theological exegesis most often takes the form of a complex paraphrase within which reference is frequently made to the Pauline text, both as anchor and as sign that the commentary has no independent life of its own. *Paraphrase* is one of the best terms to describe Barth's commentarial practice, because it is a low-level term, indicating the essentially ostensive character of what Barth has to say. In another draft preface to the first edition, Barth explains his method of paraphrase thus:

> This book does *not* consciously use *easier language* than the *Römerbrief* itself. It only wants to interpret by *paraphrasing* the thoughts of Paul, not by translating them into our "easier" thoughts. . . . The "easier" Christian way of thinking . . . does *not*, unfortunately, by any means indicate that we, after all, have arrived upon the same subject matter as Paul and the bible. If ears will be once again open to the *subject matter* with which Paul was concerned, then will his language be once again understood as well.[56]

At least in his commentary work, Barth's procedure is somewhat less synthetic than the "analysis of biblical concepts" that has been proposed as the dominant mode of exegesis in the *Church Dogmatics*.[57] *Conceptual analysis* suggests something too abstract and remote, insufficiently immediate to the text; paraphrase—even when its language is quite distinct from the language of Paul, and even when the concepts are fraught with reference to realities beyond his text—is still what Barth seeks to do in directing the reader back to the biblical material. Where concepts may take on a life of their own, detached from that which has generated them, paraphrase is firm in its intention to bring before the reader the matter of the text in its otherness, completeness, and integrity.

---

54. Ibid., 82.
55. *Romans*, 9.
56. Preface draft IA., cited by Burnett, *Karl Barth's Theological Exegesis*, 279.
57. Paul McGlasson, *Jesus and Judas: Biblical Exegesis in Barth* (Atlanta: Scholars Press, 1991), 81.

V

What I have tried to do in this chapter is to provide a prolegomenon to the study of Barth's commentarial work on Romans, and I am breaking off at the point where the real work of analyzing Barth's practice should begin. But by way of preliminary conclusion two things might be said.

The first simply repeats what I tried to stress all along, namely, that no account of Barth's work is adequate which does not take seriously his writings as biblical commentator. One of the many reasons that his work is still waiting to be received is that he has been read and criticized on the basis of only a selection of what he said, and little headway can be expected in the matter of clarifying Barth's *oeuvre*, especially in its earlier phase, unless a great deal more precise engagement with his biblical writings is undertaken.

Second, consideration of Barth's *Romans* may raise the question of the significance of biblical commentary for theology as a whole. Despite some serious contemporary counterexamples, in our own day no less than in Barth's the biblical commentary remains largely in the hands of ancient historians.[58] One of the things that made Barth speak of himself as an *Alleingänger,*[59] a man treading a lonely path, was his strong sense that the commentary belongs to a positive rather than a purely critical theological and spiritual culture. J. B. Henderson notes that "the transition from commentarial forms and modes of discourse to modern scholarship and criticism is one of the most important in the intellectual history of mankind,"[60] and that "the abandonment or suppression of commentarial forms in the intellectual culture of early modern times . . . is probably of greater significance in the intellectual transition between the mediaeval and modern worlds than most of the great ideas of the leading philosophers and scientists."[61] In important respects, what is happening in *Romans* is a rediscovery of this commentarial mode of theology. Both in his explicit treatments of the biblical text and in his other theological writings, Barth worked on the assumption that exegesis solves theological problems, and that the necessary conceptual work of dogmatics serves, and does not transcend, exegesis.

58. See, for example, Karlfried Froehlich, "Bibelkommentare—Zur Krise einer Gattung," *Zeitschrift für Theologie und Kirche* 84 (1987): 465–92.

59. Karl Barth, *Die christliche Dogmatik im Entwurf* (Zurich: Theologischer Verlag Zurich, 1982), 5.

60. John B. Henderson, *Scripture, Canon, and Commentary: A Comparison of Confucian and Western Exegesis* (Princeton: Princeton University Press, 1991), 200.

61. Ibid., 221.

Yet it would be a mistake simply to think of Barth as resting content with the positivities of a stable culture organized around a canon, or allowing the gloss to bear the whole weight of the theological enterprise. The reason for this is to be sought, once again, in the *Sache* to which the biblical text bears testimony. The matter of the gospel is for Barth far too disruptive and destabilizing to be assimilated into a textual or scribal culture. The new world of the Bible, about which Barth wrote with such astonishment in *Romans,* is the new world of *God*; exegesis cannot capture that reality, and it can never be transformed into a mere textual *positum.*[62] If scripture is present in and to the church, and is therefore a matter for exegetical and commentarial labor, it is as a text that brings to bear upon the church an act of God, and an act of God that is never directly identical with the text of scripture nor patent of exegetical reproduction. A biblical commentary is to be one of the places in which the church's theology registers the fact that its life is always open to devastation and renewal by the Word of God. From that devastation and renewal there can be no deliverance, not even a scriptural one.

---

62. *Contra* the account of Barth in George Lindbeck, "Barth and Textuality," *Theology Today* 43 (1986): 361–76, or the account of scriptural pragmatism in Peter Ochs, *Peirce, Pragmatism and the Logic of Scripture* (Cambridge: Cambridge University Press, 1998).